2002 CATALOGUE OF

EЯRORS

ON U.S. POSTAGE STAMPS

Stephen R. Datz

3 3113 02064 3252

Published by

krause
publications

700 E. State Street • Iola, WI 54990-0001
Telephone: 715/445-2214

Please call or write for our free catalog of numismatic publications.
Our toll-free number to place an order or obtain a free catalog is 800-258-0929
or please use our regular business telephone 715-445-2214
for editorial comment and further information.

Library of Congress Catalog Number: 97-80544
ISBN: 0-87349-315-X

Printed in the United States of America

CONTENTS

ACKNOWLEDGMENTS

Many individuals generously assisted in the preparation of this book. Sincere thanks are extended to all who contributed. Special thanks are due Jacques C. Schiff, Jr. for his encouragement and resources in making this book a reality. Sincere thanks also to Marvin Frey for his help and guidance in editing the section on EFOs. Among those who have helped with this or previous editions (including the late *) are:

Ken Beiner
Larry Bustillo
Mike Charles *
Robert Dowiot
Bob Dumaine
Marvin Frey
Howard P. Gates Jr. *
Stan Goldfarb

John Greenwood
Herman Herst Jr. *
John Hotchner
William S. Langs
James McDevitt
Bruce H. Mosher
Jack S. Molesworth
Jack Nalbandian

James B. Peterson
D. James Samuelson
Robert A. Siegel *
John Tison
Wm. Wallerstein *
Martin Wilkinson
Wayne Youngblood

Our sincere appreciation to the following firms for their assistance in providing auction catalogues and prices realized, or retail price lists for this edition.

Matthew Bennett, Inc.
Richard E. Drews Philatelic Auctions
EFO Collectors Club
Ivy & Mader Auctions, Inc.
Jack Nalbandian, Inc.
Regency Stamps, Ltd.
Robert A. Siegel Auction Galleries, Inc.
Sam Houston Philatelics
Jacques C. Schiff Jr., Inc.
Shreves Philatelic Galleries, Inc.
Superior Stamp & Coin Co., Inc.
Weiss Philatelics

INTRODUCTION

This work includes major error stamps lacking perforations; multicolored stamps and postal stationery lacking one or more colors that would normally be present; stamps with holograms omitted; stamps with reverse inscription omitted or inverted; and stamps and postal stationery of two or more colors in which one of the design elements was inverted during printing. Certain other stamps that resemble major errors are included and described under **Error-Like Stamps** or in the **EFOs & Other Unusual Stamps** section. Other types of errors exist, but are not within the present scope of this book.

Imperforates. To be considered an imperforate error, all traces of perforations (or die cuts) between two complete, adjacent stamps must be absent. The presence of even one perforation between stamps disqualifies it from being considered an imperforate error. The presence of incompletely impressed perforations or die cuts also disqualifies a stamp as an imperforate error. Refer to **Blind Perforations.**

The presence of a row of perforations completely within the design of one of the stamps of a pair and parallel to the row of omitted perforations, disqualifies the pair from being considered imperforate between, imperforate horizontally, or imperforate vertically, as the case may be. Perforations touching or cutting a design do not disqualify an error. Only when perforations are completely inside the border of a design does disqualification occur.

It is generally accepted that a single stray perforation hole (not part of a row) within a design does not affect an error's status as an error. An example is **IM 263.**

Some imperforates are the result of foldovers on booklets or sheet stamps. Some feel that such items should be regarded as freaks or oddities. However, our policy is to judge items on their physical appearance. If they meet the criteria set forth in a definition, they are listed without regard to how they may have been created, which in many cases cannot be known with certainty anyway.

At present, some controversy exists over whether a folding crease disqualifies an imperforate pair as a major error. In our opinion, the presence of a folding crease does not disqualify

a stamp as an error because it is not material to the fundamental condition that defines the error: the complete omission of perfs between adjacent stamps. Since the presence of creases (or other faults) does not disqualify other major errors, it is illogical to conclude that they should disqualify foldovers from being major errors.

Where the possibility for confusion exists, our policy is to describe errors according to the evidence provided by their appearance. A case in point is the description of imperforate errors arising from booklets. Pairs from booklets with natural straight edges on two opposing exterior sides are best described as imperforate vertically or horizontally (whichever the case may be) in order to distinguish them from true imperforate betweens, which possess perforations on all exterior sides, and which may arise from foldovers. In some cases, both forms of errors exist for the same issue, and confusion arises where descriptions are not specific.

Stamps with perforations omitted between the stamp and the selvage are not listed because the omitted perforations do not occur between two adjacent stamps and, therefore, do not fall within the definition of an imperforate error. Their omission is not a reflection on their desirability or collectibility.

Color-Omitted Errors. To be considered a color-omitted error, 100 percent of the affected color(s) must be absent from the design. The presence of even one dot of color disqualifies a stamp. The stamp must be able to pass scrutiny under 30-power magnification. Colors absent from a design due to a perforation shift are not color-omitted errors.

Albinos, stamps with all color(s) omitted, exist for a few issues but are not included in this work. Their omission is not a reflection on their desirability or collectibility.

Tagging is applied by a separate printing plate and, although invisible to the naked eye, is considered by some to be a "color" for purposes of defining what constitutes a properly prepared stamp. Stamps with tagging omitted are not considered major errors and are not separately listed. In some cases, the omission of tagging is mentioned because it helps to authenticate the error.

Error-Like Stamps. Traditionally, to be regarded as a "legitimate" error, a stamp must have found its way into public hands by being sold at a post office. Several kinds of stamps, usually imperforates, have found their way into the philatelic domain by other means. While not errors in the traditional sense, they are similar in appearance.

Because it is the purpose of this catalogue to be used as a reference, to aid in identification, and to foster knowledge, certain of these stamps are included herein. They are identified by one of the following references.

PRF. *(Proof).* Some early imperforates are arguably proofs, prepared in issued colors on stamp paper, either gummed or ungummed. Where the prevailing opinion is that an imperforate item was actually a stamp-like proof, the listing is identified by the symbol **PRF**.

NRI. *(Not Regularly Issued).* Some imperforates were not regularly issued. Imperforate stamps have, on occasion, been traded for services or rare items (such as the 1869 pictorial inverts) needed for the National Museum's collection. Typically, they are identical to their perforated counterparts, except for the lack of perforations. They were intentionally allowed to leave government hands, although not made available to the general public. They are identified by the symbol **NRI**.

PW. *(Printer's Waste).* In printer's terminology "make-readies" or "set-ups" is paper used to get presses up and running smoothly. It is usually discarded as waste, but occasionally finds its way into philatelic hands. On occasion, printer's waste—even after having been marked for destruction by quality control inspectors—has found its way into philatelic hands, inadvertently included in regular shipments of stamps. Most often, however, printer's waste reaches the market via a dishonest employee whose has stolen it from a printing plant or wastepaper destruction facility.

The term "printer's waste," has taken on a pejorative connotation in philately—purloined stamps. Generally, printer's waste is neither recognized nor esteemed by the philatelic community and many collectors prefer not to include printer's waste in their collections.

In some cases it is not clear how imperfect stamps (either marked for destruction or generally faulty) reached public hands. Some legitimate errors are known with destruction marks. And in some cases, printer's waste has the appearance of a perfectly legitimate error, but is known to have reached the market by having been misappropriated by someone inside a printing plant or destruction facility. In this catalogue, the term printer's waste takes the traditional connotation, that of stamps having reached the market by suspect means. They are identified by the symbol **PW**.

Errors purchased over a post office counter are perfectly legal to own. However, misappropriated stamps remain the property of the United States Government and are not legal to own. Stamps that could not have been purchased at a post office, such as full uncut sheets of booklet panes, should be avoided, as they remain government property.

Freaks and Oddities. A multitude of stamps exists containing irregularities such as perforation or color shifts, overinking or underinking, folding or other factors that make them strange in appearance. They are commonly referred to as EFOs (errors, freaks and oddities). Their value is usually, but not always, much less than that of major errors. Refer to the section on **EFOs & Other Unusual Stamps.**

FAKES

Fakes. Fakes exist for some errors. While many are crude, some are excellent and difficult to detect. Cautionary notes appear in the listings where appropriate. From a practical standpoint, the collector's best protection is dealing with knowledgeable, reputable dealers, or requiring, at least for items of significant value, that an expert certificate from a recognized expertizing body be furnished.

Imperforate Singles. Generally, imperforate singles should be avoided. Some nineteenth century issues are known as error singles. However, many nineteenth and twentieth century stamps exist with huge margins that can be trimmed to resemble imperforates. An expert certificate is necessary for imperforate singles.

Blind Perforations. Blind perforations can be ironed out and made invisible to the naked eye. This is especially true of stamps with gum soaked off. Ungummed imperforates should be examined closely under magnification. The barest trace of even one perforation, even though not punched through, disqualifies the stamp from being imperforate. Pairs of stamps offered as imperforate should be carefully checked by a knowledgeable authority.

Colors Omitted. Certain dyes used in printing are susceptible to removal or alteration by exposure to light, heat or chemicals. Many, such as the Copernicus yellow-omitted error, are easily created, therefore, expertizing is recommended. Be suspicious of "newly discovered" color-omitted errors on 20- or 30-year-old-stamps for which only a single copy is purportedly known.

Erasers have been used to remove colors from stamps, occasionally with treacherously deceptive results. Lithographed and gravure printed stamps are especially susceptible to this kind of tampering.

Because used stamps are particularly susceptible to tampering, our policy is not to list used color-omitted errors unless mint examples are also known.

Inverts. Clever fakes exist created by cutting a center design and inverting it in relation to its frame. The most clever of these do not cut entirely through the stamp's paper, so when viewed from the back, gum and paper are intact.

Used Errors. Used errors should be checked carefully. Blind perfs can be ironed out and chemical treatments or other operations performed to remove colors without having to worry about disturbing original gum, tagging, or the pristineness of the stamp. Use caution.

Expertizing. The publisher cannot give opinions regarding the genuineness of errors. The American Philatelic Expertizing Service (APEX), P.O. Box 8000, State College, PA 16803, and the Philatelic Foundation, 501 Fifth Avenue, Room 1901, New York, NY 10017, expertize error stamps. Contact them directly for information about their services before submitting a stamp for an opinion.

HOW TO USE THE CATALOGUE

Listings are divided into sections according to type of error and arranged as follows:

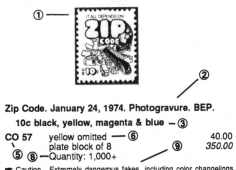

Zip Code. January 24, 1974. Photogravure. BEP.

10c black, yellow, magenta & blue — ③

CO 57	yellow omitted — ⑥		40.00
	plate block of 8	⑨	350.00
⑤ ⑧	—Quantity: 1,000+		

☛ Caution. Extremely dangerous fakes, including color changelings, exist. Certificate of authenticity essential.

1. Illustration. Illustrations bordered in black are those of actual error stamps. Illustrations of actual error stamps are used wherever possible. Where an error illustration was not available, the illustration of a normal stamp—not bordered in black—is substituted. Illustrations of normal stamps are also used in cases where black and white reproduction does not adequately reveal a color-omitted error.

2. Description. Each error is described by the subject of the stamp, date of issue, form (se-tenant, souvenir sheet, etc.), method of printing, perforation, watermark, and type. *Watermark, perforation, and type are given only when necessary to distinguish one stamp from another of similar design.* Printers are listed for stamps issued after 1980.

3. Description. Denomination and color(s) are given. Only color information necessary to identify the stamp is given for imperforate errors. For color-omitted errors, individual colors and the printing process used to apply them are given.

4. Designs. Where multiple stamp designs are contained se-tenant in an error, each individual design is identified.

5. Numbering. Errors are classified by category. Individual types within a category are identified by a prefix and number. For example: the **IM** identifies prefix imperforate errors;

the **CO** prefix identifies color(s)-omitted errors; and the **IV** prefix identifies invert errors.

A separate catalogue number is assigned to each error or variety. Multiples, such as plate blocks, Zip blocks, etc., are not separately numbered; they are regarded as varieties in form of the basic type.

Gaps in the sequence of catalogue numbers occur from time to time in order to accommodate possible future listings.

6. Form. Following the catalogue number is a listing of the error in its basic or most commonly encountered form. Other forms of the error (such as plate blocks, used copies, covers, etc.) are listed where known. The omission of a form does not necessarily imply that it does not exist, but only that it has not come to the attention of the publisher.

7. Price. Prices are in U.S. dollars and are based on the best information available at press time. Auction prices, advertised retail prices, and editors' judgments have been weighed and blended in an attempt to reflect a reasonable idea of value. **Prices are intended to reflect net retail prices, the price a consumer would expect to pay a dealer for stocking an item and making it available on demand.** Retail prices reflect a dealer's cost of overhead and investment in inventory.

Auction prices can be either higher or lower than listed prices, and vary from sale to sale. In general, auction prices tend to be lower than retail prices for plentiful items or items sold in bulk. And they tend to be higher than listed prices for items that rarely come to market, especially classic errors of premium quality.

In any case, there are no absolutes, and listed prices are not intended as such. They are intended—at best—to be a general guide to value. Note well, that because the market determines values, prices for individual items may vary—up or down—from those listed in the catalogue. This is especially true for newly discovered errors. Actual market prices also vary according to condition, especially for pre-1950 items.

Condition. Prices are for sound stamps except where noted. Damaged or faulty copies usually sell for less, especially modern issues. Hinging is to be expected on issues before

1940, and prices are for hinged copies in fine to very fine (F-VF) condition. Better copies or never hinged (NH) copies often command a premium—often substantial. After 1940, prices are for NH copies in F-VF condition.

LRS. For rare, infrequently traded items, the Last Reported Sale (where known) is indicated by the initials LRS, followed by the date in parentheses and the transaction price.

Italics. Prices in italics are the editors' estimates where no precise information is available, such as newly discovered errors or infrequently traded errors. They should be regarded as tentative and subject to fluctuation. Actual market prices for these items may be either higher or lower.

Dash. (—). A dash indicates that insufficient pricing information exists, e.g. infrequently traded items or varieties such as plate blocks, etc. *Use of this symbol does not necessarily imply rarity.*

Covers. Prices for used modern errors on cover are for timely usage. *Philatelically inspired covers are usually worth much less.*

Pricing anomalies. Many errors exist in similar quantities but have different prices. *Do not assume that there is a dependable ratio of quantity to price. There is none.* Classic errors, such as the 1869 inverts or the inverted Jenny, sell for much more than modern errors of similar quantity. This, because values for classic rarities have been established over time.

Modern errors, as a group, are more plentiful. Generally, for modern errors—other factors being equal—the greater the eye appeal, the more dramatic and visually interesting the error, the greater the price. Those with topical appeal also tend to sell for more. In many cases, plate or position error blocks do not command the premium that their normal counterparts do. That is because error plate or position multiples are generally not as much in demand among error collectors as their normal counterparts are among the general collecting population. Also, pressure often exists to break multiples, even plate blocks, because they may be more salable as individual stamps, pairs, etc.

8. Quantity. Quantities known or reliably reported to exist are listed. The number listed under quantity is for the number of error stamps irrespective of form (pairs, blocks, etc.) unless otherwise stated. A quantity of 100 listed for in imperforate error means that 50 pairs could exist, or 25 blocks of 4, or some combination. In many cases the exact quantity existing is not ascertainable and, therefore, not given. Quantities given in italics are tentative and reflect the best information available at press time, which is often sketchy. The word "new" is used to indicate that the error appeared on the market just prior to press time. It appears together with an initial reported quantity, which should be considered tentative and subject to change.

Ranges are given, e.g. 50 to 100 pairs, where the general order of magnitude, but not the specific quantity, is acknowledged.

The term "reported" is used to indicate the quantity initially reported to exist. This number, especially for recently discovered errors, is subject to change. In addition, several general terms are used to indicate quantity believed to exist where exact information is not available.

Unique. Only one copy known.
Very Rare. Fewer than 10 copies.
Rare. Fewer than 25 copies.
Very Scarce. Fewer than 50 copies.
Scarce. Fewer than 100 copies.
Few Hundred. Generally, 100-300 copies.
Several Hundred. More than 300 copies.
Few Thousand. Generally, 1,000-3,000 copies.
Several Thousand. More than 3,000 copies.
N/a. Not available. No reliable information available.

9. Notes. Information of interest to the reader. Cautionary notes, for fakes and other potential problems, are given where appropriate and indicated by the symbol ☞.

DEFINITIONS

Blind Perforations. Incompletely or partially impressed perforations, often barely indented into the paper and giving stamps the appearance of being imperforate, and perforations incompletely cut (visible on one side of a pane of stamps but not visible on the other side) by the new grinding technology.

Block. Four or more unseparated stamps arranged in a rectangle.

Booklet Pane. Small sheetlets of stamps bound into booklets between card-stock covers by staples, thread or glue. More recently, panes containing self-adhesive stamps have been issued without separate covers. They can be folded and inserted into wallet or purse, and are referred to as booklet panes.

Color Changeling. A stamp whose color(s) have been altered or eliminated by physical or chemical tampering. Certain stamp dyes are susceptible to alteration, especially bleaching by sunlight, heat, or chemicals. Color changelings are of no philatelic value.

EE Bars. Electric eye bars. Bars printed on margins of press sheets to guide them into position for perforating. These markings are normally trimmed off finished coil stamps.

EFO. See **EFOs & Other Unusual Stamps**.

Engraving. Also known as intaglio. A method of printing in which the design is engraved (recessed) into a metal plate. Ink fills the recesses and when printed, forms small ridges on the paper. Engraving can be identified by magnifying glass or by running your finger over the surface of the stamp and feeling the ridges.

Flat Press. A printing press that utilizes flat plates and prints paper one sheet at a time.

Imperforate. Lacking perforations. When used to describe a pair or multiple, imperforate means completely lacking perforations between stamps and on all sides. Stamps lacking die cuts are referred to as "die cut omitted."

Imperforate Between. Lacking perforations

between two stamps, but with perforations present on all outer sides. Pairs or multiples may be either horizontal or vertical. In the case of booklet panes, this description is applied only to those having perforations on all outer sides (as often result from foldovers). Booklet pane pairs having natural straight edges on two opposing exterior sides are described as imperforate vertically or horizontally in order to distinguish them from true imperforate betweens, i.e. possessing perforations on all outer sides. Those with a natural straight edge at bottom can be described using the criteria set forth in **Imperforates—Other Configurations.**

Vertical Pair, Imperforate Horizontally. A pair of stamps, one atop the other vertically, lacking horizontal perforations between stamps and with horizontal straight edges at top and bottom. Perforations are present all across left and right sides.

Horizontal Pair, Imperforate Vertically. A pair of stamps, side by side horizontally, lacking vertical perforations between stamps and with vertical straight edges at either side. Perforations are present all across top and bottom.

Imperforates—Other Configurations. Imperforates that do not conveniently fall into the above categories are described according to their appearance. The illustrated example is an imperforate horizontal pair with perforations at bottom and left, and straight edges at top and right.

The initial reference "imperforate" refers only to the omission of perforations between two stamps. Exterior sides are described according to the position and presence of perforations or straight edges. An item could have perforations on three sides and a straight edge on the fourth, or vice versa. This style is also appropriate for blocks or multiples, and for items imperforate horizontally or vertically on which perforations appear only part way across the exterior top or bottom or sides.

Whether each of these possible combinations constitutes a separate listing category, rather than mere sub-variety status, is not clear.

Imprint. A marginal inscription such as "American Bank Note Company." On modern issues "Use Zip Code," "Mail Early in the Day," and "Copyright USPS" often appear in margins.

Line Pair. On engraved, rotary-press coil stamps, a line is created by ink that fills the small space where the curved plates join and is printed in the same fashion as ink from the recessed stamp design.

Lithography. Also known as planographic or surface printing. This process is based on the antipathy of water and oil. A photographic image is exposed to a photosensitive plate. The area exposed becomes water insoluble. The unexposed, water-soluble area is washed away leaving an image that is receptive to ink. In some cases the inked image on the plate is transferred to a rubber-like blanket before being impressed on paper, hence the term offset printing.

Images are broken up into a series of dots in order to achieve tonal gradation. Color lithography involves the mingling of areas of dots from several plates, each printing a separate color, in order to achieve the effect of full color. Because each printing plate lays down only a single color, passes beneath several plates are necessary in order to achieve the final, full-color result. These passes may occur in several press runs or in a single press run through a large press capable of mounting and running multiple plates. Stamp production typically involves from four to seven plates (colors).

Color-omitted errors are produced when one or more plate impressions are omitted. You can observe the dot structure of lithography by examining any black-and-white or color printing, e.g. from a magazine or stamp, under a 10-power or stronger glass. You will see how the dots are used to yield tonal gradations and blend to make a variety of colors. In commercial printing four plates (colors) are typically used to achieve the full color effect: black, yellow, magenta (red) and cyan (blue). Stamp printing often employs additional plates, with a variety of specially mixed inks, in order to achieve a higher quality result.

Miscut. Cut abnormally so that portions of adjoining stamps appear together in the area normally occupied by a single design.

Pair. Two unseparated stamps.

Pane. A separate section of stamps, variously a quarter, half, or one-sixth sheet, as cut for retail sale from a press sheet.

Photogravure. Like lithography, the gravure plate is made by a photosensitive process; however, unlike lithography, the ink lies in small recesses and is very thinly applied. Tones are achieved by varying the depth of the recesses and thickness of the ink. The image is broken up into a series of fine points that keep the paper from being pressed into the recesses. The dot structure in photogravure is usually much finer than that used in lithography. You can see the difference by comparing a magazine illustration with a photogravure stamp under a 10 power magnifying glass.

Plate Number. A serial number usually appearing in the margin of a pane of stamps and, infrequently, on miscut coil or booklet stamps. Since about 1981, small plate numbers have appeared at the bottom of every nth stamp on most coil issues. Multicolored stamps usually, but not always, have a separate plate number for each color used in printing.

Rotary Press. A printing press on which the plates are curved in the form of a cylinder to facilitate continuous printing on a web of paper.

Se-tenant. Two or more different designs printed next to one another on a regular pane of stamps, a souvenir sheet, a booklet or a coil.

Splice. The splicing or joining of paper by glue or tape during stamp manufacture, typically in web-fed rotary printing. Tape splices are known in a variety of colors and types of tape, including paper and plastic. Splices are often referred to as paste-ups, a term originating from a time when most splices were made using glue or paste. At present, most, but not all, splices are made with tape. Splices on modern issues are usually the result of two webs of paper being joined during the printing process.

Strip. Three or more unseparated stamps arranged side-by-side or end-to-end.

Tagging. A luminescent coating, applied during printing, used to facilitate the facing and handling of mail by automated machinery. Usually invisible to the naked eye, it can be observed under ultraviolet light. Tagging may cover all or part of a stamp.

Transition Multiple. A pair, strip or block containing one or more color-omitted error stamps, one or more normal stamps, and in many cases, one or more stamps with color(s) partially omitted. Transition multiples are also known for some imperforate errors, where part of a pane, coil or booklet contains perforations and part does not. Transition multiples usually sell for a premium.

Double Line Watermark

USPS
Single Line Watermark

Watermark. Letters impressed on paper during manufacture to discourage counterfeiting. Paper is thinner where the watermark has been impressed and, therefore, appears lighter when immersed in watermark detecting fluid.

PRINTERS

Abbreviations for printers appearing in the listings. Before 1980 most stamps were printed by the Bureau of Engraving & Printing. Printers are listed for stamps issued after 1980. Listings for twentieth century stamps not mentioning a printer were printed by the Bureau of Engraving & Printing.

ABN American Bank Note Company
APU Ashton-Potter (USA) Ltd.
AVR Avery Dennison
BCA Banknote Corporation of America
BEP Bureau of Engraving & Printing
DBF Dittler Brothers
GGI Guilford Gravure Inc.
JWF J.W. Fergusson & Sons
KCS KCS Industries
NBC National Bank Note Company
SSP Sennett Security Products
SVS Stamp Venturers
UBN United Bank Note Co.
UCC Union Camp Corporation
USB U.S. Bank Note
3M 3M Corporation

NUMBERING CHANGES

The new catalogue number appears in bold at left followed by the old catalogue number or reason for change at right. In the case of delisted stamps, the former catalogue number appears.

IM 255A a new listing
IM 393 a new listing
IM 394 IM 393
IM 395 IM 394
IM 396 IM 395
IM 574B IM 574A
IM 574C a new listing
IM 600 a new listing
IM 601 IM 600

CO 194 CO 195
CO 195 a new listing

COAG 1 a new listing
COAG 1A COAG 1

PLATE NUMBER COIL STRIPS QUANTITIES KNOWN

Regretfully, the Census of Imperforate Plate Number Coil Strips, which had appeared in previous editions, has been discontinued effective with this edition. We took this step because recently it has become increasingly difficult to obtain reliable information about quantities of plate number coil strips. This is due, in part, to the natural reluctance of owners to disclose information that might adversely affect the value of their stamps, especially when the item in question is new and its value is still in the process of being established.

It came to our attention that quantities of some plate number coil strips were greater than those reported to us and subsequently published in our census. Because we have no way of determining the actual number, we have elected to report no number rather than an inaccurate number, especially an inaccurate low number that could only serve to justify an artificially high price.

We will continue to cite quantities with regular listings in those cases where the quantity can be reliably established. We will continue to use the abbreviation "n/a" in those cases where quantity cannot be reasonably established.

— Stephen R. Datz

IMPERFORATE ERRORS

SERIES OF 1857/61

Benjamin Franklin. July 1857. Engraved.

1c blue, type IIIa

IM 1 used hz pair, imperf between *4,750.00*
Quantity: very rare

Benjamin Franklin. 1857. Engraved.

1c blue, type V

IM 2 used vrt strip of 5, imperf hz —
Quantity: unique

Typically, nineteenth century stamps are heavily hinged, contain only partial original gum and often, small faults. Prices are for stamps in such condition unless otherwise indicated. Sound stamps, stamps with full original gum, and lightly hinged copies sell for a premium.

3c WASHINGTON DESIGNS OF THE 1857/61 SERIES

Type I. The outer frame line is intact all around.
Type II. The outer frame line is removed at the top and bottom. The side frame lines form a continuous line from stamp to stamp and extend beyond the design of the stamp.
Type III. The outer frame line is removed at top and bottom. The side frame lines extend only to the top and bottom of the stamp design.

George Washington. 1857. Engraved.

3c rose, type I

IM 3 used hz pair, imperf vrt —
Quantity: very rare

☛ Caution. Fakes exist.

IM 4 used vrt pair, imperf hz —
used single on cover **LRS** 6,600.00
Quantity: 1 pair and one single
on cover reported

IM 3 and **IM 4** were printed from the same plates as the imperforate 1851 series. Regularly issued imperforate stamps of the 1851 series should not be confused with errors of the 1857 series. Also, proofs of the 1851 series in issued colors were printed on bond paper very similar in appearance to stamp paper. The two are so similar that it is very difficult, especially for the unpracticed eye, to distinguish one from another.

3c dull red, type II

IM 5 hz pair, imperf vrt —
as above, used —
severed pair on cover **LRS (4/01)** 5,775.00
Quantity: very rare

The severed pair on cover is postmarked "Hermon, NY, Nov. 10."

IM 6 vrt pair, imperf hz —
used vrt pair, imperf hz —
used strip of 3, imperf hz, on cover —
Quantity: very rare

IM 7 used hz pair, imperf between —
Quantity: very rare

3c dull red, type III

IM 7A hz strip of 3, imperf vrt, on cover
 LRS (5/97) 8,250.00
 single, imperf vrt —
 Quantity: the two items as listed

The copy listed on cover is postmarked "Boston, Ms. Apr. 20, 1859," in red, contains two black grid cancels, and is addressed to St. Louis. The left stamp in the strip has a closed tear.

George Washington. 1857. Engraved.

 12c black

IM 8 used hz pair, imperf between *11,000.00*
 Quantity: very rare

George Washington. 1860. Engraved.

 24c gray or gray lilac

IM 9 imperf pair *16,000.00*
 single, imperf *1,250.00*
 Quantity: 2 pairs reported, singles very rare

In his book *Postage Stamps of the United States,* John Luff claims to "have seen 2 copies used on original envelopes." He thinks perhaps a pane got out. Lester Brookman claims these (24c-30c-90c) were trial printings submitted by Toppan, Carpenter & Co. to the Postmaster General and, therefore, not regularly issued.

Benjamin Franklin. 1860. Engraved.

 30c orange

IM 10 imperf pair *7,500.00*
 single, imperf *2,500.00*
 used imperf pair *1,250.00*
 Quantity: 3 unused pairs and 1 used
 pair reported; singles very rare

Refer to note following **IM 9**. Luff states that a used single, printed in the brown orange shade peculiar to imperfs, exists on cover to France.

George Washington. August 1860. Engraved.

 90c blue

IM 11 imperf pair —
 single, imperf *3,000.00*
 Quantity: 1 pair reported; singles very rare

According to Lester Brookman a used single, with "good margins," appeared in the Pelander sale of February 1943. A set of **IM 9—IM 11**, including the unique 90c pair, sold at auction for $55,000 in May 2000.

SERIES OF 1857/1860
SPECIAL PRINTING OF 1875

Engraved. Printed by the Continental Bank Note Co. on bright, white paper, without gum. Imperforates are varieties of the perforated stamps issued for the Centennial Exposition of 1876. They vary in color from **IM 9, IM 10** and **IM 11** and can thus be distinguished.

IM 12 1c Franklin, bright blue
IM 13 3c Washington, scarlet
IM 14 5c Jefferson, orange brown
IM 15 10c Washington, blue green
IM 16 12c Washington, greenish black
IM 17 24c Washington, blackish violet
IM 18 30c Franklin, yellow orange
IM 19 90c Washington, deep blue

 set of 8 pairs, imperf **LRS (89)** 71,500.00
 set of 8 imperf margin singles **LRS (85)** 41,250.00
 Quantity: singles very rare; one set
 of pairs reported; plus two pairs
 of the 1c, one pair of the 10c,
 and one pair of the 12c

SERIES OF 1861/1862

Benjamin Franklin. August 17, 1861. Engraved

1c blue

IM 20 used vrt pair, imperf hz —
Quantity: very rare

George Washington. August 17, 1861. Engraved.

3c rose red or various shades

IM 21 imperf pair, ungummed **PRF** 600.00
block of 4, imperf —
block of 8, imprint & plate
No. 11, imperf **LRS (12/99)** 1,897.50
Quantity: scarce

IM 21 typically occurs with mottled paper.

IM 22 vrt pair, imperf hz *2,750.00*
used vrt pair, imperf hz *750.00*
Quantity: rare

3c lake or carmine lake

IM 23 imperf pair 1,750.00
strip of 4, imprint & plate
No. 52, imperf **LRS (5/00)** 2,970.00
bottom block of 8, imprint & plate
No. 52, imperf **LRS (4/98)** 12,100.00
Quantity: scarce; 3 imprint blocks

Trial color proofs were printed from Plate No. 34. Imprint blocks or strips are from Plate No. 52.

George Washington. August 17, 1861. Engraved.

10c green

IM 24 used vrt pair, imperf hz —
Quantity: very rare, possibly unique

George Washington. February 20, 1863. Engraved.

24c dark gray

IM 29 vrt pair, imperf **NRI** —
used single, imperf —
Quantity: 1-3 pairs known

STAMPS WITH GRILLS

Grills, waffle-like in appearance, were impressed on stamps to break their paper fibers and permit better ink absorption, preventing washing and reuse. Several types of grills exist.

A grill: points up, grill covers entire stamp.
C grill: points up, grill measures about 13x16 mm.
F grill: points down, grill measures about 9x13 mm.

George Washington. 1867. Engraved.

3c rose, A grill

IM 30 imperf pair **PRF NRI** 1,500.00
bottom imprint block of 8,
imperf **LRS (12/99)** 6,037.50
Quantity: rare

3c rose, C grill

IM 31 imperf pair **PRF NRI** 1,750.00
imperf margin single with selvage *1,000.00*
Quantity: n/a

☞ Caution: Nineteenth century stamps often occur with large margins that can be trimmed to resemble imperforates. Single stamps, even margin copies, should be regarded with suspicion. Imperforate singles without expert certificate should be avoided.

3c red or rose red, F grill

IM 32 imperf pair **NRI** 1,000.00
Quantity: very rare

IM 33 vrt pair, imperf hz *1,000.00*
Quantity: very rare

SERIES OF 1869
SPECIAL PRINTING OF 1875

Columbus. 1875. Engraved. National Bank Note Co.

15c brown & blue

IM 35 single, imperf hz *3,500.00*
used single, imperf hz **LRS (4/01)** 7,150.00
Quantity: 5-10 unused; 2 used

A gem copy sold for $6,600 at auction in October 1998. No multiples exist.

A unique partial set of imperforate singles of the 1869 issue exists printed on gummed stamp paper that, unlike the regularly issued stamps of the series, lacks grills. The center of the 24c denomination is inverted. They were not regularly issued. The set includes the 1c, 3c, 12c, 15c (type I), 24c, 30c and 90c denominations. This group of seven sold for $94,600 in 1989.

SERIES OF 1870/1871

George Washington. April 1870. Engraved.

3c green, with grill

IM 36 imperf pair **NRI** 1,250.00
block of 16 with plate No. 44, imperf —
Quantity: very scarce

3c green, without grill

IM 37 imperf pair **NRI** 750.00
block of 10 with bottom imprint
& plate No. 11, imperf *5,500.00*
Quantity: rare

SERIES OF 1873

Benjamin Franklin. 1873. Engraved. Secret mark.

1c ultramarine

IM 38 imperf pair **LRS (3/97)** 1,155.00
used imperf pair *600.00*
Quantity: *approx 15 pairs, including
2 mint pairs*

Many are toned and creased. Price is for toned and creased pair.

Andrew Jackson. 1873. Engraved. Secret mark. White wove paper.

2c brown

IM 39 imperf pair —
Quantity: very rare

Andrew Jackson. June 21, 1875. Engraved. Secret mark. Yellowish wove paper.

2c vermilion

IM 40 imperf pair **PRF** *800.00*
imperf block of 4 —
imperf block of 16 with inscription
& plate No. 161 **LRS (4/98)** 5,225.00
Quantity: scarce; *2 plate blocks*

George Washington. 1873. Engraved. Secret mark.

3c green

IM 41 imperf pair **PRF** 850.00
Quantity: n/a

IM 42 used hz pair, imperf vrt —
Quantity: n/a

IM 43 used hz pair, imperf between *1,250.00*
Quantity: rare

3c green, with grill

IM 44 imperf pair **PRF** 750.00
Quantity: n/a

Thomas Jefferson. 1873. Engraved. Secret mark.

10c brown

IM 45 hz pair, imperf between —
used imperf pair *2,750.00*
Quantity: 2 pairs reported

SERIES OF 1879

George Washington. 1879. Engraved.

3c green

IM 46 imperf pair **PRF** *550.00*
Quantity: rare

Thomas Jefferson. 1879. Engraved. Secret mark.

10c brown

IM 47 used vrt pair, imperf between —
Quantity: rare

Commodore O.H. Perry. 1879. Engraved.

90c carmine

IM 48 imperf pair **PRF** *2,250.00*
imperf block of four —
Quantity: rare

Often contains faults. Price is for a sound copy.

George Washington. 1883. Engraved.

2c red brown

IM 49 imperf pair **NRI** —
Quantity: rare

SPECIAL PRINTING OF 1883

George Washington. 1883. Engraved. Soft porous paper.

2c pale red brown

IM 50 hz pair, imperf between **NRI** 2,000.00
top margin inscription strip of 6, center
pair imperf between **LRS (6/96)** 6,325.00
part sheet of 66 with right six pairs
imperf between - affixed to
cardboard **LRS (87)** 17,600.00
Quantity: at least 20 pairs

Price is for a sound copy.

Typically, nineteenth century stamps are heavily hinged, contain only partial original gum and often, small faults. Prices are for stamps in such condition unless otherwise indicated. Sound stamps, stamps with full original gum, and lightly hinged copies sell for a premium.

Andrew Jackson. October 1, 1883. Engraved.

4c blue green

IM 51 imperf pair **PRF** —
Quantity: scarce

Benjamin Franklin. June 11, 1887. Engraved.

1c ultramarine

IM 52 imperf pair 1,000.00
used pair, imperf **LRS (4/01)** 632.50
used strip of 3 on piece —
Quantity: rare

A horizontal strip of 3 on piece postmarked Hoboken, New Jersey,
March 25, 1890 (with toning on the left pair) and a horizontal strip on
cover postmarked Hoboken, New Jersey, have been reported.

George Washington. September 10, 1887. Engraved.

2c green

IM 54 imperf pair 1,000.00
used pair, imperf **LRS (4/01)** 2,200.00
used strip of 3, imperf —
pair on cover, imperf —
Quantity: rare unused; one used pair,
 and one used strip of 3 reported.

James A. Garfield. February 10, 1888. Engraved.

5c indigo

IM 55 imperf pair **PRF** 1,250.00
Quantity: rare

Alexander Hamilton. January 3, 1888. Engraved.

30c orange brown

IM 56 imperf pair **PRF** 1,500.00
Quantity: rare

Often contains faults.

Commodore O.H. Perry. February 28, 1888. Engraved.

90c purple

IM 57 imperf pair **PRF** 3,000.00
Quantity: rare

Usually contains faults.

Typically, nineteenth century stamps are heavily hinged, contain only
partial original gum and often, small faults. Prices are for stamps in
such condition unless otherwise indicated. Sound stamps, stamps with
full original gum, and lightly hinged copies sell for a premium.

ISSUES OF THE AMERICAN BANKNOTE COMPANY
SMALL FORMAT 1890/1893

In order to acquire rare stamps for the official collection
at the National Museum, imperforate stamps, identical to
their perforated counterparts, were exchanged for
acquisitions, such as the 1869 inverts. A total of 56
imperforate sets, mostly in pairs or blocks of four, were
released. Imperforate postage due stamps, series of
1891, were simultaneously released and appear in the
postage due section.

Some regard these stamps as proofs, however, we
regard them as stamps not regularly issued and refer to
them as such (**NRI**).

In addition to the imperforate stamps, proofs of the 2c,
4c, and 5c denominations in various shades similar to the
issued colors exist on gummed stamp paper. The 2c
denomination reportedly exists in 5 shades; the 4c, in 11
shades; and the 5c, in 13 shades. They should not be
confused with the imperforate stamps listed below.

Benjamin Franklin. February 22, 1890. Engraved.

1c dull blue

IM 58	imperf pair **NRI**	150.00
	block of 4, imperf	320.00
	plate block of 12 (No. 14), imperf	1,150.00
	Quantity: 56	

George Washington. February 22, 1890. Engraved.

2c lake (issued without gum)

IM 59	imperf pair **NRI**	100.00
	block of 4, imperf	225.00
	plate block of 12, imperf	—
	Quantity: *56+*	

2c carmine, May 12, 1890

IM 60	imperf pair **NRI**	125.00
	block of 4, imperf	275.00
	plate block of 12 (No. 18), imperf	*900.00*
	Quantity: 56	

Andrew Jackson. February 22, 1890. Engraved.

3c purple

IM 61	imperf pair **NRI**	150.00
	block of 4, imperf	350.00
	top plate block of 12 (No. 21), imperf	—
	Quantity: 56	

Pricing Note: Most examples of this series are heavily hinged, contain disturbed or partial original gum, and often contain faults. Prices are for stamps in such condition. Sound, lightly hinged stamps sell for a premium of 50% to 100% more. Never hinged copies are rare and worth a premium of 100% to 150% more.

Abraham Lincoln. June 2, 1890. Engraved.

4c dark brown

IM 62	imperf pair **NRI**	165.00
	block of 4, imperf	400.00
	Quantity: 56	

Ulysses S. Grant. June 2, 1890. Engraved.

5c chocolate brown

IM 63	imperf pair **NRI**	165.00
	block of 4, imperf	400.00
	top plate block of 12, imperf	—
	Quantity: 56	

James A. Garfield. February 22, 1890. Engraved.

6c brown red

IM 64	imperf pair **NRI**	175.00
	block of 4, imperf	420.00
	top plate block of 12 (No. 23), imperf	*1,200.00*
	Quantity: 56	

William T. Sherman. March 21, 1893. Engraved.

8c lilac

IM 65	imperf pair **NRI**	*1,250.00*
	block of 4, imperf	—
	Quantity: n/a	

Daniel Webster. February 22, 1890. Engraved.

10c green

IM 66	imperf pair NRI	225.00
	imperf block of 4	420.00
	Quantity: 56	

Henry Clay. February 22, 1890. Engraved.

15c indigo

IM 67	imperf pair NRI	500.00
	imperf block of 4	1,100.00
	plate block of 12 (No. 22), imperf	*3,750.00*
	Quantity: 56	

Thomas Jefferson. February 22, 1890. Engraved.

30c black

IM 68	imperf pair NRI	750.00
	imperf block of 4	1,650.00
	Quantity: 56	

Commodore O.H. Perry. February 22, 1890. Engraved.

90c orange

IM 69	imperf pair NRI	1,350.00
	imperf block of 4	2,500.00
	Quantity: 56	

Refer to note on pricing for this series preceding **IM 58**.

COLUMBIAN SERIES OF 1893

The B. K. Miller Collection at the New York Public Library Collection contains a complete set of imperforate horizontal pairs, 1c-$5. They were originally the property of John Wanamaker, Postmaster General 1889-1893.

Columbus Landing. January 2, 1893. Engraved.

2c purple maroon

IM 70	imperf pair, ungummed PW	1,750.00
	imperf block of 4	*5,000.00*
	Quantity: 50-100	

These stamps are from a crumpled sheet, which id printer's waste. All known copies are ungummed and defective.

SERIES OF 1894

Similar to the Series of 1890 except triangles added to the upper corners. Printed on unwatermarked paper.

George Washington. October 5, 1894. Engraved.

2c pink, type I

| IM 71 | vrt pair, imperf hz | *2,250.00* |
| | Quantity: *rare* | |

2c carmine, type I

| IM 72 | vrt pair, imperf hz | *2,000.00* |
| | Quantity: *rare* | |

| IM 73 | hz pair, imperf between | *1,750.00* |
| | Quantity: *rare* | |

2c carmine, type III

IM 74 hz pair, imperf vrt 1,500.00
Quantity: *rare*

IM 75 hz pair, imperf between 1,500.00
Quantity: *rare*

Andrew Jackson. September 24, 1894. Engraved.

3c purple

IM 76 imperf pair, ungummed **NRI** 200.00
imperf block of 4, ungummed 420.00
imperf plate block of 6, ungummed —
Quantity: 400

Abraham Lincoln. September 11, 1894. Engraved.

4c dark brown

IM 77 imperf pair, ungummed **NRI** 200.00
imperf block of 4, ungummed 420.00
imperf plate block of 6 (No. 50),
 ungummed **LRS (4/98)** 1,760.00
Quantity: 400

Ulysses S. Grant. September 28, 1894. Engraved.

5c chocolate brown

IM 78 imperf pair, ungummed **NRI** 225.00
imperf block of 4, ungummed 500.00
imperf plate block of 6, ungummed —
Quantity: 300-400

IM 79 vrt pair, imperf hz, with gum *2,000.00*
vrt strip of 3, imperf hz, with gum *2,100.00*
block of 9 with plate No. and imprint —
Quantity: uncertain, but less than
 one pane of 100

James A. Garfield. July 18, 1894. Engraved.

6c dull brown

IM 80 vrt pair, imperf hz *950.00*
block of 4, imperf hz —
plate block of 6 —
Quantity: 100

Usually with disturbed gum or faults. Price is for copy with usual disturbed gum or faults. Sound copies sell for more.

Daniel Webster. September 17, 1894. Engraved.

10c dark green

IM 81 imperf pair, ungummed **NRI** 500.00
imperf block of 4, ungummed 1,100.00
plate block of 6 —
Quantity: 400

Lester Brookman mentions that the 50c denomination was reported as a single on cover. Brookman also describes a bottom margin pair with no perforations between the bottoms of the stamps and the selvage. He also mentions that the $1 denomination (type I, broken circle around the $1) exists imperforate, but does not mention its form, i.e., imperforate horizontally, vertically, or between.

Note: IM 76, IM 77, IM 78 and **IM 81** were issued without gum. Those with gum had it added later.

Although catalogue prices are based on the best information available at press time, readers should be aware that prices for error stamps fluctuate over time, and therefore, are advised to contact dealers active in the error stamp market for timely quotes when buying or selling.

SERIES OF 1895

Similar to the Series of 1894 except with double-line watermark USPS horizontally or vertically.

Like the Series of 1890, quantities of imperforate stamps of this series reached public hands, this time via Gilbert Jones, owner of the New York Times, who accepted them in exchange for services rendered to the Bureau of Engraving and Printing. They are gummed and identical to regular stamps of the series except for the lack of perforations. It is reported that the 1c, 2c, 3c, 4c and 8c denominations exist used philatelically on cover. Some regard this issue as proofs, however, we regard them as stamps that were not regularly issued.

Benjamin Franklin. January 17, 1898. Engraved. Double-line watermark.

1c dull blue

IM 82	imperf pair **NRI**	150.00
	block of 4, imperf	320.00
	plate block of 6, imperf	*2,000.00*
	used pair on cover, imperf	—
	Quantity: 900 stamps	

IM 83	hz pair, imperf vrt	—
	plate strip of 3, imperf vrt	—
	Quantity: 1-5 pairs	

George Washington. 1895. Engraved. Double-line watermark.

2c carmine, type III

IM 84	imperf pair **NRI**	175.00
	block of 4, imperf	400.00
	plate strip of 3, (No. 319), imperf	*675.00*
	plate block of 6 (No. 319), imperf	*2,250.00*
	used pair **LRS (4/01)**	1,980.00
	Quantity: 500	

Andrew Jackson. October 31, 1895. Engraved. Double-line watermark.

3c dark purple violet

IM 85	imperf pair **NRI**	200.00
	block of 4, imperf	420.00
	used pair on cover, imperf	—
	Quantity: 300	

Abraham Lincoln. June 5, 1895. Engraved. Double-line watermark.

4c black brown

IM 86	imperf pair **NRI**	200.00
	block of 4, imperf	420.00
	used pair on cover, imperf	—
	Quantity: 300	

Ulysses S. Grant. June 11, 1895. Engraved. Double-line watermark.

5c deep reddish brown

IM 87	imperf pair **NRI**	200.00
	block of 4, imperf	420.00
	Quantity: 300	

James A. Garfield. August 31, 1895. Engraved. Double-line watermark.

6c claret brown

IM 88	imperf pair **NRI**	200.00
	block of 4, imperf	420.00
	plate block of 6, imperf	—
	Quantity: 300	

William T. Sherman. July 22, 1895. Engraved. Double-line watermark.

8c deep claret brown

IM 89	imperf pair **NRI**	300.00
	block of 4, imperf	625.00
	used pair on cover, imperf	—
	Quantity: 300	

Daniel Webster. June 7, 1895. Engraved. Double-line watermark.

10c pale dull green

IM 90	imperf pair **NRI**	225.00
	block of 4, imperf	475.00
	Quantity: 400	

Henry Clay. September 10, 1895. Engraved. Double-line watermark.

15c deep indigo

IM 91	imperf pair **NRI**	750.00
	block of 4, imperf	1,500.00
	Quantity: 100	

Thomas Jefferson. November 9, 1895. Engraved. Double-line watermark.

50c orange

IM 92	imperf pair **NRI**	750.00
	block of 4, imperf	1,500.00
	Quantity: 100	

Commodore O.H. Perry. August 12, 1895. Engraved. Double-line watermark.

$1 black, type I

IM 93	imperf pair **NRI**	1,250.00
	block of 4, imperf	2,600.00
	Quantity: 100	

James Madison. August 13, 1895. Engraved. Double-line watermark.

$2 blue

IM 94	imperf pair **NRI**	2,250.00
	block of 4, imperf	5,000.00
	Quantity: 100	

John Marshall. August 16, 1895. Engraved. Double-line watermark.

$5 dark green

IM 95	imperf pair **NRI**	2,500.00
	block of 4, imperf	5,250.00
	Quantity: 100	

Refer to the pricing note preceding **IM 82** regarding this series.

Troops Guarding Train. June 1898. Engraved.

8c violet brown

IM 96 vrt pair, imperf hz 22,500.00
 vrt strip of 4, imperf hz —
 block of 4, top or bottom plate
 number, imperf hz —
 Quantity: 25 pairs

Price is for a sound copy.

IM 97 IM 98

George Washington. November 12, 1903. Engraved.

2c carmine

IM 97 vrt pair, imperf hz 5,000.00
 block of 4, imperf hz **LRS (9/00)** 16,500.00
 Quantity: 1 pair, 1 strip of three
 and 2 blocks of four

IM 98 vrt pair, imperf between *1,250.00*
 Quantity: rare

☛ Caution. Do not confuse **IM 97** and **IM 98** with similar stamps of 1906 which were regularly issued imperforate. Expert certificate recommended.

Pairs similar to **IM 98** exist rouletted between. Panes lacking perforations between the top two rows were rouletted by the postmaster in San Francisco and sold over the counter in the normal course of business.

Hinging. Prices for stamps preceding **IM 196** are for hinged copies. Never hinged copies sell for a premium ranging from 25% to 100% or more depending on the scarcity of an item, and the scarcity of never hinged copies of an item. These guidelines do not apply to prices for ultra-rare or unique items, which may not exist never hinged.

Thomas Jefferson. April 30, 1904. Engraved.

2c carmine

IM 99 vrt pair, imperf hz 9,000.00
 as above, line pair —
 block of 4, imperf hz *18,000.00*
 plate block of 4, imperf hz —
 margin block of 4, arrow at lower
 left, imperf hz **LRS (5/98)** 28,600.00
 Quantity: 19 pairs & 3 blocks as listed

Well centered copies sell for a premium.

Benjamin Franklin. 1908. Booklet pane. Engraved. Double-line watermark.

1c green

IM 99A hz pair, imperf between **NRI** *1,000.00*
 Quantity: n/a

From a booklet pane experiment.

George Washington. February 12, 1912. Engraved. Single-line watermark. Perf 12.

1c green

IM 100 vrt pair, imperf hz *750.00*
 vrt strip of three, imperf hz —
 Quantity: rare

☛ Caution. Do not confuse this stamp with that of identical design, which was regularly issued imperforate. Expert certificate recommended.

George Washington. 1914. Engraved. Single-line watermark. Perf 10.

1c green

IM 101 vrt pair, imperf hz **LRS (4/00)** 2,820.00
used vrt pair, imperf hz —
Quantity: very rare

IM 101A vrt pair, imperf between **LRS (5/00)** 5,500.00
Quantity: 2 reported

IM 101A results from a foldover in which the upper right pair is imperf between and contains a straight edge at the top.

IM 102 booklet pane of 6, imperf,
ungummed 1,650.00
Quantity: 60 reported

Price is for a sound, well centered pane.

George Washington. 1917. Engraved. No watermark. Perf 11.

1c green

IM 103 vrt pair, imperf hz 200.00
block of 4, imperf hz 400.00
Quantity: 1 pane of 100 reported

IM 104 hz pair, imperf between 95.00
Quantity: n/a

IM 105 vrt pair, imperf between 400.00
Quantity: scarce

☛ Caution. It is possible to fabricate Nos. **IM 103—IM 108** by adding perforations to completely imperforate regularly issued stamps of identical design. Expert certificate strongly advised.

George Washington. 1917. Engraved. No watermark. Perf 11.

2c rose, type I

IM 106 vrt pair, imperf hz 150.00
Quantity: n/a

IM 107 hz pair, imperf vrt 300.00
used hz pair, imperf vrt *175.00*
Quantity: 100 pairs reported

IM 108 vrt pair, imperf between 500.00
used vrt pair, imperf between *250.00*
Quantity: *very scarce*

☛ Caution. Pairs are known with blind perfs that can be ironed out and eliminated to the naked eye, resulting in dangerous fakes. Pairs are also known with blind perfs occurring in the upper stamp due to a wandering perforating wheel. All pairs should be checked carefully. Copies lacking gum should be regarded with special caution. Expert certificate strongly advised.

22

George Washington. 1917. Engraved. No watermark. Perf. 11.

3c violet, type I

IM 109 vrt pair, imperf hz 425.00
 Quantity: *25 pairs*

3c dark violet, type II

IM 110 vrt pair, imperf hz *350.00*
 used vrt pair, imperf hz *150.00*
 Quantity: 40-50 pairs reported

George Washington. 1917. Engraved. No watermark. Perf 11.

5c blue

IM 111 hz pair, imperf between 2,250.00
 hz pair, plate No. 8902 in top
 margin, imperf between —
 Quantity: *very rare*

Benjamin Franklin. 1917. Engraved. No watermark. Perf 11.

8c olive bistre

IM 112 vrt pair, imperf between —
 used vrt pair, imperf between —
 Quantity: 1 pair unused and
 2 pair used reported

Benjamin Franklin. 1917. Engraved. No watermark. Perf 11.

20c light ultramarine

IM 113 vrt pair, imperf between *1,500.00*
 as above, used **LRS (3/99)** 1,437.50
 Quantity: rare, used pair
 possibly unique

☛ Caution. These stamps are often encountered with blind perfs that can be ironed out and eliminated to the naked eye, resulting in dangerous fakes. Copies lacking gum should be regarded with special caution. The discovery panes of this error contained mostly pairs with blind perforations and yielded only about 5 truly imperf pairs per pane. Blind-perf pairs are comparatively plentiful and can be deceptive.

Benjamin Franklin. 1917. Engraved. No watermark. Perf 11.

50c red violet

IM 114 vrt pair, imperf between —
 vrt pair, imperf between precanceled
 AKRON, OHIO LRS (9/00) 6,600.00
 Quantity: very rare

☛ Caution. Beware pairs with blind perfs.

George Washington. 1918. Offset lithography. No watermark. Perf 11.

1c gray green

IM 115 hz pair, imperf between 95.00
 Quantity: n/a

All known examples contain a straight edge on the right.

George Washington. 1919. Engraved. Rotary Press. No watermark. Design measures 19.5 to 20mm by 22 to 22.25mm. Perf 11x10.

1c green

IM 116	vrt pair, imperf hz	50.00
	used vrt pair, imperf hz	*75.00*
	block of 4, imperf hz	100.00
	top plate block of 6, imperf hz	750.00
	Quantity: 1,000+	

George Washington. 1919. Offset lithography. No watermark. Perf 12½.

1c gray green

IM 117	hz pair, imperf vrt	650.00
	block of 4, imperf vrt	—
	Quantity: n/a	

George Washington. 1919. Engraved. Rotary press. No watermark. Design measures 19.5 to 20mm by 22 to 22.25mm. Perf 11x10.

2c carmine rose, type III

IM 118	vrt pair, imperf hz	50.00
	used vrt pair, imperf hz	*125.00*
	block of 4, imperf hz	100.00
	plate block of 8, imperf hz	800.00
	Quantity: 1,000+	

| IM 119 | hz pair, imperf vrt | 850.00 |
| | Quantity: 25 pairs | |

George Washington. 1920. Offset lithography. No watermark. Perf 11.

2c carmine, type V

| IM 120 | vrt pair, imperf hz | *850.00* |
| | Quantity: 2-3 pairs reported | |

IM 121	hz pair, imperf vrt	*1,250.00*
	used hz pair, imperf vrt	—
	Quantity: n/a	

☛ Caution. Do not confuse **IM 120—IM 124** with the regularly issued imperforates of the same design.

2c carmine, type Va

| IM 122 | vrt pair, imperf between | *1,250.00* |
| | Quantity: rare | |

2c carmine, type VI

| IM 123 | vrt pair, imperf hz | — |
| | Quantity: very rare | |

| IM 124 | vrt pair, imperf between | *1,250.00* |
| | Quantity: very rare | |

George Washington. 1921. Engraved. Rotary press. No watermark. Design 19 by 22.5mm. Perf 10.

1c green

| IM 125 | hz pair, imperf between | *1,250.00* |
| | Quantity: *rare* | |

SERIES OF 1922/26

Stamps of 1922/26 series were printed by flat plate press and normally perforated 11. Designs measure 18.5 to 19mm by 22mm.

1922 Series, ½c-$5. Engraved. Flat plate press.

IM 127 ½c Nathan Hale
IM 128 1c Benjamin Franklin
IM 129 1½c Warren G. Harding
IM 130 2c George Washington
IM 133 3c Abraham Lincoln
IM 134 4c Martha Washington
IM 137 5c Theodore Roosevelt
IM 139 6c James A. Garfield
IM 140 7c William McKinley
IM 141 8c Ulysses S. Grant
IM 142 9c Thomas Jefferson
IM 143 10c James Monroe
IM 145 11c Rutherford B. Hayes
IM 147 12c Grover Cleveland
IM 150 13c Benjamin Harrison
IM 151 14c American Indian
IM 152 15c Statue of Liberty
IM 153 17c Woodrow Wilson
IM 154 20c Golden Gate
IM 156 25c Niagara Falls
IM 158 30c Buffalo
IM 159 50c Tomb of the Unknown Soldier
IM 160 $1 Lincoln Memorial
IM 161 $2 U.S. Capitol
IM 162 $5 America

blocks of 4, imperf, ungummed **NRI** —
Quantity: *unique*

The set of imperforate blocks of 4 as listed above, ½c through $5, was sold at auction in 1968 for $12,200. These stamps were not regularly issued, and as far as is known, the set of blocks is unique.

George Washington. January 15, 1923. Engraved. Flat plate press.

2c carmine

IM 131 hz pair, imperf vrt 225.00
plate block of 6, imperf vrt —
Quantity: few hundred

Exists misperfed horizontally.

IM 132 vrt pair, imperf hz 3,250.00
Quantity: 3 pairs reported

☛ Caution. It is possible to fabricate Nos. **IM 131-IM 132** regularly issued imperforate stamps of the same design. Beware fakes. Expert certificate advised.

Martha Washington. January 15, 1923. Engraved. Flat plate press.

4c brown

IM 135 hz pair, imperf between —
Quantity: reportedly unique

IM 136 vrt pair, imperf hz **LRS (11/00)** 10,450.00
Quantity: *unique*

Theodore Roosevelt. October 27, 1922. Engraved. Flat plate press.

5c blue

IM 137A imperf pair, gummed 1,500.00
imperf plate block of 6, gummed *7,500.00*
Quantity: 1 pane of 100; 2 plate blocks

IM 138 hz pair, imperf vrt *1,500.00*
Quantity: 10 pairs reported

James Monroe. January 15, 1923. Engraved. Flat plate press.

10c yellow

IM 143	imperf pair, ungummed	1,750.00
	block of 4	—
	plate block of 6 LRS (6/96)	8,800.00
	Quantity: 2 panes	

Both panes contained large areas defaced by inspector's blue pencil marks. It is estimated that only 40 to 50 unmarked pairs exist. Blue pencil marked pairs sell for less. **IM 143** was issued without gum.

Grover Cleveland. May 20, 1923. Engraved. Flat plate press.

12c brown violet

IM 148	imperf pair, gummed	—
	Quantity: rare	

IM 149	hz pair, imperf vrt	*1,250.00*
	block of 4, imperf vrt	—
	Quantity: *very scarce*	

Often without gum or with government splicing paper on reverse.

IM 144	vrt pair, imperf hz	1,250.00
	block of 4 LRS (12/99)	2,990.00
	Quantity: 50 pairs	

Most are poorly centered. Well centered pairs sell for a premium. Twenty-seven pairs contain splicing paper on the reverse or blue pencil marks on the front. All pairs originally contained penciled position numbers on the reverse. The numbers are missing on regummed pairs.

Golden Gate. May 1, 1923. Engraved. Flat plate press.

20c carmine rose

IM 155	hz pair, imperf vrt	2,000.00
	pair with plate No. 19646 at left,	
	imperf vrt LRS (9/00)	4,675.00
	block of 4, imperf vrt	—
	Quantity: 50 pairs	

Rutherford Hayes. October 4, 1922. Engraved. Flat plate press.

11c light blue

IM 146	imperf vrt pair precanceled	
	SAN FRANCISCO, CALIFORNIA	—
	imperf vrt strip of 3 precanceled	
	as above LRS (5/00)	17,600.00
	Quantity: 1 pair nearly severed by scissors	
	cut and 1 strip of 3 reported	

Niagara Falls. November 11, 1922. Engraved. Flat plate press.

25c green

IM 157	vrt pair, imperf hz	*1,000.00*
	block with plate No. 14063 at right,	
	imperf hz	—
	Quantity: rare	

The 1½c, 2c, 4c, 5c, 6c and 8c denominations of this series exist imperforate with various degrees of smearing or underinking. They are the result of impressions made during the cleaning of printing plates with solvent and are reported to have originally come on the market from a waste paper company. They are not recognized as postage stamps. They are mentioned here as a matter of record only.

Theodore Roosevelt. 1925. Engraved. Rotary press. Perf 10.

5c blue

IM 163 hz pair, imperf vrt precanceled
 PORTLAND, OREGON LRS (5/00) 9,900.00
 Quantity: *very rare, possibly unique*

Benjamin Franklin. June 10, 1927. Engraved. Rotary press. Perf 11x10½.

1c green

IM 164 vrt pair, imperf between **LRS (10/00)** 2,420.00
 as above, used —
 Quantity: very rare

IM 165 hz pair, imperf between **LRS (10/00)** 7,425.00
 Quantity: very´rare, possibly unique

George Washington. December 10, 1926. Engraved. Perf 11x10½.

2c carmine

IM 166 hz pair, imperf between —
 Quantity: very rare

IM 167 vrt pair, imperf between —
 Quantity: very rare

William McKinley. March 24, 1927. Engraved. Rotary press. Perf 11x10½.

7c black

IM 168 vrt pair, imperf between 225.00
 as above, used 75.00
 block of 4, imperf between hz —
 Quantity: n/a

☛ Caution. These stamps are known with blind perfs that can be ironed out and eliminated to the naked eye, resulting in dangerous fakes. Copies lacking gum should be regarded with special caution. Expert certificate advised.

IM 169 vrt pair, imperf between,
 precanceled **MOBILE, ALA.** 120.00
 Quantity: n/a

☛ Caution. Refer to note following **IM 168**.

Warren G. Harding. September 1, 1923. Engraved. Flat plate press. Design measures 19.25mm by 22.25mm.

2c black

IM 170	hz pair, imperf vrt	1,500.00
	Quantity: n/a	

☛ Caution. It is possible to fabricate this error from regularly issued imperforate stamps of the same design. Expert certificate strongly advised. Most pairs are centered to bottom. Price is for a copy centered to bottom. Well centered pairs sell for more.

Battle of White Plains. October 18, 1926. Engraved.

2c carmine rose

IM 171	vrt pair, imperf between	—
	Quantity: very scarce	

General Von Steuben. September 17, 1930. Engraved

2c carmine rose

IM 172	imperf pair	3,000.00
	block of 4, imperf	—
	plate block of 6, imperf	—
	Quantity: 1 pane of 100	

Hinging. Prices for stamps preceding **IM 196** are for hinged copies. Never hinged copies sell for a premium ranging from 25% to 100% or more depending on the scarcity of the item, and the scarcity of never hinged copies of the item. These guidelines do not apply to prices for ultra-rare or unique items, which may not exist never hinged.

Although catalogue prices are based on the best information available at press time, readers should be aware that prices for error stamps fluctuate over time, and therefore, are advised to contact dealers active in the error stamp market for timely quotes when buying or selling.

Yorktown Sesquicentennial. October 19, 1931. Engraved.

2c carmine & black

IM 173	hz pair, imperf vrt	4,500.00
	block of 4, imperf vrt	9,500.00
	hz block of 6, imperf vrt	—
	hz center line block of 106, imperf vrt	—
	bottom plate block of 10, imperf vrt	—
	Quantity: 1 pane of 50	

George Washington Bicentennial. June 16, 1932. Engraved.

3c violet

IM 174	vrt pair, imperf between	300.00
	used pair, imperf between **LRS (4/01)**	1,375.00
	as above, precanceled	
	PHILADELPHIA, PENNSYLVANIA	
	LRS (4/00)	880.00
	Quantity: mint n/a; at least 1 used pair,	
	3 precanceled pairs	

☛ Caution. Pairs exist with blind perforations that can be ironed out and eliminated to the naked eye, resulting in dangerous fakes. Copies lacking gum should be regarded with special caution.

William Penn. October 24, 1932. Engraved.

3c violet

IM 175	vrt pair, imperf hz	—
	Quantity: very rare	

General Tadeusz Kosciuszko. October 13, 1933. Engraved.

5c blue

IM 176 hz pair, imperf vrt 2,250.00
 block of 4, imperf vrt 5,000.00
 plate block of 8, imperf vrt —
 Quantity: 1 pane of 100 stamps

Often with heavy natural gum creases or bends.

Maryland Tercentenary. May 23, 1934. Engraved.

3c carmine rose

IM 177 hz pair, imperf between LRS (89) 6,600.00
 Quantity: unique

A single unique pair of **IM 177** exists in a block of 12 stamps, the error resulting from a foldover.

Wisconsin Tercentenary. July 7, 1934. Engraved.

3c violet

IM 178 vrt pair, imperf hz 350.00
 Quantity: n/a

IM 179 hz pair, imperf vrt 450.00
 bottom plate strip of 10, imperf vrt 2,350.00
 Quantity: approx 80 pairs reported

NATIONAL PARK SERIES OF 1934

The items listed below are errors of the fully gummed, perforated stamps of National Parks issue. They are similar in appearance to the Farley Special Printing which was issued fully imperforate and without gum.

Yosemite. July 16, 1934. Engraved.

1c green

IM 180 vrt pair, imperf hz, with gum 1,500.00
 Quantity: 16 pairs or strips of three

☛ Caution. Fakes exist. All known genuine examples are signed "S.A." (Spencer Anderson) on the reverse in indelible pencil. Those rubber stamped "Sloane" are fakes.

☛ Caution. It is possible to fabricate **IM 178-IM 186** from completely imperforate stamps of identical designs from the Farley Special Printing of 1935, which were issued without gum. In 1940, the Bureau of Engraving & Printing offered to gum Farley Special Printing sheets submitted by collectors. Therefore, presence of government gum on part-perforate stamps is not necessarily an indication of genuineness. Expert certificate advised for part-perforate error stamps that have Farley Special Printing counterparts.

Hinging. Prices for stamps preceding **IM 196** are for hinged copies. Never hinged copies sell for a premium, which can range from 25% to 100% or more depending on the scarcity of an item, and the scarcity of never hinged copies of the item. These guidelines do not apply to prices for ultra-rare or unique items, which may not exist in never hinged condition.

Although catalogue prices are based on the best information available at press time, readers should be aware that prices for error stamps fluctuate over time, and therefore, are advised to contact dealers active in the error stamp market for timely quotes when buying or selling.

Grand Canyon. July 24, 1934. Engraved.

2c red

IM 181 vrt pair, imperf hz, with gum 600.00
top plate block of 6, imperf hz,
 with gum —
Quantity: 2-3 panes

IM 182 hz pair, imperf vrt, with gum 600.00
bottom plate strip of 10,
 imperf vrt, with gum 2,500.00
Quantity: 2-3 panes

☛ Caution. Fakes exist. See second note following **IM 180**.

Mt. Rainier. August 3, 1934. Engraved.

3c violet

IM 183 vrt pair, imperf hz, with gum 450.00
bottom plate block of 6,
 imperf hz, with gum —
Quantity: 1 pane

☛ Caution. Fakes exist. See second note following **IM 180**.

Mesa Verde. September 25, 1934. Engraved.

4c brown

IM 184 vrt pair, imperf hz, with gum 650.00
Quantity: 15 pairs

Approximately 6 to 9 of the 15 known pairs have brown Post Office
paper affixed to the reverse. Copies without brown paper sell a for 50%
to 100% premium or more.

Yellowstone. July 30, 1934. Engraved.

5c blue

IM 185 hz pair, imperf vrt, with gum 700.00
plate block of 6 —
Quantity: 50 pairs

☛ Caution. Fakes exist. See second note following **IM 180**.

Acadia. October 2, 1934. Engraved.

7c black

IM 186 hz pair, imperf vrt, with gum 600.00
top plate strip of 10,
 imperf vrt, with gum LRS (4/98) 4,675.00
Quantity: 50 pairs

☛ Caution. It is possible to fabricate **IM 178-IM 186** from imperforate
stamps of the Farley Special Printing. Refer to note following **IM 180**.

PRESIDENTIAL SERIES OF 1938

Martha Washington. May 5, 1938. Engraved.

1½c brown

IM 188 hz pair, imperf between 150.00
Quantity: n/a

IM 189 hz pair, imperf between,
precanceled **SAINT LOUIS, MO.** 20.00
Quantity: few thousand

Thomas Jefferson. June 16, 1938. Engraved.

3c violet

IM 190 imperf pair *2,750.00*
Quantity: very rare

☛ The 3c Jefferson was counterfeited to defraud the post office. The printer was raided and his stock seized; nevertheless, a small number of the counterfeits, fully gummed and imperforate, escaped. Counterfeits were lithographed and thus can be distinguished from engraved genuine stamps. Gum on counterfeits lacks the gum-breaking ridges found on genuine stamps and is much more yellow than gum on genuine stamps. **IM 190** should possess large outer margins.

IM 191 hz pair, imperf between *1,100.00*
booklet pane of 6, imperf between vrt —
booklet pane, imperf between vrt, vrt
gutter between **LRS (2/99)** 2,415.00
Quantity: 10 pairs; 1 pane with gutter

☛ Refer to note following **IM 190**. The booklet pane with the vertical gutter contains 3 errors pairs plus 6 additional stamps or parts of stamps, one on either side of each error pair.

Woodrow Wilson. August 29, 1938. Engraved.

$1 purple & black

IM 192 vrt pair, imperf hz 1,500.00
top plate block of 8, imperf hz *8,500.00*
arrow block of 6, imperf hz —
Quantity: 50 pairs reported, including
the unique plate block

IM 193 vrt pair, imperf between *2,750.00*
Quantity: very rare

Woodrow Wilson. August 31, 1954. Engraved.

$1 reddish purple & black

IM 194 vrt pair, imperf hz 1,000.00
Quantity: 1-2 panes of 100 reported

IM 195 vrt pair, imperf between *7,500.00*
block of 4, imperf hz between —
Quantity: 10 pairs

IM 194 and **IM 195** were printed by the dry process on somewhat thicker paper than that of **IM 192** and **IM 193**. The gum of the 1954 stamps is smooth and clear, and the purple color is decidedly more reddish than that of the 1938 issue.

Hinging. Prices for stamps before **IM 196** are for hinged copies. Never hinged copies sell for a premium, which can range from 25% to 100% or more depending on the scarcity of an item, and the scarcity of never hinged copies of the item. These guidelines do not apply to ultra-rare or unique items. Prices for stamps after **IM 196** are for never hinged copies; hinged copies sell for less.

NATIONAL DEFENSE SERIES OF 1940

Statue of Liberty. October 16, 1940. Engraved.

1c green

IM 196 vrt pair, imperf between 500.00
 Quantity: 100-200 pairs reported

IM 197 hz pair, imperf between 35.00
 Quantity: several thousand pairs

IM 198 hz pair, imperf between, precanceled
 GLENDALE, CALIF. 75.00
 Quantity: n/a

☛ Caution. Often with blind perfs or a few punched perf holes.

Anti-aircraft gun. October 16, 1940. Engraved.

2c rose carmine

IM 199 hz pair, imperf between 40.00
 Quantity: several thousand

☛ Caution. Often with blind perfs or few punched perf holes.

Torch. October 16, 1940. Engraved.

3c violet

IM 200 hz pair, imperf between 25.00
 Quantity: several thousand

☛ Caution. Often with blind perfs or a few punched perf holes.

Mt. Palomar. August 30, 1948. Engraved.

3c blue

IM 201 vrt pair, imperf between 500.00
 plate block of 4, imperf vrt between *750.00*
 Quantity: *350+ pairs, 15+ plate*
 blocks (each with 2 pairs) reported

LIBERTY SERIES OF 1954

Statue of Liberty. June 24, 1954. Engraved.

3c deep violet

IM 202 imperf pair *2,500.00*
 block of 6, imperf —
 Quantity: 5-10 pairs reported

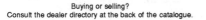

Buying or selling?
Consult the dealer directory at the back of the catalogue.

IM 203 hz pair, imperf between *2,500.00*
booklet pane of 6, as above —
Quantity: 5-10 pairs

Abraham Lincoln. July 31, 1958. Booklet pane of 6. Engraved.

4c red violet

IM 204 booklet pane of 6, imperf hz —
Quantity: *very rare, possibly unique*

IM 205 hz pair, imperf between **LRS (10/94)** 3,575.00
Quantity: *very rare, possibly unique*

IM 205 occurs as the result of a booklet pane foldover.

Theodore Roosevelt. March 1957. Engraved. BEP.

6c rose red

IM 205A imperf block of 4 **LRS (7/00)** 23,000.00
Quantity: 1 block of 4

IM 205A is of the dry printing version first released in March 1957.

Where possible, illustrations of actual error stamps have been used. They are bordered in black. Illustrations of normal stamps have been used in cases where error stamp illustrations were not available, or where an error illustration would not adequately illustrate the error. Illustrations of normal stamps appear without black border.

COIL STAMPS

George Washington. October 8, 1954. Coil. Engraved.

1c green

IM 206 imperf pair *2,250.00*
Quantity: 13 pairs reported

Thomas Jefferson. October 22, 1954. Coil. Engraved.

2c carmine rose

IM 207 imperf pair 600.00
line pair, imperf *1,200.00*
spliced pair or strip, imperf —
Quantity: 100 pairs reported

Transition multiples exist.

IM 208 imperf pair, precanceled
RIVERDALE, MD 550.00
line pair, imperf —
Quantity: 200 pairs reported

Statue of Liberty. July 20, 1954. Coil. Engraved.

3c deep violet

IM 209 imperf pair 1,500.00
line pair, imperf —
used strip of 3, imperf *850.00*
Quantity: 30 pairs reported

Abraham Lincoln. July 31, 1958. Coil. Engraved.

4c red violet

IM 210	imperf pair	90.00
	line pair, imperf	200.00
	spliced pair or strip, imperf	—
	used pair, imperf	*75.00*
	Quantity: 500+ pairs reported	

Exists miscut. Transition multiples exist and sell for a premium.

IM 211	imperf pair, precanceled	
	SEATTLE, WASH.	—
	Quantity: rare	

Paul Revere. February 25, 1965. Coil. Engraved.

25c green

IM 212	imperf pair	25.00
	line pair, imperf	50.00
	spliced pair or strip, imperf	—
	Quantity: 1,200 pairs reported	

Exists miscut. Most copies are poorly centered as illustrated. Price is for a poorly centered copy. Add a 66% premium for a well centered copy. Transition multiples exist and sell for a premium.

Jose de San Martin. February 25, 1959. Engraved.

4c blue

IM 213	hz pair, imperf between	1,500.00
	Quantity: 20 pairs reported	

Often poorly centered. Price is for a poorly centered copy.

IM 214 IM 216

Ephraim McDowell. December 3, 1959. Engraved.

4c maroon

IM 214	vrt pair, imperf hz	300.00
	plate block of 4, imperf hz	—
	Quantity: 210 pairs reported	
IM 215	vrt pair, imperf between	500.00
	Quantity: 50+ pairs reported	

Thomas G. Masaryk. March 7, 1960. Engraved.

4c blue

IM 216	vrt pair, imperf between	*3,250.00*
	Quantity: 10 pairs	

Thomas G. Masaryk. March 7, 1960. Engraved.

8c yellow, blue & red

IM 217	hz pair, imperf between	—
	Quantity: 3 pairs reported	

The term "transition multiple" refers to errors appearing in combination with normal or nearly-normal stamps. Generally, a pair, strip, or block containing one or more error stamps, one or more normal stamps, and, in the case of color-omitted errors, one or more stamps with color(s) partially omitted. Transition multiples sell for a premium.

SEATO. May 31, 1960. Engraved.

4c blue

IM 218 vrt pair, imperf between 150.00
plate block of 4, imperf hz between —
Quantity: 100-200 pairs reported

Winslow Homer. December 15, 1962. Engraved.

4c multicolored

IM 219 hz pair, imperf between *6,750.00*
hz pair with plate No.,
imperf between —
Quantity: 4 pairs reported

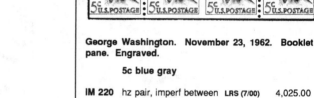

George Washington. November 23, 1962. Booklet pane. Engraved.

5c blue gray

IM 220 hz pair, imperf between **LRS (7/00)** 4,025.00
hz pair (1 stamp, 1 label),
imperf between —
booklet pane, imperf vrt between
LRS (5/98) *5,750.00*
Quantity: very rare

IM 220 results from miscut booklet panes and also exists se-tenant with label containing slogan.

COIL STAMP

George Washington. November 23, 1962. Coil. Engraved.

5c blue gray

IM 221 imperf pair 425.00
line pair, imperf *1,000.00*
spliced strip of 8 with 2 line pairs —
Quantity: *50+ pairs reported*

Transition multiples exist and sell for a premium. Exists tagged and untagged. Often with gum problems. Price is for copy with sound gum.

U. S. Flag. January 9, 1963. Engraved.

5c red & blue

IM 222 hz pair, imperf between *1,500.00*
Quantity: 3-4 pairs reported

☛ Caution. Pairs exist with blind perfs. Expert certificate advised.

Appomattox. April 9, 1965. Engraved.

5c blue & black

IM 223 hz pair, imperf vrt —
 Quantity: *very rare*

☞ Caution. Pairs exist with nearly invisible blind perfs. Expert certificate advised.

COIL STAMPS

Thomas Jefferson. January 12, 1968. Coil. Engraved.

1c green

IM 224 imperf pair 25.00
 line pair, imperf 55.00
 Quantity: 1,000+ pairs

 IM 225 IM 226

Francis Parkman. November 4, 1975. Coil. Engraved.

3c violet

IM 225 imperf pair 25.00
 line pair, imperf 45.00
 Quantity: 1,000+ pairs

IM 226 imperf pair, precanceled
 Non-Profit ORG CAR-RT SORT 6.00
 line pair, imperf 20.00
 spliced pair or strip, imperf —
 Quantity: several thousand

Exists miscut. Transition multiples exist.

Abraham Lincoln. May 28, 1966. Coil. Engraved.

4c black

IM 227 imperf pair 850.00
 line pair, imperf 1,750.00
 spliced pair or strip, imperf —
 Quantity: 100 pairs reported

Transition multiples exist and sell for a premium.

IM 227A pair, imperf between —
 Quantity: *very rare*

George Washington. September 8, 1966. Original design. Coil. Engraved.

5c blue

IM 228 imperf pair 150.00
 line pair, imperf 275.00
 spliced pair or strip, imperf —
 used pair, imperf —
 Quantity: 200 pairs reported

Often with faults. Price is for a sound copy. Exists miscut. Transition multiples exist and sell for a premium.

IM 229 imperf pair, precanceled
 MOUNT PLEASANT, IA 350.00
 line pair, imperf *1,000.00*
 imperf pair or strip, gap in bars *475.00*
 Quantity: n/a

IM 229A imperf pair, precanceled
 CHICAGO, IL *1,500.00*
 line pair, imperf —
 Quantity: *6 pairs and unique line pair reported*

| Original Design | Revised Design |

George Washington. Revised design; clean shaven. Coil. Engraved.

5c blue

IM 230 imperf pair 625.00
 line pair, imperf —
 Quantity: *50-60 pairs reported*

Franklin D. Roosevelt. December 28, 1967. Coil. Engraved. Horizontal format.

6c brown

IM 231 imperf pair 2,250.00
 line pair, imperf —
 line strip of 4, imperf **LRS (6/01)** 7,475.00
 Quantity: 25-30 pairs reported

Franklin D. Roosevelt. February 28, 1968. Coil. Engraved. Vertical format.

6c brown

IM 232 imperf pair 70.00
 line pair, imperf 125.00
 Quantity: approx 1,000 pairs

Exists miscut. Transition multiples exist.

Dwight D. Eisenhower. August 6, 1970. Coil. Engraved.

6c grayish blue

IM 233 imperf pair *1,500.00*
 line pair, imperf —
 Quantity: 20-30 pairs reported

Sometimes encountered with incomplete gum or without gum. Price is for pair with full gum, never hinged.

Dwight D. Eisenhower. May 10, 1971. Coil. Engraved.

8c dark claret

IM 234 imperf pair 40.00
 line pair, imperf 70.00
 spliced pair or strip, imperf —
 used pair, imperf —
 Quantity: 1,000+ pairs

Exists miscut. Transition multiples exist and sell for a premium.

IM 235 pair, imperf between *6,500.00*
 Quantity: 1 pair

Oliver Wendell Holmes. June 14, 1978. Coil. Engraved. Exists with wet or dry finish gum.

15c carmine or bright carmine; type I, wet gum

IM 236 imperf pair 30.00
 line pair, imperf 75.00
 used pair, imperf —
 Quantity: 600-800 pairs

Exists miscut. Transition multiples exist and sell for a premium.

| Type I | Type II |

Type I. The tip of the tie touches or almost touches the coat. The downward sloping hatch lines in the tie are more pronounced. The upper bar of the cents symbol is aligned slightly to the left of the "E" of "POSTAGE."

Type II. The tip of the tie is well clear of the coat. The downward sloping hatch lines in the tie are almost eliminated. The third upward sloping line of the tie stops well short of the right side of the tie. The upper bar in the cents symbol is aligned almost directly under the "E" of "POSTAGE."

15c carmine or bright carmine; type I, dry gum

IM 236A	imperf pair	30.00
	line pair, imperf	65.00
	Quantity: several hundred pairs	

IM 237	pair, imperf between	175.00
	line pair, imperf between	—
	Quantity: 200-250 pairs reported	

15c carmine or bright carmine; type II, dry gum

IM 237A	imperf pair	75.00
	line pair, imperf	150.00
	Quantity: 150+ pairs	

Transition multiples exist and sell for a premium.

Eugene O'Neill. January 12, 1973. Coil. Engraved.

$1 dark violet

IM 238	imperf pair	2,000.00
	line pair, imperf	*4,250.00*
	spliced pair or strip, imperf	—
	Quantity: 50 pairs, 3 line pairs reported	

Exists miscut. Transition multiples exist and sell for a premium.

Franklin D. Roosevelt. December 28, 1967. Booklet pane. Engraved.

6c brown

IM 238A	hz pair, imperf between **LRS (5/98)**	1,650.00
	Quantity: very rare, possibly unique	

IM 238A results from a foldover.

Dwight D. Eisenhower. January 28, 1972. Booklet pane. Engraved.

8c dark claret

IM 239	block of 4 (incl label "Use Zip Code"), imperf hz between	*850.00*
	booklet pane of 7 + 1 label, imperf hz between	—
	Quantity: n/a	

Where possible, illustrations of actual error stamps have been used. They are bordered in black. Illustrations of normal stamps have been used in cases where error stamp illustrations were not available, or where an error illustration would not adequately illustrate the error. Illustrations of normal stamps appear without black border.

The label "Use Zip Code" appears at the bottom left corner on normal booklet panes. It appears that **IM 239** occurs from sheets of perforated booklet panes that were separated along the perforations instead of being cut apart in the normal places. In addition, some examples are known as the result of a foldover. They are rare and sell for more.

Oliver Wendell Holmes. June 28, 1978. Booklet pane of 8. Engraved. Perf 10.

15c carmine

IM 240 booklet pane of 8, imperf
vrt between *1,750.00*
Quantity: n/a

Davy Crockett. August 17, 1967. Engraved, lithographed. BEP.

5c black, yellow & green

IM 241 vrt pair, imperf between *5,000.00*
Quantity: 3-5 pairs reported

U.S. Flag. January 24, 1968. Engraved. Design 19x22mm. Perf 11. BEP.

6c red, blue & green

IM 242 vrt pair, imperf hz 500.00
as above, used —
Quantity: *very scarce*

☛ Caution. Beware regumming. Most pairs lack gum, which was removed to eliminate faint perforation impressions. So long as impressions do not affect a stamp's paper, the stamp is considered imperforate. Check carefully for blind perfs. Price is for pair with original gum. Those without gum sell for less.

IM 243 vrt pair, imperf between 500.00
as above, used —
Quantity: less than 50 pairs reported

☛ Caution. Many offered as imperforates have traces of perforations. Check carefully.

U.S. Flag. August 7, 1970. Engraved. Design 18.25 by 21mm. Perf 11x10½. BEP.

6c red, blue & green

IM 244 hz pair, imperf between 150.00
Quantity: 100-200 pairs

Often with clipped perfs, a normal result of trimming at the Bureau of Engraving & Printing.

Buying or selling?
Consult the dealer directory at the back of the catalogue.

U.S. Flag. May 10, 1971. Engraved. Perf 11x10½. BEP.

8c red, blue & green

IM 245	imperf vertical pair	40.00
	top or bottom plate block of 20, imperf	600.00
	Quantity: 500+ pairs reported	

Price is for copy with gum. Pairs without gum sell for less. Collected in vertical pairs or blocks to distinguish it from the coil imperforate of similar design.

IM 246	hz pair, imperf between	50.00
	Quantity: 600 pairs	

COIL STAMPS

U.S. Flag. May 30, 1969. Coil. Engraved. BEP.

6c red, blue & green

IM 247	imperf pair	500.00
	spliced pair or strip, imperf	—
	Quantity: 50-100 pairs reported	

Where possible, illustrations of actual error stamps have been used. They are bordered in black. Illustrations of normal stamps have been used in cases where error stamp illustrations were not available, or where an error illustration would not adequately illustrate the error. Illustrations of normal stamps appear without black border.

U.S. Flag. May 10, 1971. Coil. Engraved. BEP.

8c red, blue & green

IM 248	imperf pair	50.00
	spliced pair or strip, imperf	—
	Quantity: 750-1000 pairs reported	

Exists miscut, including 3 strips with complete plate number showing at bottom. Transition multiples exist and sell for a premium. Although it is generally accepted that line pairs, in the traditional sense, are not created on Huck press printed stamps, pairs with coloration between stamps resembling lines exist and are collected. They sell for about double the price of regular pairs.

Walt Disney. September 11, 1968. Photogravure. UCC.

6c multicolored

IM 249	imperf pair	650.00
	block of 4, imperf	—
	Quantity: 100 pairs	

IM 250	vrt pair, imperf hz	650.00
	plate block of 4, imperf hz	—
	Quantity: 50 pairs	

IM 251 hz pair, imperf between *5,000.00*
Quantity: 5 pairs

☛ Caution. Expert certificate essential. This error can be fabricated from **IM 249**.

Waterfowl Conservation. **October 24, 1968.** **Engraved, lithographed. BEP.**

6c multicolored

IM 252 vrt pair, imperf between 475.00
Quantity: 100+ pairs

Some margins pairs contain an inspector's red crayon mark in the selvage. Its presence does not detract from value.

Christmas. **November 1, 1968.** **Engraved, lithographed. BEP.**

6c multicolored

IM 253 imperf pair, tagged 200.00
 plate block of 10, imperf, tagged —
 Quantity: 500 pairs

IM 254 imperf pair, untagged 250.00
 Quantity: 250 pairs

IM 254 often occurs with mottled gum. Those with flawless gum sell for a premium.

Grandma Moses. **May 1, 1969.** **Engraved, lithographed. BEP.**

6c multicolored

IM 255 hz pair, imperf between 200.00
 Quantity: 250 pairs reported, see note

☛ Caution. Many pairs have faint traces of blind perfs. Frequently, perf traces can be seen only on the gummed side. Pairs on cover have been reported, however, it is thought that they may have been thus used to disguise the presence of blind perfs and, therefore, when encountered, should be examined carefully. Of the quantity reported, it is not known how many pairs contain faint blind perfs.

Apollo 8. **May 5, 1969. Engraved. BEP.**

6c multicolored

IM 255A imperf pair **PW** 1,500.00
 Quantity: n/a

☛ Printer's waste. Refer to introduction.

Christmas. November 3, 1969. Engraved, lithographed. BEP.

6c multicolored

IM 256 imperf pair 1,000.00
Quantity: 25 pairs reported

Christmas. November 5, 1970. Se-tenant block of 4. Photogravure. GGI.

6c multicolored

a) Doll Carriage b) Toy Horse

IM 257 used vrt margin pair (a & b) with
plate No. 31907, imperf —
used vrt margin pair (a & b) with
Mail Early slogan, imperf —
Quantity: each pair listed is unique

Each listed pair is postmarked Washington, DC, Nov. 5, 1970.

Tom Sawyer. October 13, 1972. Engraved, lithographed. BEP.

8c multicolored

IM 258 hz pair, imperf between *5,000.00*
plate block of 4, imperf vrt between *9,500.00*
Quantity: 7 pairs reported (one
of which is damaged)

George Gershwin. February 23, 1973. Photogravure. BEP.

8c multicolored

IM 259 vrt pair, imperf hz 200.00
plate block of 12, imperf hz —
Quantity: 160-200 pairs

Robinson Jeffers. August 13, 1973. Photogravure. BEP.

8c multicolored

IM 260 vrt pair, imperf hz 250.00
Quantity: 80-100 pairs reported

Willa Cather. September 20, 1973. Photogravure. BEP.

8c multicolored

IM 261 vrt pair, imperf hz 250.00
Quantity: 80-100 pairs

Lyndon B. Johnson. August 27, 1973. Photogravure. BEP.

8c multicolored

IM 262 hz pair, imperf vrt 325.00
plate block of 12, imperf vrt —
Quantity: 128-160 pairs

Rural America. October 5, 1973. Engraved, lithographed. BEP.

8c multicolored

IM 262A used vrt pair, imperf hz **LRS (11/95)** 4,675.00
Quantity: unique

☛ Caution. Many pairs exist with blind perforations. Expert certificate essential. The listed pair is comprised of stamps 2 and 3 in a vertical strip of 5.

Christmas. November 7, 1973. Photogravure. BEP.

8c multicolored

IM 263 vrt pair, imperf between 300.00
Quantity: 50+ pairs

Pairs often contain a misplaced perforation in the design due to the nature of the error. Transition multiples exist and sell for a premium.

Crossed Flags. December 8, 1973. Engraved. BEP.

10c red & blue

IM 264 hz pair, imperf between 50.00
top or bottom plate strip of 20 —
Quantity: several hundred pairs

Also exists with Salem, Ind. local precancel: price $100.

IM 264A hz pair, imperf vrt —
hz strip of 4, imperf vrt 1,900.00
Quantity: *8 pairs reported*

Most often encountered as a strip of 4 containing two error pairs.

Where possible, illustrations of actual error stamps have been used. They are bordered in black. Illustrations of normal stamps have been used in cases where error stamp illustrations were not available, or where an error illustration would not adequately illustrate the error. Illustrations of normal stamps appear without black border.

Hinging. Prices for stamps after **IM 196** are for never hinged copies. Hinged copies sell for less.

IM 265 vrt pair, imperf — 950.00
block of 4, imperf — 1,900.00
Quantity: 35-60 pairs

Collected in vertical pairs or blocks to distinguish it from coil stamps of the same design

IM 265A vrt pair, imperf between — —
Quantity: *reportedly unique*

Jefferson Memorial. December 14, 1973. Engraved. BEP.

10c blue

IM 266 vrt pair, imperf hz — 500.00
Quantity: n/a

IM 266 is poorly centered. Price is for poorly centered copy.

IM 267 vrt pair, imperf between — *800.00*
Quantity: n/a

IM 267 occurs from miscut booklet panes.

Although catalogue prices are based on the best information available at press time, readers should be aware that prices for error stamps fluctuate over time, and therefore, are advised to contact dealers active in the error stamp market for timely quotes when buying or selling.

COIL STAMPS

Liberty Bell. October 1, 1974. Coil. Engraved. BEP.

6.3c reddish orange

IM 268 imperf pair — 175.00
line pair, imperf — —
Quantity: 200+ pairs reported

Transition multiples exist.

IM 269 imperf pair, precanceled
 WASHINGTON, DC — 90.00
 line pair, imperf — 200.00
 imperf pair or strip, gap in bars — —
 spliced pair or strip, imperf — —
 Quantity: 300-500 pairs reported

Exists miscut. Transition multiples exist and sell for a premium.

IM 270 imperf pair, precanceled
 COLUMBUS, OH — 550.00
 line pair, imperf — *1,250.00*
 imperf pair or strip, gap in bars — —
 spliced pair or strip, imperf — —
 Quantity: rare

IM 271 imperf pair, precanceled
 GARDEN CITY, NY — 850.00
 line pair, imperf — —
 Quantity: rare

Flags. December 8, 1973. Coil. Engraved. BEP.

10c red & blue

IM 272 imperf pair — 35.00
line pair, imperf — 50.00
spliced pair or strip, imperf — —
Quantity: 1,000+ pairs

Refer to note after **IM 248**. Exists miscut. Transition multiples exist and sell for a premium.

44

Jefferson Memorial. December 14, 1973. Coil. Engraved. BEP.

10c blue

IM 273	imperf pair	35.00
	line pair, imperf	65.00
	spliced pair or strip, imperf	—
	used pair, imperf	*40.00*
	Quantity: 750+ pairs	

Exists miscut. Transition multiples exist and sell for a premium.

Skylab. May 14, 1974. Engraved, lithographed. BEP.

10c multicolored

IM 274	vrt pair, imperf between	—
	Quantity: n/a	

UPU. June 6, 1974. Se-tenant block of 8. Photogravure. BEP.

10c multicolored (block of 8)

a) Terboch	e) Raphael
b) Chardin	f) Hokusai
c) Gainsborough	g) Peto
d) Goya	h) Liotard

IM 275	block of 8, imperf vrt	*8,000.00*
	plate block of 16	—
	Quantity: 4 blocks of 8, including plate block	

Collective Bargaining. March 13, 1975. Photogravure. BEP.

10c multicolored

IM 276	imperf pair **PW**	*350.00*
	Quantity: 25 pairs reported	

☛ Printer's waste, refer to introduction.

Lexington & Concord. April 19, 1975. Photogravure. BEP.

10c multicolored

IM 277	vrt pair, imperf hz	425.00
	plate block of 12, imperf hz	—
	Quantity: 60-80 pairs	

Paul Laurence Dunbar. May 1, 1975. Photogravure. BEP.

10c multicolored

IM 278	imperf pair	1,250.00
	plate block of 10, imperf **LRS (9/94)**	7,425.00
	Quantity: 15 pairs	

Apollo-Soyuz. July 15, 1975. Se-tenant pair. Photogravure. BEP.

10c multicolored

a) Spacecraft & Globe
b) Spacecraft & Emblem

IM 279 vrt pair, imperf hz 2,100.00
Quantity: 24-36 pairs

IM 279A imperf pair **PW** —
Quantity: *approximately 10 pairs*

☛ **IM 279A** occurs from printer's waste, refer to introduction. All reported pairs are faulty and without gum.

Christmas. October 14, 1975. Photogravure. BEP.

10c multicolored

IM 280 imperf pair 100.00
plate block of 12, imperf *625.00*
Quantity: several hundred pairs

Christmas. October 14, 1975. Photogravure. BEP.

10c multicolored

IM 281 imperf pair 100.00
plate block of 12, imperf —
Quantity: several hundred pairs

World Peace Through Law. September 29, 1975. Engraved. BEP.

10c multicolored

IM 281A plate block, imperf vrt **LRS (4/95)** 13,750.00
Quantity: unique plate block

The plate block (plate No. 36535) consists of 2 pairs plus parts of 2 additional stamps at left, giving it the appearance of containing nearly six stamps.

AMERICANA SERIES OF 1975/1981

Flag & Independence Hall. November 15, 1975. Engraved. Huck Press. Perf 11x10½. BEP.

13c red, blue & brown

IM 282 hz pair, imperf between 50.00
Quantity: approx 1,000 pairs

IM 282A hz pair, imperf vrt —
Quantity: *9 pairs reported*

Where possible, illustrations of actual error stamps have been used. They are bordered in black. Illustrations of normal stamps have been used in cases where error stamp illustrations were not available, or where an error illustration would not adequately illustrate the error. Illustrations of normal stamps appear without black border.

IM 283 vrt pair, imperf 500.00
 block of 4, imperf —
 top plate strip of 20 —
 Quantity: 110-130 pairs

Flag & Independence Hall. 1981. Engraved. Combination Press. Perf 11. BEP.

13c red, blue & brown

IM 284 vrt pair, imperf 135.00
 block of 4, imperf 250.00
 Quantity: 150-200 pairs reported

IM 283 was printed on the Huck Press; plate numbers appear at the top or bottom of a pane. **IM 284** was printed on the Combination Press; plate numbers appear on the left or right of the sheet. In addition, **IM 283** and **IM 284** can be distinguished from one another as follows: **IM 283** has visible gum breaking ridges on the reverse, and tagging is usually in the form of a well defined block. **IM 284** has smooth gum without ridges, and tagging, while in block form, tends to be very irregular.

IM 283 and **IM 284** are collected in vertical pairs or blocks to distinguish them from coil imperforates of the same design.

Eagle & Shield. December 1, 1975. Photogravure. BEP.

13c multicolored

IM 285 imperf pair 45.00
 block of 4, imperf 100.00
 Quantity: approx 500 pairs

Exists with color shift.

Buying or selling?
Consult the dealer directory at the back of the catalogue.

U.S. Flag. June 30, 1978. Engraved. BEP.

15c red, blue & gray

IM 286 vrt pair, imperf 17.50
 block of 4, imperf 35.00
 Quantity: 1,000+ pairs

Collected in vertical pairs or blocks to distinguish from coil imperforate of the same design. Transition multiples exist and sell for a premium.

IM 286A vrt pair, imperf hz —
 Quantity: *7 pairs reported*

IM 286B vrt pair, imperf between *500.00*
 Quantity: rare

IM 286B contains a natural straight edge at bottom. It is usually encountered in a strip of 3 or more.

Oil Lamp. September 11, 1979. Engraved, lithographed. BEP.

50c black, orange & tan

IM 287 vrt pair, imperf hz *1,750.00*
 Quantity: very rare

☛ Caution. Most pairs contain faint blind perfs and, therefore, do not qualify as errors. The blind perfs can be very deceptive. Extreme caution advised. Expert certificate necessary.

Where possible, illustrations of actual error stamps have been used. They are bordered in black. Illustrations of normal stamps have been used in cases where error stamp illustrations were not available, or where an error illustration would not adequately illustrate the error. Illustrations of normal stamps appear without black border.

BOOKLET PANE

Liberty Bell. October 31, 1975. Booklet pane. Engraved. BEP.

13c brown

IM 288 vrt pair, imperf between 300.00
booklet pane of 7 + 1 label —
Quantity: scarce

Most pairs of **IM 288** were taken from complete booklet panes with perforations all around the outside edges. The complete panes, and vertical pairs taken from these panes, are almost certainly printer's waste. There is strong evidence to support this view. The slogan label appears at the lower left rather than the upper left, where it should normally be, suggesting that imperforate between panes were separated from uncut sheets along perforation lines instead of being severed in the normal place. A few vertical pairs, imperforate between result from foldovers. They are rare, more highly prized, and sell for much more. Recent sales have been in the $1,500 range.

COIL STAMPS

Inkwell & Quill. March 6, 1981. Coil. Engraved. BEP.

1c blue (green paper)

IM 289 imperf pair 175.00
line pair, imperf 250.00
spliced pair or strip, imperf —
Quantity: 250+ pairs

Transition multiples exist and sell for a premium.

Although catalogue prices are based on the best information available at press time, readers should be aware that prices for error stamps fluctuate over time, and therefore, are advised to contact dealers active in the error stamp market for timely quotes when buying or selling.

Guitar. October 25, 1979. Coil. Engraved. BEP.

3.1c dark red (yellow paper)

IM 290 imperf pair 1,375.00
line pair, imperf —
Quantity: 30-50 pairs, 2 line pairs

Violins. June 23, 1980. Coil. Engraved. BEP.

3.5c violet (yellow paper)

IM 291 imperf pair 200.00
line pair, imperf 350.00
Quantity: 250 pairs reported

Prices are for well centered copies. Poorly centered copies sell for about half. Exists miscut. Transition multiples exist and sell for a premium.

Saxhorns. November 20, 1976. Coil. Engraved. BEP.

7.7c brown (yellow paper)

IM 292 imperf pair, precanceled
MARION, OH *1,950.00*
Quantity: 7-10 pairs reported

IM 293 imperf pair, precanceled
WASHINGTON, DC 1,650.00
line pair, imperf —
imperf pair or strip, gap in bars —
Quantity: 40-50 pairs reported

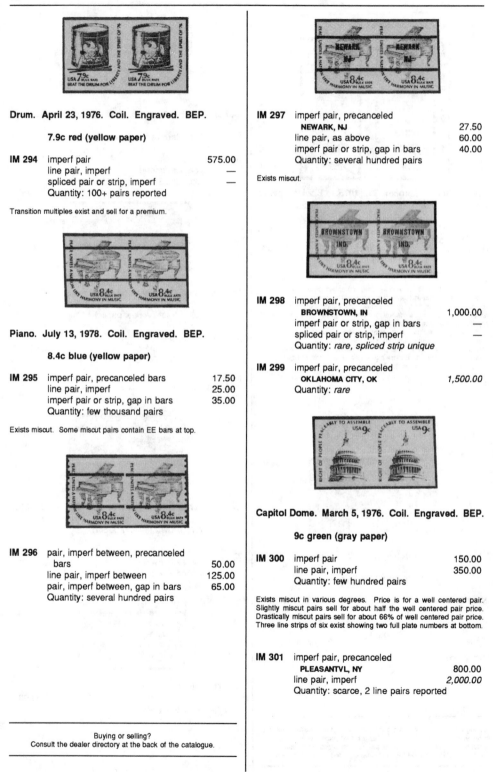

Drum. April 23, 1976. Coil. Engraved. BEP.

7.9c red (yellow paper)

IM 294	imperf pair	575.00
	line pair, imperf	—
	spliced pair or strip, imperf	—
	Quantity: 100+ pairs reported	

Transition multiples exist and sell for a premium.

Piano. July 13, 1978. Coil. Engraved. BEP.

8.4c blue (yellow paper)

IM 295	imperf pair, precanceled bars	17.50
	line pair, imperf	25.00
	imperf pair or strip, gap in bars	35.00
	Quantity: few thousand pairs	

Exists miscut. Some miscut pairs contain EE bars at top.

IM 296	pair, imperf between, precanceled bars	50.00
	line pair, imperf between	125.00
	pair, imperf between, gap in bars	65.00
	Quantity: several hundred pairs	

IM 297	imperf pair, precanceled	
	NEWARK, NJ	27.50
	line pair, as above	60.00
	imperf pair or strip, gap in bars	40.00
	Quantity: several hundred pairs	

Exists miscut.

IM 298	imperf pair, precanceled	
	BROWNSTOWN, IN	1,000.00
	imperf pair or strip, gap in bars	—
	spliced pair or strip, imperf	—
	Quantity: *rare, spliced strip unique*	

IM 299	imperf pair, precanceled	
	OKLAHOMA CITY, OK	*1,500.00*
	Quantity: *rare*	

Capitol Dome. March 5, 1976. Coil. Engraved. BEP.

9c green (gray paper)

IM 300	imperf pair	150.00
	line pair, imperf	350.00
	Quantity: few hundred pairs	

Exists miscut in various degrees. Price is for a well centered pair.
Slightly miscut pairs sell for about half the well centered pair price.
Drastically miscut pairs sell for about 66% of well centered pair price.
Three line strips of six exist showing two full plate numbers at bottom.

IM 301	imperf pair, precanceled	
	PLEASANTVL, NY	800.00
	line pair, imperf	*2,000.00*
	Quantity: scarce, 2 line pairs reported	

Buying or selling?
Consult the dealer directory at the back of the catalogue.

Justice. November 4, 1977. Coil. Engraved. BEP.

10c violet (gray paper)

IM 302	imperf pair	60.00
	line pair, imperf	125.00
	spliced pair or strip, imperf	—
	Quantity: few hundred pairs	

Exists miscut. Exists with glossy gum and with dull gum. Transition multiples exist and sell for a premium.

Torch. April 8, 1981. Coil. Engraved. BEP.

12c red brown (gray paper)

IM 303	imperf pair	165.00
	line pair, imperf	325.00
	Quantity: 250 pairs	

Flag & Independence Hall. November 15, 1975. Coil. Engraved. BEP.

13c red, blue & brown

IM 304	imperf pair	20.00
	line pair, imperf	50.00
	spliced pair or strip, imperf	—
	Quantity: several thousand pairs	

Refer to note after **IM 248**. Transition multiples exist and sell for a premium.

Liberty Bell. November 25, 1975. Coil. Engraved. BEP.

13c brown

IM 305	imperf pair	25.00
	line pair, imperf	50.00
	spliced pair or strip, imperf	—
	Quantity: few thousand pairs	

Exists miscut. Transition multiples exist and sell for a premium.

IM 306	pair, imperf between	—
	Quantity: scarce	

U.S. Flag. June 30, 1978. Coil. Engraved. BEP.

15c red, blue & gray

IM 307	imperf pair	20.00
	spliced pair or strip, imperf	—
	Quantity: several thousand pairs	

Exists miscut. Transition multiples exist and sell for a premium.

IM 308	pair, imperf between	150.00
	Quantity: 75-100 pairs	

a) b) c)

The Spirit of '76. January 1, 1976. Se-tenant strip of 3. Photogravure. BEP.

13c multicolored

a) Drummer Boy
b) Adult Drummer
c) Fifer

IM 309	imperf strip of 3 (a-c)	1,000.00
	plate block of 12, imperf	—
	vertical pair (c), imperf	850.00
	imperf single (c), white border all around	350.00
	Quantity: 3 panes of 50 yielding 45 possible strips of 3 and 15 stamps as singles or pairs.	

BICENTENNIAL SOUVENIR SHEETS

A variety of perforation and color-omitted errors exist for this series. Some sheets contain multiple errors. Only those that exist imperforate are listed here, even though they may also contain color-omitted errors. Refer to the colors-omitted section for other varieties. Gaps in the numbering system exist for possible future listings.

Surrender at Yorktown. May 29, 1976. Souvenir sheet of 5. Lithographed. BEP.

13c multicolored

IM 310	imperf souvenir sheet, untagged, tied by postmark (5/29/76) to first day display card	2,250.00
	Quantity: 1-2 reported	

IM 310A	imperf souvenir sheet, tagged	—
	Quantity: possibly unique	
IM 311	imperf souvenir sheet, untagged, USA 13c omitted on all stamps, with 5/29/76 PHILADELPHIA, PA precancel postmark	—
	Quantity: 1-2 reported	
IM 312	imperf souvenir sheet, untagged, USA 13c omitted on 2nd, 3rd & 4th stamps, with 5/29/76 PHILADELPHIA, PA precancel postmark	2,500.00
	Quantity: 1-2 reported	
IM 313	imperf souvenir sheet, USA 13c omitted on 1st & 5th stamps	450.00
	Quantity: *very rare*	
IM 314	imperf souvenir sheet, USA 13c omitted on 1st & 5th stamps, with 5/29/76 PHILADELPHIA, PA first day cancellation	—
	Quantity: very rare, possibly unique	

Declaration of Independence. May 29, 1976. Souvenir sheet of 5. Lithographed. BEP.

18c multicolored

IM 315	imperf souvenir sheet, tagged	—
	Quantity: very rare, possibly unique	
IM 316	imperf souvenir sheet, USA 18c omitted on all stamps	2,750.00
	Quantity: very rare	

Where possible, illustrations of actual error stamps have been used. They are bordered in black. Illustrations of normal stamps have been used in cases where error stamp illustrations were not available, or where an error illustration would not adequately illustrate the error. Illustrations of normal stamps appear without black border.

Washington Crossing the Delaware. May 29, 1976. Souvenir sheet of 5. Lithographed. BEP.

24c multicolored

IM 317 imperf souvenir sheet, untagged *2,750.00*
Quantity: very rare

IM 318 imperf souvenir sheet, untagged,
 USA 24c omitted on all stamps *3,500.00*
Quantity: *2-3 reported*

IM 319 imperf souvenir sheet, untagged,
 USA 24c omitted on 4th &
 5th stamps —
Quantity: very rare, possibly unique

IM 320 imperf souvenir sheet, untagged,
 USA 24c omitted on 1st, 2nd &
 3rd stamps *3,250.00*
Quantity: very rare

Washington at Valley Forge. May 29, 1976. Souvenir sheet of 5. Lithographed. BEP.

31c multicolored

IM 322 imperf souvenir sheet, untagged,
 tied by 5/29/76 PHILADELPHIA, PA
 precancel postmark to first day
 display card *2,250.00*
Quantity: *very rare*

IM 323 imperf souvenir sheet, untagged,
 USA 31c omitted from all stamps *2,500.00*
Quantity: 6-8 reported

IM 324 imperf souvenir sheet, untagged,
 USA 31c omitted on 1st, 3rd &
 5th stamps —
Quantity: *possibly unique*

IM 325 imperf souvenir sheet, untagged,
 USA 31c omitted on 2nd, 4th &
 5th stamps *2,500.00*
Quantity: very rare

Olympics. July 16, 1976. Se-tenant block of 4. Photogravure. BEP.

13c multicolored

a) Diver b) Skier
c) Runner d) Skater

IM 329 imperf block of 4 (a-d) 676.00
 plate block of 12, imperf —
 Zip block of 4, imperf —
 imperf pair (a-b) or (c-d) 275.00
 Quantity: 200+ blocks of 4 reported

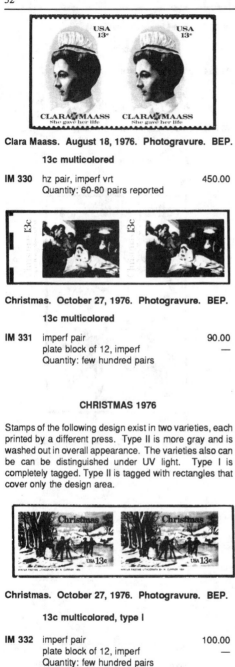

Clara Maass. August 18, 1976. Photogravure. BEP.

13c multicolored

IM 330 hz pair, imperf vrt 450.00
Quantity: 60-80 pairs reported

Christmas. October 27, 1976. Photogravure. BEP.

13c multicolored

IM 331 imperf pair 90.00
plate block of 12, imperf —
Quantity: few hundred pairs

CHRISTMAS 1976

Stamps of the following design exist in two varieties, each printed by a different press. Type II is more gray and is washed out in overall appearance. The varieties also can be can be distinguished under UV light. Type I is completely tagged. Type II is tagged with rectangles that cover only the design area.

Christmas. October 27, 1976. Photogravure. BEP.

13c multicolored, type I

IM 332 imperf pair 100.00
plate block of 12, imperf —
Quantity: few hundred pairs

13c multicolored, type II

IM 333 imperf pair 100.00
plate strip of 20, imperf —
Quantity: few hundred pairs

IM 334 vrt pair, imperf between —
Quantity: *40-60 pairs*

Washington at Princeton. January 3, 1977. Photogravure. BEP.

13c multicolored

IM 335 hz pair, imperf vrt 575.00
Quantity: 20-40 pairs

Pueblo Art. April 13, 1977. Se-tenant block or strip of 4. Photogravure. BEP.

13c multicolored

a) Hopi Pottery b) Acoma Pottery
c) Zia Pottery d) San Ildefonso Pottery

IM 336 block of 4 (a-d), imperf vrt 2,250.00
strip of 4 (a-d), imperf vrt 2,000.00
Quantity: 16 blocks of 4, 4 strips
of 4 reported

Panes of the Pueblo Pottery stamp are arranged so that the four designs are se-tenant (a-b-c-d) in a row. Additionally, rows alternate so that it is possible for the four designs to appear in a se-tenant block of four.

Although catalogue prices are based on the best information available at press time, readers should be aware that prices for error stamps fluctuate over time, and therefore, are advised to contact dealers active in the error stamp market for timely quotes when buying or selling.

Spirit of St. Louis. May 20, 1977. Photogravure. BEP.

13c multicolored

IM 337 imperf pair 1,000.00
Quantity: 85-100 pairs reported

Colorado. May 21, 1977. Photogravure. BEP.

13c multicolored

IM 338 hz pair, imperf vrt 850.00
Quantity: *35 pairs*

Butterflies. June 6, 1977. Se-tenant block of 4. Photogravure. BEP.

13c multicolored

a) Swallowtail	b) Checkerspot
c) Dogface	d) Orange-Tip

IM 339 block of 4 (a-d), plate numbers
at left, imperf hz **LRS (91)** 12,100.00
block of 4 (a-d), perfs slightly in
at lower right, imperf hz **LRS (5/98)** 12,100.00
Quantity: the 2 blocks as listed

Christmas. October 21, 1977. Photogravure. BEP.

13c multicolored

IM 340 imperf pair 70.00
plate strip of 20, imperf —
Quantity: 1,000+ pairs

Christmas. October 21, 1977. Photogravure. BEP.

13c multicolored

IM 341 imperf pair 300.00
plate block of 10, imperf —
Quantity: few hundred

Captain James Cook. January 20, 1978. Pane of 50 arranged so that each half pane contains 25 stamps of the same design. Five se-tenant pairs exist at the center of each pane. Engraved. BEP.

13c dark blue (a), green (b)

a) Captain Cook	b) Ships at Anchor

IM 342 se-tenant pair (a-b), imperf between 4,250.00
Quantity: fewer than 5 pairs reported

Although **IM 342** appears to be imperf vertically, it is properly described as imperf between because of the presence of blind perfs at left and right.

☞ Caution. Pairs of the Captain Cook portrait design exist with blind perforations that give the appearance of being imperforate.

Hinging. Prices for stamps after **IM 196** are for never hinged copies. Hinged copies sell for less.

IM 343 vrt pair (b), imperf hz —
strip of 10 containing **IM 342 & IM 343** —
Quantity: very rare

☛ Caution. Pairs of the Captain Cook portrait design exist with blind perforations that give the appearance of being imperforate.

Indian Head Penny. January 11, 1978. Engraved. BEP.

13c brown & greenish (ocher paper)

IM 344 hz pair, imperf vrt 275.00
Quantity: 300-375 pairs

Eagle & A. May 22, 1978. Photogravure. BEP.

A (15c) orange

IM 345 imperf pair 90.00
plate block of 4, imperf —
Quantity: few hundred pairs

The sheet variety of this stamp was printed by photogravure; the coil stamp was engraved. Therefore, horizontal pairs of the sheet stamp are collectible because they can be distinguished from coil stamp of same design.

IM 346 vrt pair, imperf hz *675.00*
plate block of 4, imperf hz —
Quantity: 20+ pairs reported

Most pairs exist with faint vertical perfs. Pairs with distinct perforations such as those in the illustration are much rarer.

COIL STAMP

Eagle & A. May 27, 1978. Coil. Engraved. BEP.

A (15c) orange

IM 347 imperf pair 90.00
line pair, imperf 195.00
spliced pair or strip —
Quantity: 150-200 pairs

Well centered copies are scarcer and sell for more.

Where possible, illustrations of actual error stamps have been used. They are bordered in black. Illustrations of normal stamps have been used in cases where error stamp illustrations were not available, or where an error illustration would not adequately illustrate the error. Illustrations of normal stamps appear without black border.

BOOKLET PANE

Eagle & A. May 22, 1978. Booklet pane. Engraved. BEP.

A (15c) orange

IM 348 vrt pair, imperf between *1,750.00*
Quantity: *3-4 pairs reported*

CAPEX. June 10, 1978. Souvenir sheet of 8. Engraved, lithographed. BEP.

13c multicolored

a) Cardinal	e) Moose
b) Mallard	f) Chipmunk
c) Canada Goose	g) Red Fox
d) Blue Jay	h) Raccoon

IM 349 strip of 4 (a-d), imperf vrt *7,500.00*
Quantity: *2 strips of 4*

IM 350 strip of 4 (e-h), imperf vrt —
as above, in souvenir sheet 4,750.00
Quantity: 6 strips of 4, including
those within souvenir sheets

Roses. July 11, 1978. Booklet pane of 8. Engraved. BEP.

15c green, orange & rose

IM 351 booklet pane, imperf —
imperf pair *500.00*
Quantity: 9 panes reported

Trees. October 9, 1978. Se-tenant block of 4. Photogravure. BEP.

15c multicolored

a) Giant Sequoia	b) White Pine
c) White Oak	d) Gray Birch

IM 352 block of 4 (a-d), imperf hz
LRS (10/98) 17,600.00
Quantity: unique

Madonna. October 18, 1978. Photogravure. BEP.

15c multicolored

IM 353	imperf pair	90.00
	Quantity: 300-400 pairs	

Hobby Horse. October 18, 1978. Photogravure. BEP.

15c multicolored

IM 354	imperf pair	90.00
	plate block of 12, imperf	—
	Quantity: 400-500 pairs	

IM 355	vrt pair, imperf hz	*2,000.00*
	Quantity: 4-6 pairs or strips of 3	

IM 355 contains traces of blind vertical perfs that may give it the appearance of being completely imperforate.

Martin Luther King. January 13, 1979. Photogravure. BEP.

13c multicolored

IM 356	imperf pair	*1,750.00*
	Quantity: *10 pairs reported*	

☛ Caution. Many exist with blind perfs.

Buying or selling?
Consult the dealer directory at the back of the catalogue.

Folk Art. April 19, 1979. Se-tenant block of 4. Photogravure. BEP.

15c multicolored

a) Coffeepot	b) Tea Caddy
c) Sugar Bowl	d) Coffeepot

IM 357	block of 4 (a-d), imperf hz	4,000.00
	block of 6, imperf hz	4,250.00
	Quantity: 1 pane consisting of 4 blocks of 4 and 4 blocks of 6 reported	

Endangered Flora. June 7, 1979. Se-tenant block of 4. Photogravure. BEP.

15c multicolored

a) Persistent Trillium
b) Hawaiian Wild Broadbean
c) Contra Costa Wallflower
d) Antioch Dunes Evening Primrose

IM 358	block of 4 (a-d), imperf	500.00
	plate block of 12, imperf	—
	Quantity: 100+ blocks of 4; 50+ pairs	

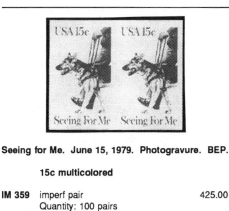

Seeing for Me. June 15, 1979. Photogravure. BEP.

15c multicolored

IM 359	imperf pair	425.00
	Quantity: 100 pairs	

IM 360	IM 361	IM 362

John Paul Jones. September 23, 1979. Photogravure. Two perforation varieties; Type I perf 11x12, Type II perf 11x11. JWF.

15c multicolored

IM 360	imperf pair **PW**	65.00
	Quantity: 500+ pairs	

☛ Printers waste, refer to introduction.

IM 361	vrt pair, type I, perf 12 vrt, imperf hz	175.00
	as above, Zip block of 4	—
	Quantity: 60-100 pairs	

IM 362	vrt pair, type II, perf 11 vrt, imperf hz	135.00
	as above, plate block of 10	—
	as above, Zip block of 4	—
	Quantity: 200-300 pairs	

The fully perforated version of this issue exists in a third variety, perf 12.

Summer Olympics. September 5, 1979. Se-tenant block of 4. Photogravure. BEP.

15c multicolored

a) Running	b) Swimming
c) Rowing	d) Horse Jumping

IM 363	block of 4 (a-d), imperf	1,500.00
	plate block of 12, imperf	*5,000.00*
	vrt pair (a & c), imperf	650.00
	vrt pair (b & d), imperf	650.00
	Quantity: 20 blocks of 4, 10 pairs	

Christmas Madonna. October 18, 1979. Photogravure. BEP.

15c multicolored

IM 364	imperf pair	90.00
	Quantity: 300-500 pairs	

IM 365	vrt pair, imperf between	2,250.00
	Quantity: *reportedly very rare*	

IM 366	vrt pair, imperf hz	675.00
	Quantity: at least 20-25 pairs	

Will Rogers. November 4, 1979. Photogravure. BEP.

15c multicolored

IM 367	imperf pair	200.00
	Quantity: several hundred pairs	

Benjamin Bannecker. February 15, 1980. Photogravure. ABN.

15c multicolored

IM 368 imperf pair **PW** 50.00
Quantity: 500+ pairs

☛ Printers waste, refer to introduction.

IM 369 hz pair, imperf vrt 775.00
Quantity: *25 pairs reported*

☛ Caution. Fakes exist made from printers waste. Expert certificate necessary.

COIL STAMP

Eagle & B. March 15, 1980. Coil. Engraved. BEP.

B (18c) violet

IM 370 imperf pair 95.00
line pair, imperf 150.00
spliced pair or strip, imperf —
used pair, imperf —
Quantity: 300-400 pairs

Well centered pairs sell for a premium.

Emily Bissell. May 31, 1980. Engraved. BEP.

15c red & black

IM 371 vrt pair, imperf hz 375.00
Quantity: 40-60 pairs

Veterans Administration. July 21, 1980. Photogravure. ABN.

15c red & blue

IM 372 hz pair, imperf vrt 450.00
Quantity: 50 pairs

Coral Reefs. August 26, 1980. Se-tenant block of 4. Photogravure. BEP.

15c multicolored

a) Brain Coral	b) Elkhorn Coral
c) Chalice Coral	d) Finger Coral

IM 373 block of 4 (a-d), imperf — 975.00
any pair, imperf — 400.00
plate block of 12, imperf — —
Quantity: 60-80 blocks of 4, 30-40 pairs

IM 374 block of 4 (a-d), imperf between vrt *3,750.00*
as above, any pair — —
Quantity: 2 blocks of 4 and 2 pairs reported

IM 375 block of 4 (a-d), imperf vrt *2,975.00*
Quantity: 4 blocks reported

☛ Caution. Blind perfs may exist. Examine carefully.

Organized Labor. September 1, 1980. Photogravure. BEP.

15c multicolored

IM 376 imperf pair — 375.00
Zip block of 4, imperf — —
Quantity: 100-150 pairs reported

Learning Never Ends. September 12, 1980. Photogravure. ABN.

15c multicolored

IM 377 vrt pair, imperf vrt — 225.00
plate block of 8, imperf vrt — —
Quantity: approx 100 pairs

Madonna. October 31, 1980. Photogravure. BEP.

15c multicolored

IM 378 imperf pair — 70.00
plate block of 12, imperf — 600.00
Quantity: 1,000+ pairs

Copies without gum sell for a substantial discount.

Drum. October 31, 1980. Photogravure. BEP.

15c multicolored

IM 379 imperf pair — 70.00
plate block of 20, imperf — *750.00*
Quantity: 1,000+ pairs

IM 379A vrt pair, imperf hz — —
Quantity: 2-3 pairs reported

IM 379B hz pair, imperf between LRS (5/99) — 7,700.00
Quantity: 2 pairs, see note

The two listed pairs of **IM 379B** are contained in a block of 15 and occupy positions 4 & 5 and 9 & 10, and the **LRS** price is for the block.

GREAT AMERICANS SERIES OF 1980

Dorothea Dix. September 23, 1983. Engraved. BEP.

1c black

IM 380 imperf pair 400.00
Quantity: *at least 100 pairs*

IM 380A **IM 380B**

IM 380A vrt pair, imperf between *3,000.00*
Quantity: 4-6 pairs

Pairs of **IM 380A** contain a natural straight edge at bottom. Perfs at top should be clear of the design.

IM 380B vrt pair, imperf hz —
Quantity: *1-4 pairs reported*

Walter Lippmann. September 15, 1985. Engraved. BEP.

6c dark orange

IM 381 vrt pair, imperf between *2,350.00*
plate block of 4 —
Quantity: 10 pairs

Pairs of **IM 381** contain a natural straight edge at bottom.

Richard Russell. May 31, 1984. Engraved. BEP.

10c Prussian blue

IM 382 vrt pair, imperf between 850.00
Quantity: 10-20 pairs

Pairs of **IM 382** contain a natural straight edge either at top or bottom.

IM 383 vrt pair, imperf hz —
Quantity: *10-17 pairs reported*

Do not confuse **IM 382** and **IM 383**. Vertical pairs of **IM 383** exist with perforations well into the stamp above the error pair. Such error pairs are considered to be imperforate horizontally, because the perforations in the third stamp do not occupy space between any stamps and are, therefore, completely extraneous to the error pair.

IM 383A hz pair, imperf between 2,000.00
Quantity: 10 pairs

IM 384 imperf pair, block tagged *1,200.00*
imperf strip of used on cover —
Quantity: *10 pairs reported*

☛ **IM 384** is block tagged. Imperf pairs without tagging exist and are printer's waste.

Sinclair Lewis. March 21, 1985. Engraved. BEP.

14c gray green

IM 385 hz pair, imperf between 8.00
Quantity: several thousand pairs

IM 386 vrt pair, imperf hz 125.00
Quantity: 200-250 pairs reported

IM 387 vrt pair, imperf between 1,750.00
Quantity: 15-20 pairs reported

John J. Audubon. April 21, 1985. Engraved. BEP.

22c dark gray blue

IM 390 vrt pair, imperf hz 2,500.00
Quantity: 10 pairs

Transition multiples exist.

IM 391 vrt pair, imperf between —
Quantity: *very rare, possibly unique*

IM 392 hz pair, imperf between *2,750.00*
Quantity: *10 pairs*

Transition multiples exist.

Jack London. May 3, 1988. Booklet pane. Engraved. BEP.

25c light blue

IM 393 hz pair, imperf between —
Quantity: new, n/a

Grenville Clark. May 20, 1985. Engraved. BEP.

39c bright purple

IM 394 vrt pair, imperf hz 575.00
strip of 3, imperf hz —
Quantity: *30-50 pairs reported*

Some copies exist with horizontal folds between stamps. Price is for copy without fold. Copies with fold sell for about one-third the price of those without folds.

IM 395 vrt pair, imperf between —
Quantity: 3-5 pairs reported

Alice Hamilton. July 11, 1995. Engraved. Dull gum. BCA.

55c gray green

IM 396 imperf pair —
Quantity: *10 pairs*

Usually in a transition strip of 10.

Flag & Grain. April 24, 1981. Engraved. BEP.

18c red, blue & brown

IM 400 imperf pair 100.00
Quantity: several hundred pairs

IM 400A vrt pair, imperf hz 850.00
block of 4, imperf hz —
Quantity: *10-15 pairs reported*

Flag & Seashore. April 24, 1981. Coil. Engraved. BEP.

18c red, blue & brown

IM 401 imperf pair 18.00
imperf strip with plate No. 2 *500.00*
imperf strip with plate No. 3 —
imperf strip with plate No. 4 —
imperf strip with plate No. 5 175.00
spliced pair or strip, imperf —
Quantity: 1,000+ pairs

Exists miscut. Price for plate No. 2 is for a strip of 4 (the longest known strip); price for plate No. 5 for strip of 6. Plate No. 2 is most commonly encountered in pairs: price $125.00. Plate number pairs of No. 5 sell for about half the price of plate strips of 6.

At the time plate number coils were first introduced, the practice of saving plate numbers in strips had not yet been established. Therefore, many early plate number imperfs are relatively plentiful in pair form, but genuinely rare in longer strips.

IM 401A hz pair, imperf between —
Quantity: *very rare*

☛ Caution. Expert certificate necessary.

Although catalogue prices are based on the best information available at press time, readers should be aware that prices for error stamps fluctuate over time, and therefore, are advised to contact dealers active in the error stamp market for timely quotes when buying or selling.

American Wildlife. March 15, 1981. Se-tenant booklet pane of 10. Engraved. BEP.

18c dark brown

IM 402 booklet pane, imperf vrt between *1,500.00*
Quantity: 15 panes reported

☛ Caution. Often with vertical row of perfs completely inside the design. Refer to the introduction for definitions of imperf errors.

Flag & Mountains se-tenant with numeral "6" in Circle of Stars. April 24, 1981. Booklet pane. Engraved. BEP.

**6c red & blue, Numeral in Circle of Stars
18c red, blue & purple, Flag & Mountains**

IM 403 booklet pane of 8 (6c & 18c),
imperf vrt between 75.00
pair (6c), imperf between —
pair (18c), imperf between —
Quantity: 1,000+ booklet panes

Eagle & C. October 11, 1981. Coil. Photogravure. BEP.

C (20c) brown

IM 404 imperf pair *1,100.00*
line strip of 4, imperf —
Quantity: *60-70 pairs, 6+ line strips*

Gum along the edges of approximately half the pairs appears to have been slightly disturbed by moisture. Price is for a pair without moisture disturbance. Those with the disturbance sell for less.

U.S. Flag. December 17, 1981. Engraved. BEP.

20c red, blue & black

IM 405	imperf vertical pair	35.00
	block of 4, imperf	75.00
	Quantity: 1,000+	

Collected in vertical pairs or blocks to distinguish it from the coil imperforate of the same design.

| IM 406 | vrt pair, imperf hz | 475.00 |
| | Quantity: very scarce | |

Transition multiples exist and sell for a premium.

U.S. Flag. December 17, 1981. Coil. Engraved. BEP.

20c red, blue & black

IM 407	imperf pair	8.00
	used pair, imperf	—
	imperf strip with plate No. 1	—
	imperf strip with plate No. 2	350.00
	imperf strip with plate No. 3	450.00
	imperf strip with plate No. 4	400.00
	imperf strip with plate No. 5	300.00
	imperf strip with plate No. 6	1,250.00
	imperf strip with plate No. 8	150.00
	imperf strip with plate No. 9	175.00
	imperf strip with plate No. 10	150.00
	imperf strip with plate No. 11	750.00
	imperf strip with plate No. 12	850.00
	imperf strip with plate No. 13	950.00
	imperf strip with plate No. 14	1,250.00
	spliced pair or strip, imperf	—
	Quantity: several thousand pairs	

Exists miscut, some with EE bars at top or marginal markings at bottom. Transition multiples exist and sell for a premium. Exists untagged.

Prices are for plate strips of 6; plate strips of 5 sell for similar prices. Generally, plate strips of 3 sell for about 50% of the plate strip of six price, and plate pairs sell for about 33% of the strip of six price. There are exceptions depending on the issue and the plate number. Refer to second note following **IM 401**.

| IM 408 | pair, imperf between | *1,000.00* |
| | Quantity: 10-15 pairs | |

☛ Caution. Fakes exist. Expert certificate necessary.

Bighorn Sheep. January 8, 1982. Booklet pane of 10. Engraved. BEP.

20c gray blue

IM 409	booklet pane of 10, imperf vrt between	95.00
	complete booklet of 2 panes,	
	imperf vrt between	185.00
	Quantity: at least 150 booklet panes	

Refer to note following **IM 402** and to introduction.

TRANSPORTATION SERIES OF 1982
COIL STAMPS

NOTE. Prices for imperf plate number coil (PNC) strips in this section are for strips of 6 unless otherwise noted. Generally, PNC strips of 5 sell for similar prices; PNC strips of 3 sell for about 50% of the strip of 6 price; and PNC pairs sell for about 33% of the strip of 6 price. There are exceptions, however, depending on issue and scarcity. Also, refer to the second note following **IM 401**.

Omnibus. August 19, 1983. Coil. Engraved. BEP.

1c violet

IM 410	imperf pair	625.00
	imperf strip with plate No. 5	—
	imperf strip with plate No. 6	—
	Quantity: 150-250 pairs	

Most plate No. strips of **IM 410** are 3 or 4 stamps in length. Longer strips are scarce.

Omnibus. November 26, 1986. Coil. Engraved. BEP.

1c violet

IM 410A imperf pair 2,400.00
 imperf strip with plate No. 1 —
 spliced pair or strip, imperf —
 Quantity: 22-24 pairs

Transition multiples exist. Plate No. 1 is known on a transition strip in which the plate number appears on a perforated stamp.

Locomotive. May 20, 1982. Coil. Engraved. BEP.

2c black

IM 411 imperf pair 50.00
 used strip of 3, imperf —
 imperf strip with plate No. 3 200.00
 imperf strip with plate No. 4 225.00
 imperf strip with plate No. 8 275.00
 imperf strip with plate No. 10 275.00
 Quantity: few thousand pairs

Transition multiples exist and sell for a premium. Prices are for plate strips of 6 with plate numbers & lines. Plate pairs sell for 33% less. Refer to second note following **IM 401**.

Stagecoach. August 19, 1982. Coil. Engraved. BEP.

4c reddish brown

IM 412 imperf pair, precanceled 2 bars
 & NON-PROFIT Org. 750.00
 imperf strip with plate No. 5 —
 imperf strip with plate No. 6 —
 imperf pair, gap in bars —
 spliced pair or strip, imperf —
 Quantity: *50-75 pairs*

Exists miscut. Transition multiples exist. The plate number appears at the top on plate number strips of plate No. 6. Plate number strips of **IM 412** exist only as strips of 3 or 4.

IM 412A imperf pair, without precancel 850.00
 imperf strip with line & plate No. 1 —
 imperf strip with line & plate No. 2 —
 spliced pair or strip, imperf —
 Quantity: 150 pairs reported

Exists miscut.

Stagecoach. August 15, 1986. Revised design. Coil. Engraved. BEP.

4c reddish brown

IM 412B imperf pair 275.00
 imperf strip with plate No. 1 *1,500.00*
 Quantity: 250 pairs

IM 412A contains a line on plate number pairs or strips. **IM 412B** contains a plate number only. Transition multiples exist.

Steam Carriage. August 31, 1990. Coil. Engraved. BEP.

4c dark purple

IM 412C imperf pair 600.00
 imperf strip with plate No. 1 —
 spliced pair or strip, imperf —
 imperf pair on first day cover —
 Quantity: *100+ pairs; 5 first day covers*

Transition multiples exist and sell for a premium. Refer to note following **IM 434** regarding first day covers.

Motorcycle. October 10, 1983. Coil. Engraved. BEP.

5c gray green

IM 413 imperf pair 2,750.00
 imperf strip of 5 with plate No. 1 —
 imperf strip of 5 with plate No. 2 —
 spliced strip, imperf —
 Quantity: 32 pairs; the 2 plate strips
 as listed above; unique spliced strip

A transition multiple exists.

Circus Wagon. August 31, 1990. Coil. Engraved. BEP.

5c red

IM 413A imperf pair 750.00
 imperf strip with plate No. 1 —
 spliced pair or strip, imperf —
 Quantity: 72-88 pairs

Transition multiples exist and sell for a premium. Wheels of the wagon are usually close to bottom or touch bottom. Price is for such a copy. Well centered copies exist and sell for more.

Circus Wagon. March 20, 1995. Coil. Photogravure. SVS.

5c carmine

IM 413B imperf pair —
 imperf strip with plate No. S2 —
 Quantity: a few hundred pairs

Some pairs possess counting numbers on the back.

Canoe. May 25, 1991. Coil. Engraved. BEP.

5c dark brownish violet & gray

IM 413C imperf pair 250.00
 imperf strip with plate No. 1 —
 imperf strip with plate No. 2 —
 imperf pair on first day cover —
 Quantity: 250+ pairs; 5 FDCs reported

Exists miscut. Transition multiples exist. Refer to note following **IM 434** regarding first day covers.

Refer to the note preceding **IM 410** and the second note following **IM 401** for information about size and pricing of plate number coil strips.

Bicycle. May 17, 1982. Coil. Engraved. BEP.

5.9c blue

IM 414 imperf pair, precanceled 2 bars 150.00
 imperf strip with plate No. 3 —
 imperf strip with plate No. 4 —
 imperf pair or strip, gap in bars —
 Quantity: 1,000+ pairs

Exists miscut, some with EE bars at top. Transition multiples exist and sell for a premium.

Tricycle. May 6, 1985. Coil. Engraved. BEP.

6c red brown

IM 416 imperf pair, precanceled 2 bars
 & **NON-PROFIT Org.** 225.00
 imperf strip with plate No. 2 1,500.00
 Quantity: 250 pairs reported

Wheel Chair. August 12, 1988. Coil. Engraved. BEP.

8.4c deep claret & red

IM 417 imperf pair 625.00
 imperf strip with plate No. 1 —
 imperf strip with plate No. 2 —
 Quantity: 100+ pairs reported

Transition multiples exist and sell for a premium.

Where possible, illustrations of actual error stamps have been used. They are bordered in black. Illustrations of normal stamps have been used in cases where error stamp illustrations were not available, or where an error illustration would not adequately illustrate the error. Illustrations of normal stamps appear without black border.

Mail Wagon. December 15, 1981. Coil. Engraved. BEP.

9.3c brownish purple

IM 418	imperf pair, precanceled 2 bars	115.00
	imperf strip with plate No. 1	*1,500.00*
	imperf strip with plate No. 2	*1,500.00*
	imperf strip with plate No. 3	—
	imperf strip with plate No. 4	—
	imperf pair or strip, gap in bars	—
	Quantity: 500 pairs	

Tractor Trailer. May 25, 1991. Coil. Engraved. BEP.

10c dark green & gray

IM 419	imperf pair	150.00
	imperf strip with plate No. 1	400.00
	Quantity: several hundred pairs	

Transition multiples exist and sell for a premium.

Canal Boat. April 11, 1987. Coil. Engraved. BEP.

10c blue

IM 419A	imperf pair	—
	imperf strip with Plate No. 1	—
	Quantity: 53 stamps	

Oil Wagon. April 18, 1985. Coil. Engraved. BEP.

10.1c slate blue

IM 420	imperf pair, precanceled 2 bars	
	& BULK RATE	85.00
	imperf strip with plate No. 1	400.00
	spliced pair or strip, imperf	
	imperf pair or strip, gap in bars	—
	Quantity: 500 pairs reported	

IM 420A	imperf pair, service inscribed	
	Bulk Rate Carrier Route Sort in red	15.00
	imperf strip with plate No. 3	200.00
	spliced pair or strip, imperf	—
	Quantity: few thousand pairs	

Hansom Cab. March 26, 1982. Coil. Engraved. BEP.

10.9c purple

IM 421	imperf pair, precanceled 2 bars	150.00
	imperf strip with plate No. 1	—
	imperf strip with plate No. 2	—
	imperf pair or strip, gap in bars	—
	Quantity: 250+ pairs reported	

Pushcart. April 18, 1985. Coil. Engraved. BEP.

12.5c dark olive green

IM 423	imperf pair, precanc bars & Bulk Rate	50.00
	imperf strip with plate No. 1	250.00
	imperf pair or strip, gap in bars	—
	Quantity: 750-1,000 pairs	

Although catalogue prices are based on the best information available at press time, readers should be aware that prices for error stamps fluctuate over time, and therefore, are advised to contact dealers active in the error stamp market for timely quotes when buying or selling.

Coal Car. July 19, 1988. Coil. Engraved. BEP.

13.2c slate green & red

IM 424	imperf pair	95.00
	imperf strip with plate No. 1	275.00
	imperf strip with plate No. 2	—
	Quantity: several hundred pairs	

Transition multiples exist and sell for a premium.

Iceboat. March 23, 1985. Coil. Engraved. BEP.

14c light blue

IM 425	imperf pair	95.00
	imperf strip with plate No.1	450.00
	imperf strip with plate No.2	450.00
	Quantity: 350+ pairs reported	

Transition multiples exist and sell for a premium.

Tugboat. July 12, 1988. Coil. Engraved. BEP.

15c violet

IM 425A	imperf pair	750.00
	imperf strip with plate No. 2	—
	Quantity: 80-100 pairs	

Transition multiples exist and sell for a premium.

Popcorn Wagon. July 7, 1988. Coil. Engraved. BEP.

16.7 rose & black

IM 426	imperf pair	175.00
	imperf strip with plate No. 1	—
	Quantity: 150-200 pairs reported	

All known copies are miscut. Transition multiples exist and sell for a premium.

Electric Auto. June 25, 1981. Coil. Engraved. BEP.

17c blue

IM 427	imperf pair	165.00
	imperf strip with plate No. 1	*1,000.00*
	imperf strip with plate No. 2	*1,000.00*
	imperf strip with plate No. 3	*1,000.00*
	imperf strip with plate No. 4	*1,000.00*
	imperf strip with plate No. 5	—
	imperf strip with plate No. 7	—
	used pair, imperf	—
	spliced pair or strip, imperf	—
	Quantity: 350-400 pairs	

Exists miscut. Plate numbers often appear at top of strip due to miscut. Transition multiples exist and sell for a premium.

IM 428	imperf pair, precanceled 2 bars	
	& **PRESORTED FIRST-CLASS**	575.00
	imperf strip with plate No. 3	—
	imperf strip with plate No. 4	
	imperf pair or strip, gap in bars	—
	spliced pair or strip, imperf	—
	Quantity: 80-100 pairs reported	

Exists miscut. A unique strip exists containing three copies of **IM 428** spliced to three copies of **IM 407**.

Buying or selling?
Consult the dealer directory at the back of the catalogue.

Dog Sled. August 20, 1986. Coil. Engraved. BEP.

17c blue

IM 429 imperf pair 425.00
 imperf strip with plate No. 2 —
 used strip of 3, imperf —
 Quantity: 100-125 pairs reported

Price for plate strip of 5 or 6 is the same. Exists miscut. Transition multiples exist and sell for a premium.

Racing Car. September 25, 1987. Coil. Engraved. BEP.

17.5c dark violet

IM 429A imperf pair 2,500.00
 imperf strip with plate No. 1 —
 Quantity: *26 pairs; 3 plate strips*
 of 6 reported

Transition multiples exist and sell for a premium.

Surrey. May 18, 1981. Coil. Engraved. BEP.

18c dark brown

IM 430 imperf pair 120.00
 imperf strip with plate No. 1 —
 imperf strip with plate No. 2 —
 imperf strip with plate No. 8 —
 imperf strip with plate No. 9 —
 imperf strip with plate No. 10 —
 imperf strip with plate No. 13 —
 spliced pair or strip, imperf —
 Quantity: 400-500 pairs reported

Exists miscut. Prices are for strips of 5 or 6 with plate number and line, except plate No. 13, which exists as a strip of 4. Also, refer to the second note following **IM 401**.

Hinging. Prices for stamps after **IM 196** are for never hinged copies. Hinged copies sell for less.

Fire Pumper. December 10, 1982. Coil. Engr. BEP.

20c red

IM 432 imperf pair 100.00
 imperf strip with plate No. 1 —
 imperf strip with plate No. 2 —
 imperf strip with plate No. 3 —
 imperf strip with plate No. 4 —
 imperf strip with plate No. 5 —
 imperf strip with plate No. 9 *1,250.00*
 imperf strip with plate No. 10 *1,250.00*
 imperf strip with plate No. 15 —
 imperf strip with plate No. 16 —
 Quantity: 600-800 pairs

Exists miscut. Transition multiples exist and sell for a premium. Prices are for strips of 6 with plate number and line. Plate Nos. 1, 2, 4 and 5 are most commonly encountered in plate number pairs: price $200-$375. Plate strips of 3 or 4 generally sell for about 33%-50% of plate strips of 6.

Cable Car. October 28, 1988. Coil. Engraved. BEP.

20c blue violet

IM 433 imperf pair 50.00
 imperf strip with plate No. 2 275.00
 spliced pair or strip, imperf —
 Quantity: 1,000+ pairs

Transition multiples exist and sell for a premium.

Cog Railway. June 9, 1995. Coil. Engraved. BEP.

20c dark gray green

IM 433A imperf pair 95.00
 imperf strip with plate No. 1 225.00
 Quantity: 400+ pairs

Mail Car. August 16, 1988. Coil. Engraved. BEP.

21c olive green & red

IM 434 imperf pair 45.00
imperf strip with plate No. 1 300.00
imperf pair on first day cover —
Quantity: 1,000+ pairs, 36 FDCs reported

Current Postal Service policy allows a grace period of 30 days (in some cases longer) after a stamp is issued during which covers may be submitted for first day cancellation. Because of this policy, controversy exists about the legitimacy of items that cannot conclusively be proved to have been postmarked on the actual first day of issue. Some regard imperfs on first day covers as contrived curiosities; others regard them as legitimately collectible. The publisher takes no position in this matter other than to report the existence of the covers.

Lunch Wagon. April 12, 1991. Coil. Engraved. BEP.

23c blue

IM 435 imperf pair 125.00
imperf strip with plate No. 2 —
imperf strip with plate No. 3 —
spliced pair or strip, imperf —
Quantity: 400-500 pairs reported

Exists miscut; some miscut pairs show EE bars at top. Transition multiples exist and sell for a premium. The gum on strips of plate No. 3 is mottled.

Breadwagon. November 22, 1986. Coil. Engr. BEP.

25c yellow brown

IM 436 imperf pair 10.00
imperf strip with plate No. 1 —
imperf strip with plate No. 2 225.00
imperf strip with plate No. 3 225.00
imperf strip with plate No. 4 225.00
imperf strip with plate No. 5 —
imperf pair, used —
spliced pair or strip, imperf —
Quantity: few thousand pairs

Exists miscut, some with EE bars at top or marginal markings at bottom. Transition multiples exist and sell for a premium. Exists untagged.

IM 437 pair, imperf between 500.00
strip of three pairs with plate No. 2 —
Quantity: *10 pairs reported*

Ferryboat. June 2, 1995. Coil. Engraved. BEP.

32c blue

IM 438 imperf pair 575.00
imperf strip with plate No. 2 —
imperf strip with plate No. 3 —
imperf strip with plate No. 5 —
Quantity: *70-80 pairs reported*

Exists miscut, some with EE bars at top or marginal markings at bottom.

IM 438A pair, imperf between —
Quantity: *n/a*

Expert certificate necessary.

Seaplane. April 20, 1990. Coil. Engraved. BEP.

$1 red & gray blue

IM 439 imperf pair 2,850.00
imperf strip with plate No. 1 —
imperf pair, used —
Quantity: 54 mint stamps; 1 strip
of 9 used & 1 strip of 4 used

Of the 54 mint stamps, 22 are in a strip containing plate No. 1 and the balance, in pairs.

Refer to the note preceding **IM 410** and the second note following **IM 401** for information about size and pricing of plate number coil strips.

Where possible, illustrations of actual error stamps have been used. They are bordered in black. Illustrations of normal stamps have been used in cases where error stamp illustrations were not available, or where an error illustration would not adequately illustrate the error. Illustrations of normal stamps appear without black border.

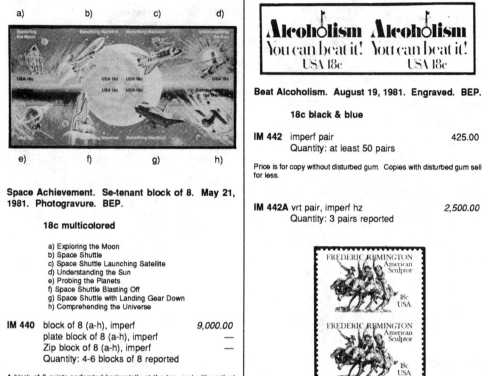

a) b) c) d)

e) f) g) h)

Space Achievement. Se-tenant block of 8. May 21, 1981. Photogravure. BEP.

18c multicolored

a) Exploring the Moon
b) Space Shuttle
c) Space Shuttle Launching Satellite
d) Understanding the Sun
e) Probing the Planets
f) Space Shuttle Blasting Off
g) Space Shuttle with Landing Gear Down
h) Comprehending the Universe

IM 440	block of 8 (a-h), imperf	*9,000.00*
	plate block of 8 (a-h), imperf	—
	Zip block of 8 (a-h), imperf	—
	Quantity: 4-6 blocks of 8 reported	

A block of 8 exists perforated horizontally at the top, and with vertical perforations extending about one-third the way down from the top. This creates four imperf stamps (e-h) along the bottom row and four imperf horizontally (a-e, b-f, c-g, and d-h) pairs.

Year of the Disabled. June 29, 1981. Photogravure. BEP.

18c multicolored

IM 441	vrt pair, imperf hz	*2,750.00*
	plate block of 4, imperf	—
	Quantity: 10 pairs reported	

☛ Caution. Beware pairs with blind horizontal perfs. Error pairs contain blind vertical perforations, which are normal.

Beat Alcoholism. August 19, 1981. Engraved. BEP.

18c black & blue

IM 442	imperf pair	425.00
	Quantity: at least 50 pairs	

Price is for copy without disturbed gum. Copies with disturbed gum sell for less.

IM 442A	vrt pair, imperf hz	*2,500.00*
	Quantity: 3 pairs reported	

Frederic Remington. October 9, 1981. Engraved. BEP.

18c brown, dark green & gray

IM 443	vrt pair, imperf between	250.00
	Quantity: 200 pairs reported	

☛ Caution. Pairs or strips of 3 exist with blind perfs.

Madonna. October 28, 1981. Photogravure. BEP.

(20c) multicolored

IM 444	imperf pair	110.00
	Quantity: few hundred pairs	

IM 444A	vrt pair, imperf hz	*1,550.00*
	block of 4, imperf hz	—
	Quantity: 4-5 pairs reported	

Christmas Toys. October 28, 1981. Photogravure. BEP.

(20c) multicolored

IM 445 imperf pair 225.00
Quantity: 200-300 pairs

IM 446 vrt pair, imperf hz —
Quantity: *10-15 pairs*

IM 446 results from blind perfs at left and right.

b)

a) c) d)

Cactus. December 11, 1981. Se-tenant block of 4. Engraved, lithographed. BEP.

20c multicolored

a) Barrel Cactus b) Agave
c) Beavertail Cactus d) Saguaro

IM 447 vrt pair (d only), imperf LRS (2/96) 6,600.00
single (d), imperf —
Quantity: 2 pairs, 1 single

The vertical imperf pair (d only) is contained in a block of 8.

Love. February 1, 1982. Photogravure. BEP.

20c multicolored

IM 448 imperf pair 250.00
plate block of 4, imperf —
Quantity: 150-200 pairs

Horizontal pairs usually sell for more than vertical pairs.

State Birds & Flowers. April 14, 1982. Se-tenant pane of 50. Photogravure. BEP.

20c multicolored.

IM 449 pane of 50, imperf LRS (3/97) 23,100.00
imperf pair —
Quantity: 4 panes

Of the four panes, two are completely imperf, one contains some blind perfs, and one was cut into pairs. The pane containing blind perfs realized $11,000 at auction in 1989.

Netherlands/USA. April 20, 1983. Photogravure. BEP.

20c multicolored

IM 450 imperf pair 300.00
Quantity: 94 pairs reported

Consumer Education. April 27, 1982. Coil. Engraved. BEP.

20c light blue

IM 451 imperf pair 95.00
imperf strip with plate No. 1 *750.00*
imperf strip with plate No. 2 *750.00*
imperf strip with plate No. 3 *1,750.00*
imperf strip with plate No. 4 *1,750.00*
Quantity: several hundred pairs

Prices are for strips of 6 with plate number and line. Plate strips of 5 sell for similar prices. Plate pairs are much more common: price $275.00. Plate strips of 3 sell for about 33% the plate strip of 6 price. Exists miscut. Transition multiples exist and sell for a premium.

72

America's Libraries. July 13, 1982. Engraved. BEP.

20c red & black

IM 452 vrt pair, imperf hz 275.00
 Quantity: 100-120 pairs

Touro Synagogue. August 22, 1982. Photogravure. BEP.

20c multicolored

IM 453 imperf pair *2,750.00*
 Quantity: 25 pairs

Ponce de Leon. October 2, 1982. Photogravure. BEP.

20c multicolored

IM 454 imperf pair 475.00
 plate block of 20, imperf —
 Quantity: 125+ pairs reported

IM 454A vrt pair, imperf between —
 Quantity: rare

Puppy & Kitten. November 3, 1982. Photogravure. BEP.

13c multicolored

IM 455 imperf pair 600.00
 Quantity: 75-100 pairs reported

Some pairs are faulty. Price is for a sound pair. Faulty pairs sell for considerably less.

Madonna. October 28, 1982. Photogravure. BEP.

20c multicolored

IM 456 imperf pair 150.00
 plate block of 20, imperf —
 Quantity: few hundred pairs

IM 457 hz, imperf vrt —
 Quantity: 3-6 pairs reported

IM 457A vrt pair, imperf hz —
 plate block of 4, imperf hz **LRS (6/98)** 4,025.00
 Quantity: very rare

The plate block contains blind perforations on its sides and at bottom.

Where possible, illustrations of actual error stamps have been used. They are bordered in black. Illustrations of normal stamps have been used in cases where error stamp illustrations were not available, or where an error illustration would not adequately illustrate the error. Illustrations of normal stamps appear without black border.

**Christmas Winter Scenes. October 28, 1982.
Se-tenant block of 4. Photogravure. BEP.**

20c multicolored

a) Snowman b) Sledding
c) Christmas tree d) Skating

IM 458 block of 4 (a-d), imperf 2,800.00
 Quantity: 20 blocks of 4

☛ Caution. Beware blocks with blind perforations.

IM 459 block of 4 (a-d), imperf hz —
 Quantity: rare

**Balloons. March 31, 1983. Se-tenant block of 4.
Photogravure. BEP.**

20c multicolored

a) Intrepid
b) Hot Air Ballooning
c) Hot Air Ballooning
d) Explorer II

IM 460 block of 4 (a-d), imperf 4,750.00
 plate block of 4, imperf —
 Zip block of 4, imperf —
 copyright block of 4, imperf —
 Quantity: 10 blocks of 4

In addition to the above, five blocks of 4 (a-d) exist with perforations on
the three exterior sides of the right stamp (d) and a vertical row of blind
perforations between stamps (b-c) and the right stamp (d). Price
$4,500.00.

**Civilian Conservation Corps. April 5, 1983.
Photogravure. BEP.**

20c multicolored

IM 461 imperf pair 3,000.00
 plate block of 4, imperf —
 Quantity: 7 pairs, including
 those in the plate block

IM 461A vrt pair, imperf hz —
 Quantity: unique

IM 461A results from blind perfs at its sides.

**Volunteer Lend A Hand. April 30, 1983. Engraved.
BEP.**

20c black & red

IM 462 imperf pair 450.00
 Quantity: 25-50 pairs reported

Some copies have an underinked appearance. Price is for underinked
copy. Solidly colored copies sell for more.

Hinging. Prices for stamps after **IM 196** are for never hinged copies.
Hinged copies sell for less.

Scott Joplin. June 9, 1983. Photogravure. BEP.

20c multicolored

IM 463 imperf pair 450.00
 Quantity: 50 pairs reported

Santa Claus. October 28, 1983. Photogravure. BEP.

20c multicolored

IM 464 imperf pair 150.00
 plate bock of 6, imperf 450.00
 Quantity: 150+ pairs

Love. January 31, 1984. Photogravure. BEP.

20c multicolored

IM 465 hz pair, imperf vrt 175.00
 Quantity: 150-175 pairs

Carter G. Woodson. January 31, 1984. Photogravure. ABN.

20c multicolored

IM 466 hz pair, imperf vrt *1,750.00*
 Quantity: 25 pairs reported

Summer Olympics. May 4, 1984. Photogravure. BEP.

 a) Diving b) Long Jump
 c) Wrestling d) Canoeing

20c multicolored

IM 466A block of 4, imperf vrt —
 pair c & d, imperf vrt —
 Quantity: 2 blocks of 4, 1 pair

The discovery pane contained the listed stamps in a strip of ten at left. The pane also contained a row of blind perfs between rows 7 and 8.

Douglas Fairbanks. May 23, 1984. Engraved, photogravure. BEP.

20c multicolored

IM 467 hz pair, imperf vrt —
 Quantity: *reportedly unique*

Preserving Wetlands. July 2, 1984. Engraved. BEP.

20c blue

IM 468 hz pair, imperf vrt 375.00
 hz strip of 3, imperf vrt 450.00
 Zip block, imperf vrt —
 Quantity: 95-120 pairs

Smokey. August 13, 1984. Photogravure. BEP.

20c multicolored

IM 469 hz pair, imperf between 275.00
 plate block of 4, vrt imperf
 between —
 Quantity: 100-125 pairs

IM 469A hz pair, imperf vrt *1,600.00*
 Quantity: 20-25 pairs

IM 470 vrt pair, imperf between 225.00
 Quantity: 160-200 pairs

IM 471 block of 4, imperf hz & vrt
 (internally) between *5,750.00*
 Quantity: 6 blocks of 4 (including
 1 faulty block)

The term "transition multiple" refers to errors appearing in combination with normal or nearly-normal stamps. Generally, a pair, strip, or block containing one or more error stamps, one or more normal stamps, and, in the case of color-omitted errors, one or more stamps with color(s) partially omitted. Transition multiples sell for a premium.

Roberto Clemente. August 17, 1984. Photogravure. BEP.

20c multicolored

IM 472 hz pair, imperf vrt 2,000.00
 hz strip of 3, vrt imperf —
 Quantity: 20 pairs, 3 strips of
 3 reported

Family Unity. October 1, 1984. Photogravure. BEP.

20c multicolored

IM 473 hz pair, imperf vrt 525.00
 Quantity: 50 pairs

IM 473A hz pair, imperf between —
 Quantity: n/a

IM 473B vrt pair, imperf between —
 Quantity: n/a

IM 473B occurs with a natural straight edge at bottom.

Christmas. October 30, 1984. Photogravure. BEP.

20c multicolored

IM 473C hz pair, imperf vrt 925.00
 Quantity: 25 pairs

Most copies are poorly centered as in the illustration. Price is for a poorly centered copy.

Hispanic Americans. October 31, 1984. Photogravure. BEP.

20c multicolored

IM 474 vrt pair, imperf hz 2,250.00
 Quantity: 20 pairs reported

Eagle & D. February 1, 1985. Photogravure. BEP.

D (22c) green

IM 475 imperf vrt pair 40.00
 block of 4, imperf 80.00
 plate block of 4, imperf 125.00
 Zip block of 4, imperf 100.00
 copyright block of 4, imperf 100.00
 Quantity: 1,000+

IM 476 vrt pair, imperf hz *1,300.00*
 Quantity: 4 pairs reported

Hinging. Prices for stamps after **IM 196** are for never hinged copies. Hinged copies sell for less.

Eagle & D. February 1, 1985. Coil. Photogravure. BEP.

D (22c) green

IM 477	imperf pair	45.00
	imperf strip with plate No. 1	500.00
	imperf strip with plate No. 2	750.00
	spliced pair or strip, imperf	—
	Quantity: 1,000+	

Prices are for plate strips of 6. Plate strips of 5 sell for similar prices. Plate strips of 3 or 4 for sell for 33%-50% the price of plate strips of 6. Strips exist spliced with a variety of kinds and colors of cellophane, masking, and paper tapes, and the sell for a premium. Exists miscut. Exists untagged; quantity 200 pairs; price $125.00.

Eagle & D. February 1, 1985. Booklet pane of 10. Photogravure. BEP.

D (22c) green

IM 477A booklet pane of 10, imperf
hz between —
Quantity: 2 panes

Flag & Capitol. March 29, 1985. Coil. Engraved. BEP.

22c red, blue & black

IM 478	imperf pair	12.50
	imperf strip with plate No. 1	500.00
	imperf strip with plate No. 2	150.00
	imperf strip with plate No. 3	*1,000.00*
	imperf strip with plate No. 4	*750.00*
	imperf strip with plate No. 5	675.00
	imperf strip with plate No. 6	*750.00*
	imperf strip with plate No. 7	500.00
	imperf strip with plate No. 8	200.00
	imperf strip with plate No. 10	500.00
	imperf strip with plate No. 11	*1,250.00*
	imperf strip with plate No. 12	350.00
	imperf strip with plate No. 13	*750.00*
	imperf strip with plate No. 15	900.00
	imperf strip with plate No. 17	—
	imperf strip with plate No. 18	650.00
	imperf strip with plate No. 19	400.00
	imperf strip with plate No. 20	950.00
	imperf strip with plate No. 22	450.00
	spliced pair or strip, imperf	—
	Quantity: few thousand pairs	

Prices are for plate strips of 5 or 6. Strips of 3 or 4 sell for 33%-50% of the strip of 6 price. Exists miscut, some with EE bars at top or marginal markings at bottom. Transition multiples exist and sell for a premium.

Special Olympics. March 5, 1985. Photogravure. BEP.

22c multicolored

| IM 479 | vrt pair, imperf hz | 500.00 |
| | Quantity: 60-80 pairs reported | |

Love. April 17, 1985. Photogravure. BEP.

22c multicolored

IM 480	imperf pair	*1,500.00*
	Quantity: 15 pairs imperf, 5 pairs	
	partially imperf, see note	

Some pairs (often in transition strips) contain perfs at left, and on top and bottom of the left stamp. Often with paper crease. Price is for sound pair. Creased pairs sell for about 33% of sound pairs.

Sea Shells. April 4, 1985. Se-tenant booklet pane of 10. Engraved. BEP.

22c multicolored

a) Frilled Dogwinkle
b) Reticulated Helmet
c) New England Neptune
d) Calico Scallop
e) Lightning Whelk

| IM 481 | booklet pane, imperf vrt between | 600.00 |
| | Quantity: 30-40 booklets reported | |

Panes removed from booklets usually contain tab faults. Price is for pane with tab faults.

Rural Electrification. May 11, 1985. Engraved, photogravure. BEP.

22c multicolored

IM 481A vrt pair, imperf between —
Quantity: *reportedly unique*

Abigail Adams. June 14, 1985. Photogravure. BEP.

22c multicolored

IM 482 imperf pair 250.00
Quantity: 150-200 pairs

Transition multiples exist and sell for a premium.

Poinsettia. October 31, 1985. Photogravure. BEP.

22c multicolored

IM 483 imperf pair 120.00
block of 4, imperf 250.00
plate block of 4, imperf —
Zip block of 4, imperf —
Quantity: 250-300 pairs

Madonna. October 31, 1985. Photogravure. BEP.

22c multicolored

IM 484 imperf pair 80.00
plate block of 4, imperf 200.00
Zip block of 4, imperf —
Quantity: 300-400 pairs

COIL STAMP

George Washington. November 6, 1985. Coil. Photogravure. BEP.

18c multicolored

IM 485 imperf pair, precanceled **PRESORTED FIRST-CLASS** 775.00
imperf strip with plate No. 3333 —
spliced pair or strip, imperf —
Quantity: 50-100 pairs reported

Exists miscut. Transition multiples exist and sell for a premium.

IM 486 imperf pair, without precancel 950.00
imperf strip with plate No. 1112
Quantity: 30-40 pairs reported

Arkansas. January 3, 1986. Photogravure. ABN.

22c multicolored

IM 487 vrt pair, imperf hz —
Quantity: 25 pairs reported

Texas. March 2, 1986. Photogravure. ABN.

22c multicolored

IM 488 hz pair, imperf vrt 1,100.00
Quantity: 25 pairs

Public Hospitals. April 11, 1986. Photogravure. BEP.

22c multicolored

IM 489 vrt pair, imperf hz 300.00
Quantity: 50-75 pairs

IM 489A hz pair, imperf vrt *1,250.00*
Quantity: *20 pairs*

Duke Ellington. April 29, 1986. Photogravure. ABN.

22c multicolored

IM 490 vrt pair, imperf hz 900.00
plate block of 4, imperf hz —
used strip of 3, imperf hz *375.00*
Quantity: 40-60 pairs

Presidents. May 22, 1986. Souvenir sheet of 9. Engraved, lithographed. BEP.

22c multicolored

IM 490A imperf sheet of 9 LRS (2/93) *10,450.00*
Quantity: *very rare, possibly unique*

Where possible, illustrations of actual error stamps have been used. They are bordered in black. Illustrations of normal stamps have been used in cases where error stamp illustrations were not available, or where an error illustration would not adequately illustrate the error. Illustrations of normal stamps appear without black border.

Wood Carving. October 1, 1986. Se-tenant block of 4. Photogravure. ABN.

22c multicolored

a) Highlander Figure b) Ship Figurehead
c) Nautical Figure d) Cigar Store Indian

IM 491 block of 4 (a-d), imperf vrt 1,450.00
pair (a-b or c-d), imperf vrt 300.00
Quantity: 20 blocks of 4;
5 pairs each a-b & c-d

Madonna. October 14, 1986. Photogravure. BEP.

22c multicolored

IM 491A imperf pair *750.00*
Quantity: *25-50 pairs reported*

William Faulkner. August 3, 1987. Engraved. BEP.

22c green

IM 491B imperf single, used **PW** —
Quantity: rare

☞ Caution. Genuine imperforate used singles of this issue are from printer's waste and are not tagged. Beware tagged used singles trimmed to resemble imperforates.

Flag & Fireworks. November 30, 1987. Booklet pane of 20. Photogravure. BEP.

22c multicolored

IM 491C vert pair, imperf btwn **LRS (6/97)** 1,980.00
Quantity: unique

IM 491C occurs as a result of a foldover.

COIL STAMP

Earth. March 22, 1988. Coil. Photogravure. BEP.

E (25c) multicolored

IM 492 imperf pair 70.00
imperf strip with plate No. 1111 *475.00*
imperf strip with plate No. 1211 —
imperf strip with plate No. 1222 —
imperf strip with plate No. 2222 —
spliced pair or strip, imperf —
Quantity: 1,000+ pairs

Prices are for plate strips of 6. Exists miscut. The plate number on plate strips of No. 1222 appear at the top due to a miscut. Transition multiples exist and sell for a premium.

Flag Over Yosemite. May 20, 1988. Coil. Block tagging. Engraved. BEP.

25c red, ultramarine & cobalt green

IM 493	imperf pair	25.00
	imperf strip with plate No. 2	600.00
	imperf strip with plate No. 3	425.00
	imperf strip with plate No. 4	—
	imperf strip with plate No. 5	700.00
	imperf strip with plate No. 7	500.00
	imperf strip with plate No. 8	750.00
	imperf strip with plate No. 9	750.00
	spliced pair or strip, imperf	—
	Quantity: several thousand pairs	

Exists miscut. Transition multiples exist and sell for a premium.

Flag Over Yosemite. February 14, 1989. Coil. Same design as IM 493. Phosphor tagging. Engraved. BEP.

IM 494	imperf pair	10.00
	imperf strip with plate No. 2	175.00
	imperf strip with plate No. 3	*750.00*
	imperf strip with plate No. 5	*750.00*
	imperf strip with plate No. 6	*900.00*
	imperf strip with plate No. 7	700.00
	imperf strip with plate No. 8	700.00
	imperf strip with plate No. 9	375.00
	imperf strip with plate No. 10	375.00
	imperf strip with plate No. 11	*600.00*
	imperf strip with plate No. 13	—
	imperf strip with plate No. 14	350.00
	imperf strip with plate No. 15	—
	imperf pair on first day cover	—
	spliced pair or strip, imperf	—
	Quantity: several thousand pairs	

Exists miscut, some with EE bands at top or marginal markings at bottom. Exists untagged. Transition multiples exist and sell for a premium. Prices are for plate strips of 6.
Block tagging on **IM 493** is rectangular in shape covering the design. Phosphor tagging on **IM 494** covers the entire stamp. Refer to note following **IM 434** regarding first day covers.

IM 494A	pair, imperf between	450.00
	strip of 6 with plate No. 9	—
	strip of 6 with plate No. 14	—
	Quantity: *35+ pairs reported*	

Expert certificate advised.

Honeybee. September 2, 1988. Coil. Engraved, lithographed. BEP.

25c multicolored

IM 495	imperf pair	50.00
	imperf strip with plate No. 1	250.00
	imperf strip with plate No. 2	250.00
	imperf pair on first day cover	—
	spliced pair or strip, imperf	—
	Quantity: several hundred pairs; 6 first day covers	

Exists miscut, some with EE bars at top. Some pairs contain lines that resemble Cottrell press lines. Prices are for plate strips of 6. Refer to the note following **IM 434** regarding first day covers.

☛ Caution. Pairs exist with blind perfs.

IM 496	pair, imperf between	—
	strip with plate No. 1, imperf between	—
	Quantity: *10 pairs, 1-2 plate number strips reported*	

Pheasant. April 29, 1988. Booklet pane of 10. Engraved, lithographed. ABN.

25c multicolored

IM 497	vrt pair, imperf between **PW**	—
	Quantity: several hundred pairs	

☛ Printer's waste. A few pairs exist as the result of a foldover. They are not printer's waste and see for substantially more.

IM 498	vrt pair, imperf hz **PW**	50.00
	booklet pane, imperf hz	—
	Quantity: several hundred pairs	

☛ Printer's waste. Refer to introduction. Caution: **IM 498** can be created by trimming perfs from top and bottom of **IM 497**.

IM 499	imperf pair **PW**	—
	Quantity: n/a	

☛ Printer's waste. Refer to introduction.

South Carolina. May 23, 1988. Photogravure. ABN.

25c multicolored

IM 499A hz strip of 3, imperf vrt **LRS (9/92)** 10,450.00
Quantity: unique strip of 3

Love. July 4, 1988. Photogravure. BEP.

25c multicolored

IM 499B imperf pair *3,250.00*
Quantity: *5 pairs or strips 3*

Antarctic Explorers. August 25, 1988. Se-tenant block of 4. Photogravure. ABN.

25c multicolored

a) Nathaniel Palmer b) Charles Wilkes
c) Richard Byrd d) Lincoln Ellsworth

IM 500 block of 4, imperf hz *3,000.00*
plate block of 4, imperf hz —
Quantity: 10 blocks of 4,
 5 singles (a & c)

Special Occasions. October 22, 1988. Booklet pane of 6. Photogravure. ABN.

25c multicolored

a) Flowers b) Bird in mailbox

IM 501 booklet pane, imperf —
Quantity: unique

Montana. January 15, 1989. Engraved, litho. BEP.

25c multicolored

IM 501A imperf pair **PW** 275.00
Quantity: a few hundred pairs

All known copies are without gum. At least one block of 4 exists with "First Day of Issue" postmark. It is almost certainly contrived.

Hemingway. July 17, 1989. Photogravure. ABN.

25c multicolored

IM 501B vrt pair, imperf hz —
Quantity: *24-36 pairs reported*

Pairs are typically centered to the right or left.

Astronauts on Moon. July 20, 1989. Engraved, lithographed. BEP.

$2.40 multicolored

IM 502 imperf pair 750.00
 plate block of 4, imperf —
 Quantity: 200 pairs

Christmas. October 19, 1989. Photogravure. Perf 11. ABN.

25c multicolored

IM 503 vrt pair, imperf hz *850.00*
 Quantity: *20+ pairs reported*

Christmas. October 19, 1989. Booklet pane of 10. Photogravure. Perf 11½. BEP.

25c multicolored

IM 504 vrt pair, imperf hz —
 booklet pane, imperf hz —
 Quantity: *2 panes reported*

IM 503 and **IM 504** can be distinguished in several ways. One of the easiest is to compare the color of the large package at the front and bottom of the sleigh. It is a light brown color on **IM 503** and dark maroon color on **IM 504**.

IM 504A imperf pair —
 block of 4, imperf **LRS (12/98)** 1,265.00
 Quantity: rare

Hinging. Prices for stamps after **IM 196** are for never hinged copies. Hinged copies sell for less.

Eagle & Shield. November 10, 1989. Photogravure. Self-adhesive. Straight die cut. ABN.

25c multicolored

IM 505 pair, die cut omitted 300.00
 plate block of 4, die cut omitted —
 Quantity: n/a

IM 505A pair, die cut omitted between 575.00
 Quantity: *27-36 pairs*

Love. January 18, 1990. Photogravure. USB.

25c multicolored

IM 506 imperf pair 800.00
 Quantity: 50 pairs

American Indian Headdresses. July 6, 1990. Se-tenant booklet pane of 10. Engraved, lithographed. BEP.

25c multicolored

IM 506A booklet pane of 10, imperf hz —
 Quantity: *very rare, possibly unique*

Although catalogue prices are based on the best information available at press time, readers should be aware that prices for error stamps fluctuate over time, and therefore, are advised to contact dealers active in the error stamp market for timely quotes when buying or selling.

84

Dwight D. Eisenhower. October 13, 1990. Photogravure. BEP.

25c multicolored

IM 507 imperf pair 2,250.00
plate block of 4, imperf —
Quantity: *20 pairs*

Greetings. October 18, 1990. Photogravure. ABN.

25c multicolored

IM 507A vrt pair, imperf hz 1,100.00
Quantity: 19 sound pairs, 1 faulty pair

Flower. January 22, 1991. Photogravure. Perf 13. USB.

F (29c) multicolored

IM 508 vrt pair, imperf 700.00
Quantity: *20-30 pairs reported*

IM 508 is collected in vertical pairs or blocks in order to distinguish it from the imperforate coil stamp of the same design.

IM 509 hz pair, imperf vrt *1,250.00*
Quantity: *5 pairs reported*

Flower. January 22, 1991. Coil. Photogravure. BEP.

F (29c) multicolored

IM 510 imperf pair 35.00
imperf strip with plate No. 1111 225.00
imperf strip with plate No. 1222 —
imperf strip with plate No. 2211 —
imperf strip with plate No. 2222 225.00
imperf pair on first day cover —
spliced pair or strip, imperf —
Quantity: 1,000+; 20 first day covers

Prices are for plate strips of 5 or 6. Exists miscut. Transition multiples exist and sell for a premium. Refer to note following **IM 434** regarding first day covers.

Makeup Rate Stamp. January 22, 1991. Lithographed. ABN.

(4c) red & olive gold

IM 511 vrt pair, imperf hz 100.00
plate block of 4, imperf hz —
Quantity: 400+ pairs

IM 511A imperf pair 75.00
plate block of 4, imperf —
Quantity: 300+ pairs

IM 511A is likely printer's waste.

Switzerland. February 22, 1991. Photogravure. ABN.

50c multicolored

IM 511B vrt pair, imperf hz 2,000.00
Quantity: 20 pairs

Flag & Mt. Rushmore. March 29, 1991. Coil. Engraved. BEP.

29c red, dark blue & dark purple

IM 512	imperf pair	20.00
	imperf strip with plate No. 1	450.00
	imperf strip with plate No. 2	—
	imperf strip with plate No. 3	375.00
	imperf strip with plate No. 4	350.00
	imperf strip with plate No. 6	350.00
	imperf strip with plate No. 7	250.00
	imperf strip with plate No. 9	—
	spliced pair or strip, imperf	—
	Quantity: 1,000+ pairs	

Exists miscut, some with EE bars at top. Prices are for plate strips of 6. Transition multiples exist and sell for a premium.

Flower. April 5, 1991. Booklet pane of 10. Photogravure. KCS.

29c multicolored

IM 514	hz pair, imperf vrt	250.00
	booklet pane, imperf vrt	1,850.00
	Quantity: 10-15 panes reported	

IM 514 contains natural straight edges on right and left sides.

IM 515	hz pair, imperf between	—
	Quantity: 3-5 pairs reported	

IM 515 results from a foldover.

IM 516	vrt pair, imperf hz	—
	booklet pane, imperf hz	—
	Quantity: 2-3 panes reported	

Pairs of **IM 516** contain a natural straight edge on either the right or the left side.

Wood Duck. April 12, 1991. Booklet pane of 10. Photogravure. BEP.

29c multicolored & black numeral

IM 517	vrt pair, imperf hz	200.00
	booklet pane of 10, imperf hz	1,000.00
	Quantity: 20 panes reported	

Wood Duck. April 12, 1991. Booklet pane of 10. Photogravure. KCS.

29c multicolored & red numeral

IM 518	vrt pair, imperf between	—
	Quantity: 2-3 reported	

IM 518 results from a foldover.

IM 518A imperf pair **LRS (6/97)**	3,960.00
Quantity: 2 pairs reported	

U.S. Flag & Olympic Rings. April 21, 1991. Booklet pane of 10. Photogravure. KCS.

29c multicolored

IM 519 vrt pair, imperf between *300.00*
 booklet pane of 10, imperf between —
 Quantity: *9-10+ panes reported*

Vertical strips of 3 are known containing a pair imperf between plus an additional perforated stamp, raising the possibility that they originate from unsevered press sheets. At least one pane containing two full pairs as a result of a foldover is known and is worth more.

IM 519A vrt pair, imperf hz —
 Quantity: new, n/a

Love. May 9, 1991. Photogravure. USB.

29c multicolored

IM 520 imperf pair *2,500.00*
 Quantity: 25 pairs reported

Fishing Flies. May 31, 1991. Booklet pane of 5. Photogravure. ABN.

29c multicolored

 a) Royal Wulff
 b) Jock Scott
 c) Apte Tarpon Fly
 d) Lefty's Deceiver
 e) Muddler Minnow

IM 520A hz pair (c), imperf vrt **PW** —
 Quantity: *5-6 pairs reported*

☛ Printer's waste, refer to introduction. All pairs reported possess a vertical crease between stamps.

Cole Porter. June 8, 1991. Photogravure. ABN.

29c multicolored

IM 521 vrt pair, imperf hz 575.00
 Quantity: 50-60 pairs reported

Hand & Torch. June 25, 1991. Booklet pane of 18. Photogravure. Self-adhesive. Straight die cut. AVR.

29c black, green & gold

IM 521A pair, die cut omitted **LRS (5/96)** 3,740.00
 Quantity: 1 pane of 18

Desert Storm. July 2, 1991. Photogravure. SVS.

29c multicolored

IM 522 vrt pair, imperf hz 1,750.00
 plate block of 4, imperf hz —
 Quantity: 20-30 pairs reported

Express Mail. June 16, 1991. Engraved, lithographed. ABN.

$9.95 black (engraved); black, yellow, red & cyan (lithographed)

IM 522A imperf pair, black (engraved) omitted **PW** —
Quantity: at least 40 pairs

☛ Printer's waste, refer to introduction.

Eagle & Olympic Rings. July 7, 1991. Engraved, lithographed. ABN.

$2.90 multicolored

IM 523 vrt pair, imperf hz —
Quantity: 4 pairs, 4 strips of 3

Boat. August 8, 1991. Coil. Photogravure. ABN.

19c multicolored

IM 524 imperf pair with gum **PW** 75.00
imperf pair without gum **PW** 40.00
imperf strip with plate No. A1112 —
imperf strip with plate No. A7767 275.00
Quantity: few thousand pairs

Exists drastically miscut with printer's registration marks and color bars at bottom. Miscuts sell for a premium. Pairs and strips from plate number A1112 are without gum, reportedly spoiled by water.

☛ Printer's waste. Refer to the introduction.

Jan E. Matzeliger. September 15, 1991. Photogravure. ABN.

29c multicolored

IM 525 hz pair, imperf vrt 1,600.00
Quantity: *50 pairs*

IM 526 vrt pair, imperf hz 1,500.00
Quantity: 40-60 pairs

IM 526A imperf pair *500.00*
Quantity: 50-100 pairs

Christmas. October 17, 1991. Photogravure. ABN.

29c multicolored

IM 527 hz pair, imperf vrt 275.00
Quantity: 80-100 pairs

Exists with rows of misplaced horizontal perforations.

IM 528 vrt pair, imperf hz 500.00
Quantity: 50-80 pairs reported

Santa in Chimney. October 17, 1991. Booklet pane of 4. Photogravure. ABN.

(29c) multicolored

IM 528A booklet pane, imperf PW —
Quantity: n/a

☞ **IM 528A-528D** are printer's waste. **IM 528A** contains 2 design types. The 2 stamps at left contain part of an extra brick on the left side of the top row of bricks. The two stamps at right do not.

Santa & Package. October 17, 1991. Booklet pane of 4. Photogravure. ABN.

(29c) multicolored

IM 528B booklet pane, imperf PW —
Quantity: n/a

Santa & Sack. October 17, 1991. Booklet pane of 4. Photogravure. ABN.

(29c) multicolored

IM 528C booklet pane, imperf PW —
Quantity: n/a

Santa & Sleigh. October 17, 1991. Booklet pane of 4. Photogravure. ABN.

(29c) multicolored

IM 528D booklet pane, imperf PW —
Quantity: n/a

Eagle & Shield, Bulk Rate-USA. December 13, 1991. Coil. Photogravure. ABN.

(10c) multicolored

IM 529 imperf pair —
imperf strip with plate No. A43335 —
Quantity: *10-25 reported*

Most **IM 529** are contained in plate number strips, most of which are transitional. Pairs are very rare. Three plate number strips of 6 or 7 have been reported, one of which is damaged. One of the plate number strips is a transition strip in which the plate number appears on a perforated stamp.

Eagle & Shield, USA-Bulk Rate. May 29, 1993. Coil. Untagged. Photogravure. BEP.

(10c) multicolored

IM 530 imperf pair 25.00
imperf strip with plate No. 11111 125.00
imperf strip with plate No. 22221 —
imperf strip with plate No. 22222 175.00
spliced pair or strip, imperf —
Quantity: several thousand pairs

Exists miscut. Transition multiples exist and sell for a premium. Exists tagged.

Love. February 6, 1992. Photogravure. ABN.

29c multicolored

IM 532 hz pair, imperf vrt 750.00
Quantity: 50 pairs

Although catalogue prices are based on the best information available at press time, readers should be aware that prices for error stamps fluctuate over time, and therefore, are advised to contact dealers active in the error stamp market for timely quotes when buying or selling.

Flag & White House. April 23, 1992. Coil. Engraved. BEP.

29c red & gray blue

IM 533	imperf pair	17.50
	used pair, imperf	—
	imperf strip with plate No. 1	—
	imperf strip with plate No. 2	—
	imperf strip with plate No. 3	500.00
	imperf strip with plate No. 4	150.00
	imperf strip with plate No. 5	—
	imperf strip with plate No. 6	—
	imperf strip with plate No. 7	400.00
	imperf strip with plate No. 8	400.00
	imperf strip with plate No. 9	400.00
	imperf strip with plate No. 10	—
	imperf strip with plate No. 11	—
	imperf strip with plate No. 12	—
	imperf strip with plate No. 13	—
	spliced strip or pair, imperf	—
	Quantity: 1,000+ pairs	

☛ Caution. Beware blind perfs. Exists miscut. Imperforate strips from the edge of the printing web (plate No. 6) exist. They contain various printed elements: production bars, markings and/or plate numbers. At press time, 3 strips the length of a coil of 100 stamps were known, all from plate No. 6. Transition strips exist and sell for a premium.

IM 534	pair, imperf between	95.00
	Quantity: 250+ pairs reported	

☛ Exercise extreme caution. Rolls from which this error arises contain imperf pairs, imperf between pairs, and many ostensibly imperf between pairs with blind perfs. Check carefully to make sure that imperf between pairs are completely free of blind perfs between stamps. Exists with plate Nos. 3 or 4.

Flag & Pledge. September 8, 1992. Booklet pane of 10. Photogravure. BEP.

29c multicolored; black denomination

IM 534A	imperf pair	—
	Quantity: 10 pairs, including 4	
	with destruction marks	

COLUMBUS SOUVENIR SHEETS OF 1992

Voyages of Columbus. May 22, 1992. Souvenir sheet of 3. Engraved, lithographed. BEP.

5c chocolate, 30c orange brown & 50c slate blue

IM 534B	souvenir sheet of 3, imperf PW		*450.00*
	Quantity: n/a		

Voyages of Columbus. May 22, 1992. Souvenir sheet of 3. Engraved, lithographed. BEP.

1c deep blue, 4c ultramarine & $1 salmon

IM 534C	souvenir sheet of 3, imperf PW		*450.00*
	Quantity: n/a		

Imperforate Columbus souvenir sheets appeared on the market several years after original issue, and, by all indications, from a single source. Many contain faults—including wrinkles, edge faults, and offsets—not normally encountered on issued sheets, which were assembled and enclosed in printed envelopes. During manufacture, the Bureau of Engraving and Printing exercised extra vigilance precisely to avoid releasing faulty sheets and errors. Prior to discovery of the imperforate sheets, virtually no other Columbus souvenir sheet EFOs had surfaced. So, while one might expect to encounter a random error, the appearance of multiple copies of all six sheets over a short period of time leaves little doubt that they are printer's waste.

Voyages of Columbus. May 22, 1992. Souvenir sheet of 3. Engraved, lithographed. BEP.

10c brown black, 15c dark green & $2 purple

IM 534D souvenir sheet, imperf **PW** *450.00*
 Quantity: n/a

Voyages of Columbus. May 22, 1992. Souvenir sheet of 3. Engraved, lithographed. BEP.

6c violet, 8c magenta & $3 olive green

IM 534E souvenir sheet of 3, imperf **PW** *450.00*
 Quantity: n/a

Voyages of Columbus. May 22, 1992. Souvenir sheet of 3. Engraved, lithographed. BEP.

2c brown violet, 3c green & $4 crimson lake

IM 534F souvenir sheet of 3, imperf **PW** *450.00*
 Quantity: n/a

Voyages of Columbus. May 22, 1992. Souvenir sheet of 1. Engraved, lithographed. BEP.

$5 black

IM 534G souvenir sheet, imperf **PW** *450.00*
 Quantity: n/a

Hummingbirds. June 15, 1992. Booklet pane of 5. Photogravure. ABN.

29c multicolored

 a) Ruby-throated hummingbird
 b) Broad-bellied hummingbird
 c) Costa's hummingbird
 d) Rufous hummingbird
 e) Calliope hummingbird

IM 534H booklet pane of 5, imperf **PW** —
 Quantity: n/a

☛ Printer's waste, refer to introduction.

Buying or selling?
Consult the dealer directory at the back of the catalogue.

Eagle & Shield. September 25, 1992. Pane of 17 plus label. Photogravure. Self-adhesive. Straight die cut. BCA.

29c multicolored, brown numeral

IM 535 pair, die cut omitted 175.00
pane of 17, die cut omitted 1,500.00
Quantity: 30-40 panes

IM 535 is often encountered with a fold or minor faults. Price is for a sound copy.

Wild Animals. October 1, 1992. Booklet pane of 5. Photogravure. SVS.

29c multicolored

a) Giraffe
b) Giant Panda
c) Flamingo
d) King Penguins
e) White Bengal Tiger

IM 536 booklet pane, imperf 3,500.00
Quantity: *6 panes reported*

Panes contain normal booklet bend between stamps b & c and gum disturbance from removal from booklet.

Chrome USA. October 9, 1992. Coil. Photogravure. BEP.

23c multicolored, deep blue background

IM 537 imperf pair 85.00
imperf strip with plate No. 1111 250.00
Quantity: 300-500 pairs

Christmas Toys. October 22, 1992. Se-tenant booklet pane of 4. Photogravure. ABN.

29c multicolored

a) Toy Horse b) Locomotive
c) Carriage d) Toy Ship

IM 538 booklet pane of 4, imperf hz
LRS (9/95) 6,875.00
Quantity: unique

IM 538A booklet pane of 4, imperf **PW** —
Quantity: n/a

Garden Flowers. May 15, 1993. Booklet pane of 5. Engraved, lithographed. BEP.

29c multicolored

a) Hyacinth
b) Daffodil
c) Tulip
d) Iris
e) Lilac

IM 539 booklet pane, imperf *2,750.00*
Quantity: 12-16 panes reported

Price is for pane with usual booklet bend between stamps b & c. A transition pane exists.

National Postal Museum. July 30, 1993. Engraved, lithographed. ABN.

29c multicolored

a) Ben Franklin
c) Charles Lindbergh
b) Pony Express
d) Stamps & Barcode

IM 540 block of 4, imperf 3,500.00
strip of 4, imperf —
plate block of 4, imperf —
Quantity: 8 blocks of 4; 2 strips reported

Country & Western Singers. September 25, 1993. Booklet pane of 4. Photogravure. ABN.

32c multicolored

a) Hank Williams
b) Carter Family
c) Patsy Cline
d) Bob Wills

IM 540A booklet pane, imperf —
Quantity: n/a

Often with disturbed gum or wrinkles.

Madonna. October 21, 1993. Booklet pane of 4. Engraved, lithographed. KCS.

29c multicolored

IM 541 imperf pair —
booklet pane of 4, imperf —
Quantity: 4 panes reported

Young Readers' Classics. October 23, 1993. Engraved, lithographed. ABN.

29c multicolored

a) Huckleberry Finn
c) Rebecca
b) Little Women
d) Little House

IM 542 block of 4, imperf *3,000.00*
strip of 4, imperf *1,750.00*
Quantity: *10-20 blocks of 4;*
2-4 strips of 4

Pine Cone. November 5, 1993. Booklet pane of 18. Engraved. Self-adhesive. Straight die cut. BCA.

29c multicolored

IM 543 pair, die cut omitted between —
used pair, die cut omitted between *150.00*
Quantity: *14-20 pairs reported*

Love. February 14, 1994. Booklet pane of 10. Photogravure. ABN.

29c multicolored

IM 544 imperf pair —
booklet pane of 10, imperf —
Quantity: n/a

IM 544A hz pair, imperf between *400.00*
 Quantity: n/a

Wonders of the Sea. October 3, 1994. Se-tenant block of 4. Lithographed. BCA.

29c multicolored

a) Motorboat & Buoy b) Sailing Ship
c) Wheel on Sea Floor d) Coral Outcropping

IM 546 block of 4, imperf 1,650.00
 plate block of 4, imperf —
 Quantity: *48-60 blocks of 4*

Garden Flowers. April 28, 1994. Booklet pane of 5. Engraved, lithographed. BEP.

29c multicolored

a) Lily
b) Zinnia
c) Gladiola
d) Marigold
e) Rose

IM 545 booklet pane of 5, imperf 2,000.00
 Quantity: *16-20 panes reported*

Panes contain normal booklet bend between stamps b & c and tab faults from removal from booklet and are priced as such.

Legends of the West. October 18, 1994. Se-tenant pane of 20. Photogravure. SVS.

32c multicolored

IM 546A pane of 20, partially imperf —
 Quantity: *reportedly unique*

Locomotives. July 28, 1994. Booklet pane of 5. Photogravure. SVS.

29c multicolored

a) Hudson's General
b) McQueen's Jupiter
c) Eddy's No. 242
d) Ely's No. 10
e) Buchanan's No. 999

IM 545A pane of 5, imperf —
 Quantity: *3 panes reported*

Panes contain normal booklet bend between stamps b and c.

Madonna. October 20, 1994. Booklet pane of 10. Engraved, lithographed. BEP.

29c multicolored

IM 547 imperf pair 600.00
booklet pane of 10, imperf 2,500.00
Quantity: *10+ panes reported*

Transition panes exist.

Greetings. October 20, 1994. Lithographed. APU.

29c multicolored

IM 548 imperf pair —
Quantity: *at least 10 pairs*

Christmas Stocking. October 20, 1994. Booklet pane of 20. Lithographed. APU.

29c multicolored

IM 549 vrt pair, imperf hz —
booklet pane, imperf hz —
Quantity: at least 8 panes

Hinging. Prices for stamps after **IM 196** are for never hinged copies. Hinged copies sell for less.

Dove, G Make-Up Rate. December 13, 1994. Lithographed. ABN.

(3c) bright blue, red & tan

IM 550 imperf pair 175.00
plate block of 4, imperf —
Quantity: *few hundred*

IM 550A imperf pair, bright blue omitted **PW** —
Quantity: *new, 100+ pairs*

☛ Printer's waste, refer to introduction. May contain traces of blue, expert certificate recommended.

Flag & G. December 13, 1994. Photogravure. BEP.

G (20c) yellow background, black G

IM 550C imperf pair —
Quantity: 35 stamps

☛ Caution. The discovery pane of 100 contained 35 imperforate examples plus many others with blind perfs. Certificate advised.

Flag & G. December 13, 1994. Coil. Photogravure. BEP.

G (32c) multicolored; black G

IM 551 imperf pair 300.00
imperf strip with plate No. 1111 —
Quantity: *100-150 pairs reported*

IM 552 pair, imperf between —
Quantity: n/a

Flag & G. December 13, 1994. Booklet pane of 10. Photogravure. KCS.

G (32c) multicolored; red G

IM 553 hz pair, imperf between —
Quantity: *2-3 pairs reported*

IM 553 results from a foldover; at least two of the pairs have a natural straight edge at the bottom. A booklet containing two panes, each with an error pair, sold at auction for $1,155.00 in July 1995.

IM 554 hz pair, imperf vrt —
Quantity: *very rare*

One pair of **IM 554** is known attached to the top selvage of a booklet. It contains straight edges on both right and left sides, and if detached from the booklet selvage, would have the appearance of an imperf pair.

Flag & G. December 13, 1994. Booklet pane of 10. Photogravure. ABN.

G (32c) multicolored; blue G

IM 555 imperf pair —
booklet pane, imperf —
Quantity: *2 panes reported*

Flag & Porch. May 19, 1995. Pane of 100. Photogravure. Water activated. Blue 1995 date. SVS.

32c multicolored

IM 556 imperf pair 75.00
Quantity: *500+ pairs*

Often collected in vertical pairs to distinguish it from coil imperforates of similar design. Transition multiples exist.

Flag & Porch. May 19, 1995. Coil. Photogravure. Water activated. Red 1995 date. BEP.

32c multicolored

IM 557		
imperf pair		35.00
imperf strip with plate No. 11111		—
imperf strip with plate No. 22222		—
imperf strip with plate No. 33333		—
imperf strip with plate No. 44444		350.00
imperf strip with plate No. 45444		—
imperf strip with plate No. 66646		—
imperf strip with plate No. 66666		—
imperf strip with plate No. 77767		350.00
imperf strip with plate No. 78767		—
imperf strip with plate No. 91161		—
imperf strip with plate No. 99969		—
spliced pair or strip, imperf		—
imperf pair on first day cover		—
Quantity: 1,000+ pairs		
5 FDCs		

Exists miscut. Transition multiples exist and sell for a premium. Refer to the note following **IM 434** regarding first day covers.

Flag & Porch. May 21, 1996. Coil. Photogravure. Self-adhesive. Serpentine die cut. Red 1996. BEP.

32c multicolored

IM 558		
pair, die cut omitted		35.00
die cut omitted strip, plate No. 11111		—
die cut omitted strip, plate No. 23222		—
die cut omitted strip, plate No. 44444		—
die cut omitted strip, plate No. 45444		—
die cut omitted strip, plate No. 55555		—
die cut omitted strip, plate No. 66666		—
die cut omitted strip, plate No. 78777		—
die cut omitted strip, plate No. 88888		175.00
die cut omitted strip, plate No. 89898		—
die cut omitted strip, plate No. 99999		—
die cut omitted strip, plate No. 11111A		—
die cut omitted strip, plate No. 13231A		—
die cut omitted strip, plate No. 22222A		—
die cut omitted strip, plate No. 44444A		—
die cut omitted strip, plate No. 55555A		—
die cut omitted strip, plate No. 66666A		—
die cut omitted strip, plate No. 88888A		—
spliced pair or strip, die cut omitted		—
Quantity: 1,000+		

Exists miscut.

Flag & Porch. May 19, 1995. Booklet pane of 10. Photogravure. Water activated. Red 1995 date. BEP.

32c multicolored

IM 561 booklet pane of 10, imperf —
Quantity: *8-10 panes*

Flag & Porch. April 18, 1995. Booklet pane of 20. Photogravure. Self-adhesive. Serpentine die cut. Small blue 1995 date. AVR.

32c multicolored

IM 562 pair, die cut omitted —
booklet pane of 20, die cut omitted
between 2nd & 3rd row —
Quantity: very rare

The backing paper of the self-adhesive error booklet pane contains the normal roulette for fold. It does not affect the status of the error.

Flag & Porch. May 21, 1996. Booklet pane of 10. Photogravure. Self-adhesive. Serpentine die cut. Red 1996 date. BEP.

32c multicolored

IM 564 booklet pane of 10, die cut omitted 250.00
Quantity: 50+ panes reported

The backing paper of **IM 564** contains the normal roulette for fold. It does not affect the status of the error.

Pink Rose. June 2, 1995. Booklet pane of 20. Photogravure. Self-adhesive. Serpentine die cut. SVS.

32c black, pink & olive green

IM 565 hz pair, die cut omitted btwn —
hz pair, 1 stamp & 1 label, die cut
omitted between —
Quantity: 12 pairs, 2 pairs with label

An intact booklet pane containing six error stamp pairs and one stamp-and-label error pair sold at auction for $4,840 in August 2000.

Yellow Rose. August 1, 1997. Coil. Photogravure. Self-adhesive. Serpentine die cut. Black 1997 date. BEP.

32c black, magenta, yellow & olive green

IM 565A pair, die cut omitted		90.00
die cut omitted strip, plate No. 1112		—
die cut omitted strip, plate No. 1122		—
die cut omitted strip, plate No. 2223		—
die cut omitted strip, plate No. 4455		—
die cut omitted strip, plate No. 5555		*750.00*
die cut omitted strip, plate No. 5556		*750.00*
die cut omitted strip, plate No. 5566		*750.00*
die cut omitted strip, plate No. 5666		*750.00*
die cut omitted strip, plate No. 6666		*750.00*
die cut omitted strip, plate No. 7777		*750.00*
Quantity: 450+ pairs		

Exists miscut. Plate number strips of 5556 exist miscut only. Transition multiples exist and sell for a premium.

IM 565B pair, die cut & black omitted —
strip with plate No. 445, black omitted —
Quantity: *30 stamps*

IM 565C pair, die cut, black, yellow
& olive green omitted —
strip with magenta plate No. 4 —
strip with magenta plate No. 7 —
Quantity: *22+ stamps*

The initial discovery of **IM 565B** and **IM 565C** consisted of two rolls of 100 with die cutting omitted on all stamps and colors omitted on some. The first roll contained 5 normally colored stamps, 11 black omitted, 15 black, yellow and olive green omitted, and the balance of the roll with all colors omitted. The first roll contained only a single occurrence of plate number, the digit "7" in magenta, the black, yellow and olive green digits being omitted. The second roll contained 68 normally colored stamps, 1 black partially omitted, 19 black omitted, 1 black, yellow and olive green partially omitted, 6 black, yellow and olive green omitted, and 5 with all colors omitted. The second roll contained three strips with full plate No. 4455 and one strip with plate No. 445, the black being omitted. A third roll exists with die cuts, but miscut. It is listed in the Color Omitted section under **CO 199** and **CO 200**. A later find also yields a strip of **IM 565C** with a single digit "4."

Western Butte. March 10, 1995. Coil. Photogravure. SVS.

(5c) multicolored

IM 566 imperf pair 650.00
imperf strip with plate No. S1111 —
Quantity: *58-80 pairs reported*

Some pairs have counting numbers on the back.

Mountain. March 16, 1996. Coil. Photogravure. SVS.

(5c) multicolored; blue-gray mountains

IM 568 imperf pair 450.00
 imperf strip with plate No. S111 —
 spliced pair or strip, imperf —
 Quantity: 109 pairs,
 10 plate No. strips

Transition multiples exist. Some pairs have counting numbers on the back.

Cherub. May 12, 1995. Booklet pane of 10. Engraved, lithographed. Water activated. Design measures 19mm by 22½mm. BEP.

32c multicolored

IM 571 imperf pair —
 pane of 10, imperf —
 Quantity: *2 panes*

The two panes each contain a black rejection mark.

Cherub. January 20, 1996. Booklet pane of 20. Engraved, lithographed. Self-adhesive. Serpentine die cut. BCA.

32c multicolored

IM 572 pair, die cut omitted 300.00
 pane of 20, die cut omitted —
 Quantity: several panes

Recreational Sports. May 20, 1995. Se-tenant strip of 5. Lithographed. BCA.

32c multicolored

a) Golf b) Volleyball c) Softball d) Bowling e) Tennis

IM 573 strip of 5, imperf *2,750.00*
 Quantity: *8-12 strips of 5*

The se-tenant designs vary in order of appearance from vertical strip to vertical strip within a pane.

Marilyn Monroe. June 1, 1995. Pane of 20. Photogravure. SVS.

32c multicolored

IM 574 imperf pair 625.00
 pane of 20, imperf 6,250.00
 Quantity: *15-20 imperforate panes;*
 3 partially imperforate panes

Due to the nature of the grinding process used to perforate this issue, perforations on partially perforated panes can appear in odd configurations such as a single row, multiple rows, or in a corner affecting only a few stamps. Because of the possible variety of partially perforated panes, no attempt has been made to list each one individually. A partially perforated pane sold for $3,737.50 in March 2000.

Challenger. June 22, 1995. Engraved, lithographed. APU.

$3 multicolored

IM 574A hz pair, imperf between —
Quantity: at least 6-10 pairs

☛ Caution. Beware pairs with deceptive blind perfs between stamps. Expert certificate strongly recommended.

IM 574B imperf pair —
Quantity: new, n/a

☛ Caution. Beware pairs with blind perfs. Expert certificate recommended.

Blue Jay. June 15, 1995. Booklet pane of 10. Lithographed. Self-adhesive. Serpentine die cut. SVA.

20c multicolored

IM 574C pane of 10, die cut omitted —
Quantity: new, n/a

Civil War. June 29, 1995. Se-tenant pane of 20. Photogravure. SVS.

32c multicolored

IM 575 pane of 20, imperf 2,000.00
pane of 20, partially imperforate —
Quantity: *20-40 imperforate panes; 4-5 partially imperforate panes*

Refer to the note following **IM 574**. Often encountered with light fingerprints on gum.

Women's Suffrage. August 26, 1995. Engraved, lithographed. APU.

32c multicolored

IM 576 imperf pair 1,500.00
plate block of 4, imperf —
Quantity: *20 pairs reported*

Often in transition strips.

Where possible, illustrations of actual error stamps have been used. They are bordered in black. Illustrations of normal stamps have been used in cases where error stamp illustrations were not available, or where an error illustration would not adequately illustrate the error. Illustrations of normal stamps appear without black border.

Buying or selling?
Consult the dealer directory at the back of the catalogue.

Garden Flowers. September 19, 1995. Booklet pane of 5. Engraved, lithographed. BEP.

32c multicolored

a) Aster
b) Chrysanthemum
c) Dahlia
d) Hydrangea
e) Rudbeckia

IM 577 booklet pane of 5, imperf —
Quantity: reportedly unique

The single known pane of this error contains a rejection mark at top.

Santa & Children. September 30, 1995. Se-tenant block of 4. Lithographed. APU.

32c multicolored

| a) Santa & Chimney | b) Child & Jumping Jack |
| c) Child & Tree | d) Santa & Sled |

IM 578 block of 4 (a-d), imperf 650.00
strip of 4 (a-d), imperf 650.00
Quantity: *75+ blocks of 4,*
15 strips of 4

Comics. October 1, 1995. Se-tenant pane of 20. Photogravure. SVS.

32c multicolored

IM 579 pane of 20, imperf —
pane of 20, partially imperf —
Quantity: *1-2 imperforate pane,*
3 partially imperforate panes

Refer to note following **IM 574**.

Midnight Angel. October 19, 1995. Booklet pane of 20. Lithographed. Self-adhesive. Serpentine die cut. BCA.

32c multicolored

IM 579A pane of 20, die cut omitted from
third horizonal row & from the top
of the fourth horizonal row —
Quantity: *15-20 reported*

Also exists as a horizontal pair (one stamp and one reorder label) with die cut omitted between as the result of a foldover.

Although catalogue prices are based on the best information available at press time, readers should be aware that prices for error stamps fluctuate over time, and therefore, are advised to contact dealers active in the error stamp market for timely quotes when buying or selling.

Note. Quantities for listings appearing for the first time in this edition are marked "new." They are tentative and subject to change.

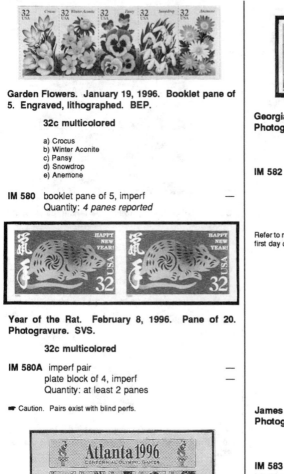

Garden Flowers. January 19, 1996. Booklet pane of 5. Engraved, lithographed. BEP.

32c multicolored

a) Crocus
b) Winter Aconite
c) Pansy
d) Snowdrop
e) Anemone

IM 580 booklet pane of 5, imperf —
Quantity: *4 panes reported*

Year of the Rat. February 8, 1996. Pane of 20.
Photogravure. SVS.

32c multicolored

IM 580A imperf pair —
plate block of 4, imperf —
Quantity: at least 2 panes

☞ Caution. Pairs exist with blind perfs.

Olympics. May 2, 1996. Se-tenant pane of 20.
Photogravure. SVS.

32c multicolored

IM 581 pane of 20, imperf *1,400.00*
pane of 20, partially imperf —
Quantity: 60+ panes

Refer to note following **IM 574**.

Georgia O'Keeffe. May 23, 1996. Pane of 15.
Photogravure. SVS.

32c multicolored

IM 582 imperf pair 175.00
pane of 15, imperf —
imperf pair on first day cover —
Quantity: 75-90 panes; 8 first
day covers

Refer to note following **IM 574**. Refer to note following **IM 434** regarding first day covers.

James Dean. June 24, 1996. Pane of 20.
Photogravure. SVS.

32c multicolored

IM 583 imperf pair 375.00
pane of 20, imperf —
pane of 20, partially imperf —
Quantity: *30+ panes*

Refer to note following **IM 574**.

IM 583A imperforate, tan omitted —
Quantity: new, 15 stamps

IM 583B imperforate, tan & red omitted —
Quantity: new, 5 stamps

IM 583A and **IM 583B** occur in a single imperforate pane. The top row of 5 contains the tan and red omitted examples. The bottom 3 rows contain the tan omitted examples. Five combination pairs containing one each of **IM 583A** and **IM 583B** are possible.

Buying or selling?
Consult the dealer directory at the back of the catalogue.

Christmas Scenes. October 8, 1996. Se-tenant in booklet pane of 20. Lithographed. Self-adhesive. Serpentine die cut. APU.

Madonna. November 1, 1996. Booklet pane of 20. Engraved, lithographed. Self-adhesive. Serpentine die cut. BEP.

32c multicolored

a) Family at Fireside
b) Christmas Tree
c) Santa & Chimney
d) Shoppers

32c multicolored

IM 584	strip of 4, die cut omitted	—
	block of 6, die cut omitted	—
	pane of 20, die cut omitted	3,000.00
	Quantity: *6-7 panes reported*	

IM 586	pair, die cut omitted	75.00
	pane of 20, die cut omitted	—
	Quantity: *50-75 panes*	

Designs are staggered, so the order of appearance in strips or blocks may vary. The illustration is cropped from the upper left corner of a pane. Strips of 4 contain each of the designs. However due to the layout, blocks of 6 are necessary to obtain all 4 designs in block form. Blocks may contain gutters. The backing paper of the self-adhesive error booklet pane contains the normal roulette for fold. It does not affect the status of the error. Price is for an unfolded pane.

Swan. February 4, 1997. Booklet pane of 20. Lithographed. Self-adhesive. Serpentine die cut. BCA.

32c multicolored

IM 587	imperf pair	175.00
	pane of 20, imperf	—
	Quantity: 15-20 panes reported	

Christmas Scenes. October 8, 1996. Se-tenant pane of 20. Lithographed. Water activated. Perforated. APU.

32c multicolored

a) Santa & Chimney
b) Shoppers
c) Family at Fireside
d) Christmas Tree

IM 585	strip of 4, c & d imperf	—
	plate block of 8	—
	Quantity: 1 strip, 1 block	
	& 1 plate block	

Statue of Liberty. February 1, 1997. Booklet pane of 20. Self-adhesive. Serpentine die cut. AVR.

32c multicolored

| IM 588 | pane of 20, die cut omitted | — |
| | Quantity: n/a | |

Perforations appear between stamps a, b & c. In addition, perforations appear at top and bottom of stamps a, b & c. Stamp d lacks perforations on all sides.

Botanical Prints. March 3, 1997. Se-tenant booklet pane of 20. Photogravure. Self-adhesive. Serpentine die cut. SVS.

a) Citron b) Flowering Pineapple

32c multicolored

IM 589 vrt pair, die cut omitted btwn 500.00
Quantity: *28 pairs reported*

Error pairs in the initial discovery panes result from die cuts shifted downward one row from the top.

Dinosaurs. May 1, 1997. Pane of 15. Lithographed. APU.

32c multicolored

IM 590 pane, bottom half imperf **LRS (4/01)** 4,400.00
pane, top half imperf **LRS (4/01)** 6,325.00
Quantity: *3 panes; 1 with bottom
imperf and 2 with top imperf reported*

Celebrate the Century 1910s. February 3, 1998. Se-tenant pane of 15. Engraved, lithographed. APU.

32c multicolored

IM 592 pane of 15, five stamps imperf —
Quantity: unique

The error pane is the result of a perforation shift upward leaving 5 stamps without perforations. They are: Jim Thorpe, First Crossword Puzzle, Jack Dempsey, Construction Toys, and Child Labor Reform.

The term "transition multiple" refers to errors appearing in combination with normal or nearly-normal stamps. Generally, a pair, strip, or block containing one or more error stamps, one or more normal stamps, and, in the case of color-omitted errors, one or more stamps with color(s) partially omitted. Transition multiples sell for a premium.

Ring-necked Pheasant. July 31, 1998. Coil. Photogravure. Self-adhesive. Serpentine die cut. BEP.

20c multicolored

IM 594	pair, die cut omitted	*200.00*
	die cut omitted strip, plate No. 1111	—
	spliced pair or strip, die cut omitted	—
	Quantity: *70 pairs reported*	

Exists miscut. At press time, of the two known rolls, one was drastically miscut (yielding 50 pairs) and one was normal (yielding about 20 pairs).

Hat & H. November 9, 1998. Coil. Photogravure. Self-adhesive. Serpentine die cut. BEP.

(33c) multicolored

IM 596	pair, die cut omitted	95.00
	die cut omitted strip, plate No. 1111	—
	die cut omitted strip, plate No. 1131	—
	die cut omitted strip, plate No. 2222	—
	die cut omitted strip, plate No. 3333	—
	used pair, die cut omitted	—
	Quantity: 200+ pairs	

IM 597	pair, die cut & black omitted	—
	die cut omitted strip, plate No. 111	—
	Quantity: *20 stamps reported*	

Red, blue and gray digits appear on the plate strip.

Uncle Sam. November 9, 1998. Coil. Photogravure. Self-adhesive. Serpentine die cut. BEP.

22c multicolored

IM 598	pair, die cut omitted	—
	die cut omitted strip, plate No. 1111	—
	Quantity: new, n/a	

Love. January 28, 1999. Photogravure. Booklet pane of 20. Self-adhesive. Die cut to shape. AVR.

33c multicolored

IM 599	pane of 20, die cut omitted	—
	Quantity: new, n/a	

Flag Over City. February 25, 1999. Coil. Water activated. BEP.

33c multicolored

IM 600	imperf pair	—
	imperf strip with plate No. 1111	—
	Quantity: new, 9 pairs & one plate number strip reported	

Flag Over City. February 25, 1999. Coil. Photogravure. Self-adhesive. Serpentine die cut. Red 1999 date. BEP.

33c multicolored

IM 601	pair, die cut omitted	65.00
	die cut omitted strip, plate No. 1111	—
	die cut omitted strip, plate No. 6666	—
	die cut omitted strip, plate No. 7777	—
	die cut omitted strip, plate No. 8888	—
	die cut omitted strip, plate No. 9999	—
	die cut omitted strip, plate No. 2222A	—
	die cut omitted strip, plate No. 4444A	—
	die cut omitted strip, plate No. 5555A	—
	Quantity: several hundred pairs	

Exists miscut.

Coyote & Roadrunner. April 6, 2000. Pane of 10. Photogravure. Self-adhesive. Serpentine die cut. BCA.

33c multicolored

IM 602	pane of 10, die cut omitted	—
	Quantity: n/a	

Imperforate single stamps exist on the right panel of one variety of the booklet combination. They were regularly issued and are not errors.

Coral Pink Rose. April 7, 2000. Booklet pane of 20. Photogravure. Self-adhesive. Serpentine die cut. SSP.

33c multicolored

IM 604	hz pair, die cut omitted vrt	—
	block, die cut omitted vrt	—
	Quantity: 9-10 pairs	

The discovery examples were contained in blocks that resulted from miscutting.

Hubble Telescope. April 10, 2000. Se-tenant pane of 20. Photogravure. SSP.

33c multicolored

a) Galaxy NGC 1316
b) Eagle Nebula
c) Ring Nebula
d) Lagoon Nebula
e) Egg Nebula

IM 605	hz strip of 5, imperf	—
	pane of 20, imperf	—
	Quantity: new, at least 2 panes	

Designs are staggered, so their order of appearance in strips may vary.

Note. Quantities for listings appearing for the first time in this edition are marked "new." They are tentative and subject to change.

Exploring the Solar System. July 11, 2000. Pane of 5. Photogravure. SSP.

$1 multicolored

a) Solar Corona
b) Solar Core
c) Sun over Earth
d) Solar Flare
e) Sun in Sky

IM 606 pane of 5, imperf —
Quantity: *new, 1 pane*

Statue of Liberty. December 15, 2000. Coil. Photogravure. Self-adhesive. Serpentine die cut. BEP.

(34c) multicolored

IM 608 pair, die cut omitted —
die cut omitted strip, plate No. 1111 —
Quantity: new, n/a

Statue of Liberty. February 7, 2001. Booklet pane. Photogravure. Self-adhesive. Serpentine die cut. AVR.

34c multicolored

IM 610 pair, die cut omitted —
pane of 20, die cut omitted —
Quantity: new, n/a

Note. Quantities for listings appearing for the first time in this edition are marked "new." They are tentative and subject to change.

105

AIR MAIL STAMPS

Beacon on Sherman Hill. July 25, 1928. Engraved.

5c red & blue

IMA 1 vrt pair, imperf between vrt strip
of 3, imperf between **LRS (81)** *7,100.00*
Quantity: very rare, likely unique

Winged Globe. February 10, 1930. Engraved. Flat plate press. BEP.

5c violet

IMA 2 hz pair, imperf between *5,000.00*
bottom strip of 5 with plate No.,
left pair imperf between *6,000.00*
Quantity: very rare

Eagle & Shield. May 14, 1938. Engraved. BEP.

6c red & blue

IMA 3 vrt pair, imperf hz 325.00
plate block of 4, imperf hz 1,250.00
top plate block of 10 1,750.00
vrt line pair, imperf hz 450.00
pair on cover postmarked 5/15/38 *300.00*
pair on cover postmarked
1/18/39 **LRS (9/00)** 1,430.00
Quantity: 1,000 pairs

IMA 4 hz pair, imperf vrt *12,500.00*
hz strip of 5, left pair imperf vrt *12,500.00*
top plate block of 10, left 6
stamps imperf vrt **LRS (9/94)** 36,800.00
Quantity: 5 pairs

Transport Plane. June 25, 1941. Engraved. BEP.

6c carmine red

IMA 5 hz pair, imperf between 1,500.00
plate strip of 10, containing
two error pairs —
Quantity: 20 pairs

Often sold in strips of 5 containing one error pair and three normal stamps. Usually with inspector's blue crayon mark, which is often lightened due to attempted erasure. Price is for pair or strip with crayon mark.

Where possible, illustrations of actual error stamps have been used. They are bordered in black. Illustrations of normal stamps have been used in cases where error stamp illustrations were not available, or where an error illustration would not adequately illustrate the error. Illustrations of normal stamps appear without black border.

Hinging. Prices for stamps after **IMA 6** are for never hinged copies. Hinged copies sell for less.

Statue of Liberty at New York. August 30, 1947. Engraved. BEP.

15c green

IMA 6 hz pair, imperf between 2,250.00
as above, block of 4 —
Quantity: 20 pairs

All known pairs are poorly centered.

Jet & Numeral. August 19, 1960. Booklet pane. Engraved. BEP.

7c carmine

IMA 6A vrt pair, imperf between —
Quantity: 2 known

IMA 6A occurs as a result of a foldover.

Statue of Liberty. June 28, 1961. Engraved, lithographed. BEP.

15c orange & black

IMA 7 hz pair, imperf vrt **LRS (79)** 11,500.00
strip of 5, 3 stamps & margin at
left imperf vrt **LRS (5/00)** 7,150.00
strip of 5, 3 stamps at left
imperf vrt **LRS (81)** 15,400.00
Quantity: 3 as listed above

Runway of Stars. January 5, 1968. Coil. Engraved. BEP.

10c red

IMA 8 imperf pair 600.00
line pair, imperf 950.00
spliced pair, imperf —
Quantity: 100+ pairs

Runway of Stars. January 5, 1968. Booklet pane of 8. Engraved. BEP.

10c red

IM 8A vrt pair, imperf between —
Quantity: possibly unique

IM 8A occurs as the result of a foldover.

Jet Aircraft. May 7, 1971. Coil. Engraved. BEP.

11c red

IMA 9 imperf pair 250.00
line pair, imperf 425.00
spliced pair, imperf —
Quantity: fewer than 200 pairs reported

Exists miscut. Slightly miscut pairs usually sell for less than listed pairs; dramatically miscut pairs often sell for more than listed pairs. Transition multiples exist.

Winged Envelope. December 27, 1973. Coil. Engraved. BEP.

13c red

IMA 10 imperf pair 75.00
line pair, imperf 150.00
Quantity: 500+ pairs

Phillip Mazzei. October 13, 1980. Photogravure. BEP.

40c multicolored

IMA 11 imperf pair 3,500.00
Quantity: 15 pairs

IMA 11A hz pair, imperf vrt —
Quantity: very rare, possibly unique

Blanche Stuart Scott. December 30, 1980. Photogravure. BEP.

28c multicolored

IMA 11B imperf pair —
Quantity: n/a

Olympics. Se-tenant block of 4. June 17, 1983. Photogravure. BEP.

28c multicolored

a) Gymnastics	b) Hurdles
c) Basketball	d) Soccer

IMA 12 block of 4 (a-d), imperf vrt *7,500.00*
as above, plate block of 4 —
Quantity: the 2 blocks as listed

Olympics. Se-tenant block of 4. April 8, 1983. Photogravure. BEP.

40c multicolored

a) Shot Put	b) Gymnastics
c) Swimming	d) Weight Lifting

IMA 13 block of 4 (a-d), imperf 1,250.00
plate block of 4, imperf —
copyright block of 4, imperf —
vrt pair (a & c) or (b & d), imperf 400.00
Quantity: 30-40 blocks of 4,
20-30 pairs reported

Alfred V. Verville. February 13, 1985. Photogravure. BEP.

33c multicolored

IMA 14 imperf pair 850.00
plate block of 4, imperf —
Quantity: 50-100 pairs

Junipero Serra. August 22, 1985. Photogravure. BEP.

44c multicolored

IMA 17 imperf pair *1,500.00*
Quantity: *19 pairs reported*

Often encountered with disturbed gum or small faults. Price is for a sound copy. Those with faults sell for about 50% less.

Lawrence & Elmer Sperry. February 13, 1985. Photogravure. BEP.

39c multicolored

IMA 15 imperf pair 1,850.00
plate block of 4, imperf —
Quantity: 25 pairs reported

Reportedly, 14 of the 25 pairs are sound. Price is for a sound copy; those with faults sell for 50% or less depending on the degree of the fault.

Harriet Quimby. April 27, 1991. Photogravure. BEP.

50c multicolored

IMA 18 vrt pair, imperf hz 2,000.00
plate block of 4, imperf hz *4,750.00*
Quantity: 25 pairs

Many pairs contain a light, cyan wiper-blade mark. Price is for copy without wiper mark. Those with wiper mark sell for slightly less.

Transpacific Airmail 1935. February 15, 1985. Photogravure. BEP.

44c multicolored

IMA 16 imperf pair 800.00
plate block of 4, imperf —
Quantity: 75 pairs reported

Vertical pairs exist with perforations at bottom between stamp and selvage.

Grand Canyon. June 20, 2000. Lithographed. Self-adhesive. Serpentine die cut. BCA.

60c multicolored

IMA 19 pair, die cut omitted —
Quantity: *new, 6 pairs reported*

IMA 20 vrt pair, die cut omitted hz —
Quantity: *new, 2 pairs reported*

SPECIAL DELIVERY

Messenger & Tablet. October 10, 1894. Engraved.

10c blue

IMSD 1 hz pair, imperf LRS (11/93) 4,675.00
vrt block of 6, without gum,
imperf LRS (86) 8,800.00
Quantity: very rare

Messenger & Tablet. October 16, 1895. Engraved. Double line watermark.

10c blue

IMSD 2 imperf pair *4,500.00*
sheet margin single, imperf *2,000.00*
Quantity: very rare

Motorcycle Messenger. November 29, 1927. Engraved. Rotary press.

10c violet

IMSD 3 hz pair, imperf between 300.00
plate block of 4, imperf vrt between 850.00
Quantity: 80-100 pairs

Many pairs are poorly centered. Price is for a poorly centered pair. Well centered pairs sell for more.

Great Seal of the United States. February 10, 1936. Engraved.

16c red & blue

IMSD 4 hz pair, imperf vrt *3,750.00*
center line block of 4, imperf
vert LRS (6/97) 8,625.00
Quantity: 10 pairs reported

POSTAGE DUE

SERIES OF 1879

Numeral. September 9, 1879. Engraved.

10c light brown

IMPD 1 imperf pair *2,000.00*
Quantity: rare

SERIES OF 1891

Numeral. 1891. Engraved.

1c bright claret

IMPD 2 imperf pair NRI *400.00*
Quantity: 46 stamps

Numeral. 1891. Engraved.

2c bright claret

IMPD 3 imperf pair NRI *400.00*
Quantity: 46 stamps

Numeral. 1891. Engraved.

3c bright claret

IMPD 4 imperf pair **NRI** *400.00*
Quantity: 46 stamps

Numeral. 1891. Engraved.

5c bright claret

IMPD 5 imperf pair **NRI** *400.00*
Quantity: 46 stamps

Numeral. 1891. Engraved.

10c bright claret

IMPD 6 imperf pair **NRI** *400.00*
Quantity: 46 stamps

Numeral. 1891. Engraved.

30c bright claret

IMPD 7 imperf pair **NRI** *400.00*
Quantity: 46 stamps

Numeral. 1891. Engraved.

50c bright claret

IMPD 8 imperf pair **NRI** *400.00*
Quantity: 46 stamps

See note for issues of the American Banknote Company, 1890/1893.

Numeral. August 14, 1894. Engraved.

1c deep claret

IMPD 9 imperf pair 250.00
block of 4, imperf —
Quantity: n/a

Usually encountered without gum. Price is for copy without gum.

IMPD 10 vrt pair, imperf hz —
Quantity: n/a

OFFICIAL STAMPS

Post Office Department. Numeral. 1873. Engraved.

15c black

IMO 1 imperf pair —
Quantity: rare

War Department. George Washington. 1879. Engraved.

3c rose red

IMO 2 imperf pair *900.00*
 Quantity: rare

COIL STAMPS

Official Mail. January 12, 1983. Coil. Engraved. BEP.

20c black, red & blue

IMO 3 imperf pair 2,000.00
 imperf strip with plate No. 1 —
 spliced strip, imperf —
 Quantity: fewer than 25 pairs reported

Official Mail. June 11, 1988. Coil. Engraved. BEP.

25c black, red & blue

IMO 5 imperf pair 1,850.00
 Quantity: 40-50 pairs, 1 used pair

Official Mail. May 24, 1991. Pane of 100. Lithographed. BEP.

23c black, red & blue

IMO 6 imperf pair **PW** 100.00
 block of 4, imperf —
 plate block of 4, imperf —
 Quantity: few hundred pairs

Printer's waste, refer to introduction. Gutter pairs and blocks exist.

MIGRATORY BIRD HUNTING STAMPS

Mallards. July 1934. Engraved. BEP.

$1 blue

IMWF 1 imperf pair **PW** *15,000.00*
 vrt pair with plate No. 129199, imperf —
 vrt strip of 3, imperf *20,000.00*
 imperf single **LRS (12/99)** 4,950.00
 Quantity: 28 stamps

Most copies of **IMWF 1** exist without gum and with faults. It is reported that 19 of the 28 stamps are off the market and will end up in the National Postal Museum.

IMWF 2 vrt pair, imperf hz **PW** *15,000.00*
 vrt block of 8, imperf hz —
 Quantity: very rare

IMWF 2 is known to exist with gum on the front of the stamp. Some experts believe that it is likely that copies of **IMWF 1** have been created by trimming the perforations off and removing the gum from the front of **IMWF 2**.

COLOR OMITTED ERRORS

Red Cross. May 21, 1931. Engraved. BEP.

2c black & red

CO 1 red omitted —
Quantity: 2 reported

CO 1 results from a paper fold that prevented the application of the red cross.

Ernst Reuter. December 29, 1959. Engraved. BEP.

8c ocher, carmine & ultramarine

CO 1A ocher omitted *3,750.00*
Quantity: 3

CO 1B ultramarine omitted *3,750.00*
Quantity: 3

CO 1C ocher & ultramarine omitted *4,000.00*
Quantity: 2

CO 1A-CO 1C all result from a single pane that passed through the printing press with a sizable piece of extraneous paper adhering to the top of it. When overlaying flap of paper was removed, certain stamps were left with only a partial impression, including those listed above with colors omitted. **CO 1A** occurs in positions 10, 20 and 30; **CO 1B** occurs in positions 17, 36 and 46; and **CO 1C** occurs in positions 27 and 37. The intact pane sold for $11,550 in May 1996. The pane has since been broken up. A block of 6 (positions 38-40 and 46-48) that included two error stamps sold at auction for $5,463 in April 2001.

The term "transition multiple" refers to errors appearing in combination with normal or nearly-normal stamps. Generally, a pair, strip, or block containing one or more error stamps, one or more normal stamps, and, in the case of color-omitted errors, one or more stamps with color(s) partially omitted. Transition multiples sell for a premium.

Water Conservation. April 18, 1960. Engraved. BEP.

4c orange brown, green & ultramarine

CO 1D orange brown omitted **LRS (6/97)** 5,280.00
Quantity: 4

American Music. October 15, 1964. Engraved. BEP.

5c black, red & blue (gray paper)

CO 2 blue omitted 950.00
Quantity: 20-40 reported

Transition multiples exist and sell for a premium.

☛ Caution. Should contain no traces of blue. Copies with traces of blue do not qualify as major errors.

Florida Settlement. August 28, 1965. Engraved. BEP.

5c black, red & ocher

CO 3 ocher omitted 300.00
Quantity: 300-400

☛ Caution. A shift in the ocher can give the stamp the appearance of having the color omitted. Examine carefully.

Ten vertical transition pairs exist, each with an error stamp at top and a normal stamp at bottom.

Marine Corps Reserve. August 29, 1966. Engraved, lithographed. BEP.

 5c black & ocher (engraved); red & blue (lithographed)

CO 4 black & ocher omitted LRS (5/95) 15,400.00
 Quantity: unique

Savings Bonds. October 26, 1966. Engraved, lithographed. BEP.

 5c black, red & dark blue (engraved); light blue (lithographed)

CO 5 black, red & dark blue (engraved)
 omitted *5,250.00*
 Quantity: 6 reported

Transition multiples exist and sell for a premium.

CO 5A dark blue (engraved) omitted —
 Quantity: *unique*

Davy Crockett. August 17, 1967. Engraved, lithographed. BEP.

 5c black & gray green (engraved); yellow & green (lithographed)

CO 6 gray green (engraved) omitted —
 Quantity: unique

CO 7 black & gray green (engraved) omitted —
 Quantity: unique

CO 8 yellow & green (litho) omitted —
 Quantity: unique

The Space Capsule stamp is known with the red flag omitted from the capsule. However, red litho dots are present elsewhere on the stamp, so it is not considered to be a 100% color-omitted error. Nevertheless, it is still a collectible variety, most often encountered as a block of nine with red omitted from the center stamp: price $195.00

Hemisfair '68. March 30, 1968. Engraved, lithographed. BEP.

 6c white (engraved); red & Prussian blue (lithographed)

CO 10 white omitted 1,250.00
 Quantity: 100

Hinging. Prices for stamps after **CO 1** are for never hinged copies. Hinged copies sell for less.

Walt Disney. September 11, 1968. Photogravure. UCC.

6c black, yellow, magenta, blue & ocher

CO 11	black omitted	2,000.00
	as above, plate block of 4	—
	Quantity: 35 reported	

CO 12	blue omitted	2,100.00
	as above, plate block of 4	—
	Quantity: 35 reported	

CO 13	ocher omitted	600.00
	as above, plate block of 4	—
	Quantity: 400-500	

Transition multiples exist for numbers **CO 11—CO 13**. They sell for a premium.

John Trumball. October 18, 1968. Engraved, lithographed. BEP.

6c black (engraved); magenta & ocher (litho)

| CO 13A | black (engraved) omitted | — |
| | Quantity: 2 | |

The 2 error stamps resulted from a foldover on the lower right corner of a pane of 50. Two stamps above and 2 stamps to the left of the color omitted pair contain partial omission of engraved black in varying degrees. The pane sold for $20,900 in May 2000.

The term "transition multiple" refers to errors appearing in combination with normal or nearly-normal stamps. Generally, a pair, strip, or block containing one or more error stamps, one or more normal stamps, and, in the case of color-omitted errors, one or more stamps with color(s) partially omitted. Transition multiples sell for a premium.

Waterfowl Conservation. October 24, 1968. Engraved, lithographed. BEP.

6c black (engraved); yellow, red, blue & blue green (lithographed)

CO 14	red & blue omitted	800.00
	as above, plate block of 4	—
	used, red & blue omitted	—
	Quantity: 100	

☞ Caution. Fakes exist. Expert certificate recommended for both unused and used copies.

CO 15 CO 16

Christmas Angel. November 1, 1968. Engraved, lithographed. BEP.

6c black, red, blue & brown (engraved); yellow (lithographed)

CO 15	yellow omitted	55.00
	as above, plate block of 10	—
	Quantity: 1,000+	

☞ Caution. Beware copies with yellow partially omitted.

Grandma Moses. May 1, 1969. Engraved, lithographed. BEP.

6c black & Prussian blue (engraved); yellow, red, blue & blue green (lithographed)

CO 16	black & Prussian blue omitted	750.00
	as above, plate block of 4	—
	Quantity: 150	

Usually with mottled gum. Price is for copy with good gum. Deduct 33% for copy with mottled gum.

Professional Baseball. September 24, 1969. Engraved, lithographed. BEP.

6c black (engraved); yellow, red & green (lithographed)

CO 17 black omitted 950.00
Quantity: 300+

Price is for a well centered copy; poorly centered copies sell for less. Exists with tagging ghosts. Transition multiples exist and sell for a premium.

Christmas. November 3, 1969. Engraved, lithographed. BEP.

6c dark green & dark brown (engraved); yellow, red, & light green (lithographed)

CO 18 yellow omitted *2,250.00*
Quantity: very rare

CO 19 light green omitted 25.00
Quantity: 1,000+

CO 20 yellow, red & light green omitted 800.00
as above, used —
Quantity: 50-60 unused, 6 copies used reported

CO 20A yellow & red omitted *3,000.00*
Quantity: *very rare*

☛ Caution. Specks of red often present on **CO 20** and **CO 20A**. Expert certificate advised. Transition multiples exist for **CO 18** and **CO 20** and sell for a premium.

CO 21 CO 22

Christmas Nativity Scene. November 5, 1970. Photogravure. GGI.

6c black, magenta, blue & ocher

CO 21 black omitted 525.00
Quantity: 50 reported

☛ Caution. Many copies similar to the error exist with partial black. However, in order to qualify as a major error no trace of black should be visible under 30-power magnification. Expert certificate advised. Transition multiples exist and sell for a premium.

Christmas Precancel. November 5, 1970. Photogravure.

6c black, magenta, blue & ocher, precanceled with black bars

CO 22 blue omitted *1,500.00*
transition multiple, blue omitted —
Quantity: 15 reported

The term "transition multiple" refers to errors appearing in combination with normal or nearly-normal stamps. Generally, a pair, strip, or block containing one or more error stamps, one or more normal stamps, and, in the case of color-omitted errors, one or more stamps with color(s) partially omitted. Transition multiples sell for a premium.

Christmas Toys. November 5, 1970. Se-tenant block of 4. Photogravure. GGI.

6c black, magenta, blue & ocher

a) Doll carriage	b) Toy Horse
c) Tricycle	d) Locomotive

CO 23 block of 4, black omitted —
block of 4, black omitted on a & c —
any single, black omitted 2,300.00
Quantity: 2 blocks, 5-6 of each single reported

Some singles are unused on piece and, due to the rarity of the issue, sell for nearly the same price as mint copies.

Landing of Pilgrims. November 21, 1970. Engraved, lithographed. BEP.

6c black (engraved); yellow, red & blue (lithographed)

CO 24 yellow omitted 850.00
Quantity: 200

U.S. Flag. May 10, 1971. Engraved. BEP.

8c red, blue & slate green

CO 24A slate green omitted 400.00
Quantity: 100

Wool. January 19, 1971. Engraved, lithographed. BEP.

6c greenish blue, dark brown, olive green (engraved); yellow, cyan, orange, olive green (lithographed)

CO 24B greenish blue (engraved) omitted —
Quantity: 6-8 reported

CO 24B results from an upward shift of the engraved greenish blue portion of the design (the words "United States"). On some examples, the color is not completely shifted off the stamp and therefore, does not qualify as the error. Expert certificate advised. Transition multiples exist.

Wildlife Conservation. June 12, 1971. Se-tenant block of 4. Engraved, lithographed. BEP.

8c black, dark brown & dark green (engraved); red, blue, buff, olive green & bluish green (lithographed)

a) Trout	b) Alligator
c) Polar Bear	d) California Condor

CO 25 block of 4, olive & bluish green omitted from a & b 4,500.00
as above, plate block of 4 —
Quantity: 8 blocks including unique plate block

CO 26 block of 4, red omitted from a, c & d 9,500.00
used single (a), LRS (11/96) 1,320.00
Quantity: very rare, possibly unique, used single unique

Due to color schemes used in the four designs, some colors are normally not present on every stamp. For example, lithographic red was not used in the alligator design and, therefore, cannot be considered to have been omitted.

☞ Caution. The red head of the condor may appear to be omitted if shifted to the lower left. Expert certificate advised.

CO 27 CO 28

CO 30 CO 31

American Revolution Bicentennial. July 4, 1971. Engraved, lithographed.

 8c black & gray (engraved); red & blue (lithographed)

CO 27 black & gray omitted 650.00
 Quantity: 100-150

CO 28 gray omitted 1,100.00
 Quantity: rare

CO 28 often occurs in pairs or larger multiples with gray completely omitted from one stamp, and gray and black partially omitted from others. They sell for a premium.

Emily Dickinson. August 28, 1971. Engraved, lithographed. BEP.

 8c black & light olive green (engraved); dark olive green, red & flesh tone (lithographed); (greenish paper)

CO 30 black & light olive green omitted 750.00
 as above, plate block of 4 —
 Quantity: 150

CO 31 pair, flesh tone omitted on one *6,500.00*
 Quantity: 3-4

Some examples of **CO 31** appear to have light olive green omitted, but traces are visible under magnification.

Space Achievement. August 2, 1971. Se-tenant pair. Engraved, lithographed. BEP.

 8c black (engraved); yellow, red, blue & gray (lithographed)

 a) Earth & Sun b) Lunar Vehicle

CO 29 pair, red & blue omitted 1,400.00
 single (b), red & blue omitted 600.00
 plate block of 4, red & blue omitted —
 Quantity: 40 pairs, 10 singles reported

☛ Caution. The flag on the lunar lander is often shifted into the lander and not visible. Examine carefully.

Where possible, illustrations of actual error stamps have been used. They are bordered in black. Illustrations of normal stamps have been used in cases where error stamp illustrations were not available, or where an error illustration would not adequately illustrate the error. Illustrations of normal stamps appear without black border.

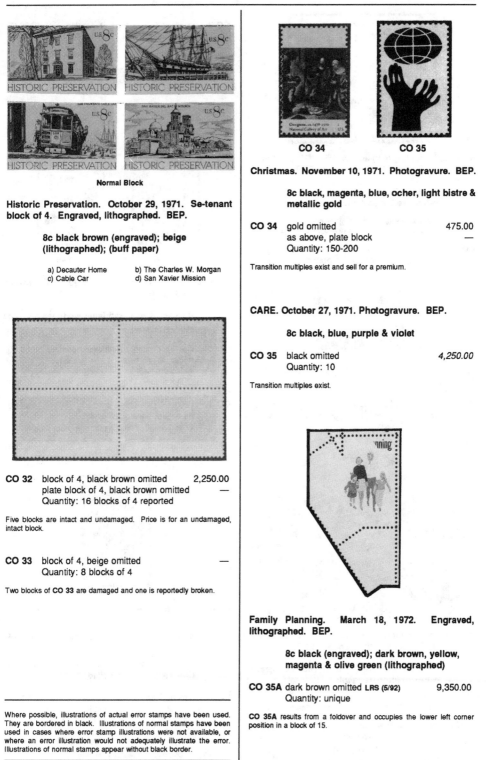

Normal Block

Historic Preservation. October 29, 1971. Se-tenant block of 4. Engraved, lithographed. BEP.

8c black brown (engraved); beige (lithographed); (buff paper)

a) Decauter Home
c) Cable Car
b) The Charles W. Morgan
d) San Xavier Mission

CO 32 block of 4, black brown omitted 2,250.00
plate block of 4, black brown omitted —
Quantity: 16 blocks of 4 reported

Five blocks are intact and undamaged. Price is for an undamaged, intact block.

CO 33 block of 4, beige omitted —
Quantity: 8 blocks of 4

Two blocks of **CO 33** are damaged and one is reportedly broken.

Where possible, illustrations of actual error stamps have been used. They are bordered in black. Illustrations of normal stamps have been used in cases where error stamp illustrations were not available, or where an error illustration would not adequately illustrate the error. Illustrations of normal stamps appear without black border.

CO 34 **CO 35**

Christmas. November 10, 1971. Photogravure. BEP.

8c black, magenta, blue, ocher, light bistre & metallic gold

CO 34 gold omitted 475.00
as above, plate block —
Quantity: 150-200

Transition multiples exist and sell for a premium.

CARE. October 27, 1971. Photogravure. BEP.

8c black, blue, purple & violet

CO 35 black omitted *4,250.00*
Quantity: 10

Transition multiples exist.

Family Planning. March 18, 1972. Engraved, lithographed. BEP.

8c black (engraved); dark brown, yellow, magenta & olive green (lithographed)

CO 35A dark brown omitted LRS (5/92) 9,350.00
Quantity: unique

CO 35A results from a foldover and occupies the lower left corner position in a block of 15.

National Parks Centennial. April 5, 1972. Se-tenant block of 4. Engraved, lithographed. BEP.

> **2c black & dark blue (engraved); black, yellow, red, blue & tan (lithographed)**
>
> a) Wrecked Hull b) Lighthouse
> c) Shorebirds d) Shorebirds & Grass

CO 36 block of 4, black (litho) omitted 2,750.00
Quantity: 25 blocks of 4 reported

Mt. McKinley. July 28, 1972. Engraved, lithographed. BEP.

> **15c black, light blue, dark brown (engraved); yellow, magenta, gray, gray green, brown (lithographed)**

CO 36A yellow omitted —
Quantity: reportedly unique

Wildlife Conservation. September 20, 1972. Se-tenant block of 4. Engraved, lithographed. BEP.

> **8c black (engraved); yellow, red, blue, green & brown (lithographed)**
>
> a) Fur Seal b) Cardinal
> c) Brown Pelican d) Bighorn Sheep

CO 37 block of 4, brown omitted 4,000.00
as above, plate block of 4 —
single (c or d), brown omitted —
Quantity: 8-16 blocks of 4 reported

CO 38 block of 4, blue & green omitted *4,750.00*
as above, plate block of 4 —
Quantity: 8 blocks of 4 reported

CO 38A block of 4, red & brown omitted *4,250.00*
Quantity: 16 blocks of 4 reported

CO 39 CO 40

Tom Sawyer. October 13, 1972. Engraved, lithographed. BEP.

> **8c black & deep red (engraved); yellow, red, blue, & gray (lithographed)**

CO 39 black & deep red (engraved) omitted 1,650.00
as above, plate block of 4 (plate No.
 also omitted) —
Quantity: 150

CO 40 yellow & gray (litho) omitted 2,250.00
as above, plate block of 4 —
Quantity: 50, including unique plate block

Christmas Angels. November 9, 1972. Photogravure. BEP.

> **8c black, yellow, magenta, blue, gray & pink**

CO 41 black omitted —
multiple, black omitted on one *4,500.00*
Quantity: 10 pairs reported

CO 42 pink omitted 150.00
pair, one with pink omitted —
plate block of 12, pink omitted —
Quantity: several hundred

Transition multiples exist and sell for a premium.

Pharmacy. **November 10, 1972.** **Engraved, lithographed. BEP.**

8c black (engraved); yellow, blue, purplish red & orange (lithographed)

CO 44 blue & orange omitted 750.00
as above, plate block of 4 —
Quantity: 150 reported

CO 45 blue omitted 2,000.00
Quantity: very rare

CO 45A orange omitted *2,000.00*
plate block of 4, 2 stamps with
orange omitted **LRS (5/99)** 3,960.00
Quantity: *very rare*

☛ Caution. Expert certificate necessary for **CO 45A**. Transition pairs exist and sell for a premium.

Stamp Collecting. **November 17, 1972.** **Engraved, lithographed. BEP.**

8c brown & black (engraved); black & greenish blue (lithographed)

CO 46 black (litho) omitted 650.00
as above, plate block of 4 —
Quantity: 80-100

The lithographed black part of the design consists of a pattern of dots printed on the greenish blue field. They are visible under magnification on the normal stamp.

Boston Tea Party. **July 4, 1973. Se-tenant block of 4. Engraved, lithographed. BEP.**

8c black (engraved); black, yellow, red & blue (lithographed)

a) Tea Cast Overboard b) Ship
c) Boat & Keel d) Pier

CO 47 block of 4, black (engraved)
omitted 1,350.00
hz pair (a & c) or (b & d) black
(engraved) omitted 450.00
Quantity: 32 blocks of 4 reported
including one without gum; sets
of horizontal pairs also exist

CO 48 block or 4, black (litho) omitted 1,250.00
as above, Zip block —
Quantity: 32 blocks 4

CO 49 CO 50

Copernicus. April 23, 1973. Engraved, lithographed. BEP.

8c black (engraved); yellow (lithographed)

CO 49	yellow omitted	950.00
	as above, plate block of 4	—
	as above, Zip block of 4	—
	Quantity: 100	

☛ Caution. Extremely dangerous fakes, including color changelings, exist. Genuine copies of this error each have an APS certificate. Expert certificate absolutely essential. Copies without certificates should be avoided.

| CO 50 | black omitted | 1,000.00 |
| | Quantity: 100 | |

Progress in Electronics. July 10, 1973. Engraved, lithographed. BEP.

8c black (engraved); orange, dark brown, tan, green & light violet (lithographed)

CO 51	tan & light violet omitted	1,250.00
	as above, plate block 4	—
	Quantity: 50	

CO 52	black omitted	450.00
	as above, plate block of 4	—
	Quantity: 300-400	

Progress in Electronics. July 10, 1973. Engraved, lithographed. BEP.

15c black (engraved); yellow, brown, gray & gray green (lithographed)

| CO 53 | black omitted | 1,350.00 |
| | Quantity: 50 | |

Rural America. October 5, 1973. Engraved, lithographed. BEP.

8c black, brown red & dark blue (engraved); yellow, green, orange brown & brown (lithographed)

| CO 54 | green & orange brown omitted | 900.00 |
| | Quantity: 100 | |

Rural America. August 16, 1974. Engraved, lithographed. BEP.

10c black & dark blue (engraved); yellow, red, gray blue & brown (lithographed)

| CO 55 | black & dark blue (engraved) omitted | 750.00 |
| | Quantity: 100 | |

Where possible, illustrations of actual error stamps have been used. They are bordered in black. Illustrations of normal stamps have been used in cases where error stamp illustrations were not available, or where an error illustration would not adequately illustrate the error. Illustrations of normal stamps appear without black border.

Crossed Flags. December 8, 1973. Engraved. BEP.

10c red & blue

CO 56	blue omitted	165.00
	pair, one normal & one with	
	blue omitted	200.00
	single used on cover, blue omitted	—
	Quantity: 100-125 singles or pairs	
	with one normal attached; 2-3 used	

Often with tagging ghosts.

Zip Code. January 24, 1974. Photogravure. BEP.

10c black, yellow, magenta & blue

CO 57	yellow omitted	50.00
	as above, plate block of 8	450.00
	Quantity: 1,000+	

☛ Caution. Extremely dangerous fakes, including color changelings, exist. Beware used copies. Expert certificate essential.

Horse Racing. May 4, 1974. Photogravure. BEP.

10c black, yellow, magenta, blue, red & ultramarine

CO 58	ultramarine omitted	850.00
	as above, Zip block of 4	—
	Quantity: 50-100	

CO 59	red omitted	—
	Quantity: 1-4 reported	

☛ Caution. To be considered a major error all traces of red must be absent under 30-power magnification. Many copies containing traces of red exist, therefore, expert certificate is advised.

Mineral Heritage. June 13, 1974. Se-tenant block of 4. Engraved, lithographed. BEP.

10c black, red, violet (engraved); yellow, light blue, gray, brown & green (lithographed)

a) Amethyst	b) Rhodochrosite
c) Tourmaline	d) Petrified Wood

CO 60	block of 4, light blue omitted (a-d),	
	yellow omitted (a & d)	1,750.00
	single a or d, yellow & lt blue omitted	—
	single b or c, light blue omitted	—
	Quantity: 24-28 blocks of 4	

Light blue (the lithographed background color) was printed on all four stamps. Lithographic yellow was printed only on stamps a and d, therefore its absence on stamps b and c is not the result of an error.

☛ Caution. Dangerous fakes exist.

CO 61	single b, black & red (engraved) omitted	—
	Quantity: 4	

CO 62	single c, black & violet (engraved) omitted	—
	Quantity: 4	

The error stamps **CO 61** and **CO 62** result from a single pane in which one se-tenant row, containing the two designs, lacked the engraved colors, black (inscription) and red or violet (mineral color) respectively.

Normal Stamp **Error Stamp**

Kentucky Settlement. June 15, 1974. Engraved, lithographed. BEP.

10c black & dark green (engraved); black, light red, blue, light green & tan (lithographed)

CO 63 black & dark green (engraved), black, green & blue (litho) omitted 3,750.00
Quantity: 29 reported including those in strips of 3 or 10

Exists in strips of 3 containing one normal, one with colors partially omitted and one with listed colors completely omitted. Also exists in strips of 10 (with various stages of colors omitted) which tend to sell for a substantial premium.

CO 64 black (litho) omitted 750.00
as above, plate block of 4 —
used single, black omitted —
Quantity: 100-150 including 2 plate blocks

Transition multiples exist and sell for a premium.

CO 64A dark green (engraved) omitted *3,750.00*
Quantity: *very rare*

CO 64B dark green (engraved) & black (litho) omitted —
Quantity: *very rare*

Hinging. Prices for stamps after **CO 1** are for never hinged copies. Hinged copies sell for less.

CO 65 **CO 66**

Energy Conservation. September 23, 1974. Engraved, lithographed. BEP.

10c black (engraved); yellow, blue, purple, orange (lithographed).

CO 65 blue & orange omitted 850.00
Quantity: approx 100

CO 66 orange & green omitted 700.00
plate block of 4
Quantity: 150-200

One pane of 50 has disturbed gum.

CO 67 green omitted 875.00
Quantity: approx 100

Christmas. October 23, 1974. Photogravure. BEP.

10c black, yellow, magenta, blue, & very light buff

CO 68 buff omitted 10.00
pane of 50, buff omitted 300.00
Quantity: 75-100 panes of 50

☛ Caution. The buff color is a very light, transparent shade. Error stamps are extremely difficult to distinguish from normal stamps. Expert certificate strongly advised. Many prefer to collect this error in intact pane form because the omission of buff is more readily evident due to the absence of the buff plate number in the selvage.

Pioneer - Jupiter. February 28, 1975. Engraved, lithographed. BEP.

 10c yellow & dark blue (engraved); dark yellow, red & blue (lithographed)

CO 69 dark blue omitted 850.00
 Quantity: 200 reported

CO 70 dark yellow & red omitted 1,250.00
 Zip block of 4 —
 Quantity: 50-100 reported

CO 70A dark yellow omitted **LRS (7/97)** 3,520.00
 Quantity: reportedly unique

CO 70A contains traces of red visible under magnification. To the naked eye, it is similar in appearance to CO 70.

Mariner 10. April 4, 1975. Engraved, lithographed. BEP.

 10c black (engraved); red, blue & brown (lithographed)

CO 71 red omitted 425.00
 plate block of 4, red omitted —
 Quantity: 300-400

☛ Caution. The red star may be shifted down and hidden in the spacecraft giving the appearance of being the error stamp. Examine carefully.

CO 72 blue & brown omitted *2,000.00*
 Quantity: 50

Haym Salomon. March 25, 1975. Photogravure. BEP.

 10c black, yellow, red, blue & gray; green inscription on reverse

CO 75 red omitted 250.00
 Quantity: 300+

☛ Caution. Expert certificate advised.

Refer to the **Reverse Inscription Omitted** section for this and other issues with reverse inscriptions omitted.

D. W. Griffith. May 27, 1975. Engraved, lithographed. BEP.

 10c dark brown (engraved); yellow, magenta, & cyan (lithographed)

CO 77 dark brown omitted 625.00
 Quantity: 100-150

☛ Caution. Color variations and color shifts on this stamp are common and can be mistaken for the color-omitted error. Expert certificate advised.

Although catalogue prices are based on the best information available at press time, readers should be aware that prices for error stamps fluctuate over time, and therefore, are advised to contact dealers active in the error stamp market for timely quotes when buying or selling.

200 Years of Postal Service. September 3, 1975. Se-tenant block of 4. Photogravure. BEP.

10c black, yellow, red (2 plates), blue & ultramarine

a) Locomotive	b) Stagecoach
c) Satellite	d) Biplane

CO 78 block of 4, red (10c denomination) omitted 7,500.00
as above, pair —
any single —
Quantity: 6-8 blocks of 4 reported, 2 pairs of each reported

Two plates were used for red: one for the denomination, the other for design elements. Only the red denomination is omitted; red printed from the second plate appears elsewhere on the stamp.

Banking & Commerce. October 6, 1975. Se-tenant pair. Engraved, lithographed. BEP.

10c dark brown, green, greenish gray (engraved); yellow, blue & brown (lithographed)

a) Banking	b) Commerce

CO 79 pair, blue & brown omitted 2,250.00
single a or b, blue & brown omitted 500.00
Quantity: 16-32 pairs; 8-16 singles

CO 79A pair, yellow, blue & brown omitted 2,750.00
Quantity: 16 pairs, 8 singles (a)

Buying or selling?
Consult the dealer directory at the back of the catalogue.

AMERICANA SERIES OF 1975/1981

CO 80 CO 81

Eagle & Shield. December 1, 1975. Photogravure. BEP.

13c black, yellow, red, blue, brown & olive green

CO 80 yellow omitted 150.00
pair, one with yellow omitted 200.00
Quantity: 500

☛ Caution. Dangerous fakes exist. Beware used stamps offered as CO 80. Expert certificate strongly advised.

Flag. June 30, 1978. Engraved. BEP.

15c red, blue & gray

CO 81 gray omitted 525.00
pair, one with gray omitted 900.00
Quantity: 100-200

☛ Caution. Stamps with gray partially omitted exist.

Lamp. September 11, 1979. Engraved, lithographed. BEP.

50c black (engraved); orange & tan (lithographed)

CO 82 black omitted 300.00
transition pair or strip 375.00
Quantity: 120-150 reported

Transition multiples exist with some stamps showing partial omission of black. Transition multiples sell for a premium.

The term "transition multiple" refers to errors appearing in combination with normal or nearly-normal stamps. Generally, a pair, strip, or block containing one or more error stamps, one or more normal stamps, and, in the case of color-omitted errors, one or more stamps with color(s) partially omitted. Transition multiples sell for a premium.

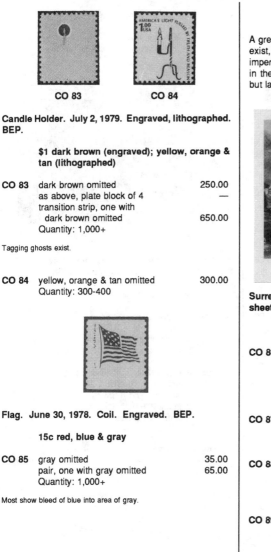

CO 83 CO 84

Candle Holder. July 2, 1979. Engraved, lithographed. BEP.

$1 dark brown (engraved); yellow, orange & tan (lithographed)

CO 83 dark brown omitted 250.00
 as above, plate block of 4 —
 transition strip, one with
 dark brown omitted 650.00
 Quantity: 1,000+

Tagging ghosts exist.

CO 84 yellow, orange & tan omitted 300.00
 Quantity: 300-400

Flag. June 30, 1978. Coil. Engraved. BEP.

15c red, blue & gray

CO 85 gray omitted 35.00
 pair, one with gray omitted 65.00
 Quantity: 1,000+

Most show bleed of blue into area of gray.

BICENTENNIAL SOUVENIR SHEETS

A great variety of color-omitted and imperforate varieties exist, many with multiple errors. Those that are imperforate in addition to having colors omitted are listed in the imperforates section. Those normally perforated but lacking one or more colors are listed below.

Surrender at Yorktown. May 29, 1976. Souvenir sheet of 5. Lithographed. BEP.

13c multicolored

CO 86 yellow (USA 13c) omitted
 on 1st & 5th stamps 450.00
 as above, used, 5/29/76 Philadelphia,
 PA first day cancellation —
 Quantity: rare

CO 87 yellow (USA 13c) omitted on
 5th stamp *550.00*
 Quantity: very rare

CO 88 brown (USA 13c) omitted on 2nd
 stamp, orange (USA 13c) omitted
 on 3rd & 4th stamps *500.00*
 Quantity: very rare

CO 89 orange (USA 13c) omitted on 3rd
 & 4th stamps 750.00
 Quantity: very rare

For imperforate varieties of Bicentennial souvenir sheets with color(s) omitted refer to the imperforates section of the catalogue.

Where possible, illustrations of actual error stamps have been used. They are bordered in black. Illustrations of normal stamps have been used in cases where error stamp illustrations were not available, or where an error illustration would not adequately illustrate the error. Illustrations of normal stamps appear without black border.

128

**The Declaration of Independence. May 29, 1976.
Souvenir sheet of 5. Lithographed.**

18c multicolored

CO 94 brown (USA 18c) omitted on 1st
 & 3rd stamps 600.00
 Quantity: rare

CO 95 orange (USA 18c) omitted on 2nd &
 5th stamps, yellow (USA 18c)
 omitted on 4th stamp 450.00
 Quantity: rare

CO 96 orange (USA 18c) omitted on 2nd &
 5th stamps 500.00
 Quantity: rare

CO 97 yellow (USA 18c) omitted
 on 4th stamp 500.00
 Quantity: rare

CO 98 black (screened dots for contrast in
 mural) omitted *2,250.00*
 Quantity: very rare

CO 99 all process colors omitted, sheet
 blank except for USA 18c, tagging
 & perfs **LRS (5/99)** 3,300.00
 Quantity: very rare

The term "process colors" refers to those colors which were reduced to
a pattern of dots and printed atop one another to achieve the effect of
full color. The denominations and "USA" were added by a separate
operation and printed in "solid color" rather than in a pattern of dots. The
difference in printing can be seen on a normal sheet by examination
under 10-power magnification.

CO 100 brown (USA 18c) omitted
 on 1st stamp 500.00
 Quantity: very rare

CO 101 yellow omitted (background color) —
 Quantity: very rare, possibly unique

CO 102 orange (USA 18c) omitted on 2nd
 stamp, yellow (USA 18c) omitted
 on 4th stamp —
 Quantity: very rare, possibly unique

CO 103 brown (USA 18c) omitted
 on 3rd stamp —
 Quantity: very rare

**Washington Crossing the Delaware. May 29, 1976.
Souvenir sheet of 5. Lithographed. BEP.**

24c multicolored

CO 104 blue (USA 24c) omitted on 1st
 stamp, light blue (USA 24c)
 omitted on 2nd & 3rd stamps 500.00
 Quantity: very rare

CO 105 blue (USA 24c) omitted on 1st
 stamp, light blue (USA 24c)
 omitted on 2nd & 3rd stamps,
 with 5/29/76 Philadelphia, PA
 first day cancellation 500.00
 Quantity: very rare

CO 106 white (USA 24c) omitted on 4th
 & 5th stamps 450.00
 Quantity: very rare

CO 107 white (USA 24c) omitted on 4th
 & 5th stamps with 5/29/76
 Philadelphia, PA first day
 cancellation, perforations inverted 450.00
 Quantity: very rare

CO 108 all process colors omitted, sheet
 blank except for 24c, tagging & perfs 3,750.00
 Quantity: reportedly unique

Refer to the note after **CO 99**.

Hinging. Prices for stamps after **CO 1** are for never hinged copies.
Hinged copies sell for less.

129

Washington at Valley Forge. May 29, 1976. Souvenir sheet of 5. Lithographed. BEP.

31c multicolored

CO 110 gray (USA 31c) omitted on 1st
 & 3rd stamps 400.00
Quantity: rare

CO 111 gray (USA 31c) omitted on 1st
 & 3rd stamps, white (USA 31c)
 omitted on 5th stamp —
Quantity: very rare

CO 112 brown (USA 31c) omitted on 2nd
 & 4th stamps *600.00*
Quantity: rare

CO 113 brown (USA 31c) omitted on 2nd
 & 4th stamps, white omitted
 on 5th stamp 500.00
Quantity: rare

CO 114 white (USA 31c) omitted on
 5th stamp 450.00
Quantity: rare

CO 115 gray (USA 31c) omitted on 1st
 stamp, brown (USA 31c) omitted
 on 4th stamp, white (USA 31c)
 omitted on 5th stamp —
Quantity: very rare

CO 116 brown (USA 31c) omitted on 4th
 stamp, white (USA 31c) omitted
 on 5th stamp —
Quantity: very rare

Note: Bicentennial souvenir sheets containing both imperforate and color-omitted errors are listed in the imperforates section.

CO 117 black (screened process dots in mural)
 omitted 2,000.00
Quantity: very rare

In process color printing a printed screen of black dots is often used to intensify contrast and add crispness to the finished illustration.

Benjamin Franklin. June 1, 1976. Engraved, lithographed. BEP.

13c dark blue (engraved); yellow, light blue & brown (lithographed)

CO 118 light blue omitted 250.00
 as above, plate block of 4 —
Quantity: 800-1000 reported

Carl Sandburg. January 6, 1978. Engraved. BEP.

13c black & dark brown

CO 119 dark brown omitted —
Quantity: 10

Usually in transition strip or pair as illustrated.

CAPEX. June 10, 1978. Souvenir sheet of 8. Engraved, lithographed. BEP.

13c black & dark green (engraved); black, yellow, red, blue, brown & light green (lithographed)

a) Cardinal b) Mallard c) Canada Goose d) Blue Jay e) Moose f) Chipmunk g) Red Fox h) Raccoon

CO 120 souvenir sheet of 8, all lithographed colors omitted **7,500.00**
as above, with plate No. —
Quantity: 6 souvenir sheets reported

CO 121 single (d or h), engraved black omitted —
Quantity: very rare

Christmas. October 18, 1979. Photogravure. BEP.

15c black, yellow, magenta, green, tan & purple

CO 123 yellow & green omitted, black misaligned 550.00
Quantity: 150

CO 124 yellow, green & tan omitted, black misaligned 625.00
Quantity: 250

Misalignment of black color occurs on all copies of **CO 123** and **CO 124**. Ten pairs exist containing one each of **CO 123** and **CO 124**: price $1,500.

The term "transition multiple" refers to errors appearing in combination with normal or nearly-normal stamps. Generally, a pair, strip, or block containing one or more error stamps, one or more normal stamps, and, in the case of color-omitted errors, one or more stamps with color(s) partially omitted. Transition multiples sell for a premium.

CO 125 CO 126

General Bernardo Galvez. July 23, 1980. Engraved, lithographed. BEP.

15c dark brown, claret & light gray-blue (engraved); light yellow, red, blue & brown (lithographed)

CO 125 dark brown, claret & light gray-blue (engraved) omitted 750.00
Quantity: 50

CO 126 light yellow, red, blue & brown (litho) omitted 1,300.00
Quantity: 50

Christmas. October 31, 1980. Photogravure. BEP.

15c black, yellow, red, green & buff

CO 126A buff omitted 25.00
plate block of 20, buff omitted 450.00
Quantity: several hundred

This error is very subtle and difficult to see. Certificate recommended.

Flag over Supreme Court. December 17, 1981. Engraved. BEP.

20c black, red & blue

CO 127 black omitted 300.00
Quantity: n/a

Transition multiples exist and sell for a premium.

CO 128 blue omitted 75.00
 Quantity: few hundred

☛ Caution. Stamps exist with colors partially omitted. Transition multiples exist and sell for a premium.

COIL STAMP

Flag over Supreme Court. Coil. December 17, 1981. Engraved. BEP.

20c black, red & blue

CO 129 black omitted 50.00
 pair, 1 normal, 1 black omitted 90.00
 Quantity: 1,000+

CO 130 blue omitted *1,500.00*
 Quantity: *very rare*

Edna St. Vincent Millay. July 10, 1981. Engraved, lithographed. BEP.

18c black (engraved); black, yellow, magenta, blue, gray & buff (lithographed)

CO 132 black (engraved) omitted 325.00
 as above, plate block of 4 —
 as above, Zip block of 4 —
 used, black omitted
 Quantity: 500+

Hinging. Prices for stamps after **CO 1** are for never hinged copies. Hinged copies sell for less.

Frederic Remington. October 9, 1981. Engraved, lithographed. BEP

18c dark brown (engraved); light brown & gray green (lithographed)

CO 133 dark brown (engraved) omitted 450.00
 as above, plate block of 4 —
 Quantity: 300-400

Yorktown - Virginia Capes. October 16, 1981. Se-tenant pair. Engraved, lithographed. BEP.

18c black (engraved); red, light blue, dark blue, brown & tan (lithographed)

a) Yorktown b) Virginia Capes

CO 134 pair, black (engraved) omitted 400.00
 as above, plate block of 4 —
 as above, Zip block of 4 —
 single a or b, black (engraved) omitted 150.00
 Quantity: 80 pairs, 10 of each single reported

Cactus. December 11, 1981. Se-tenant block of 4. Engraved, lithographed. BEP.

20c dark green & dark blue (engraved); yellow, red, dark brown, tan, light green & cyan (lithographed)

a) Barrel Cactus b) Agave
c) Beavertail Cactus d) Saguaro

CO 134A block of 4, dark brown (litho) omitted —
 Quantity: 20 blocks of 4

132

Love. February 1, 1982. Photogravure. BEP.

20c yellow, magenta, blue, violet & olive green

CO 135 blue omitted 225.00
Quantity: 50-100 well centered
150-200 poorly centered

Price is for well centered copy. Copies from some panes are centered high with the design running slightly off at the top; for those deduct 33%.

State Birds & Flowers. April 14, 1982. Se-tenant pane of 50. Photogravure. BEP.

20c black, yellow, magenta & cyan

CO 135C black omitted —
Quantity: 2 stamps (1 each as described below)

Each of the two error stamps is contained in a horizontal transition pair. One pair contains the Rhode Island stamp (black completely omitted) and the South Carolina stamp (black partially omitted); the other pair contains the New Hampshire stamp (black completely omitted) and the New Jersey stamp (black partially omitted).

The Barrymores. June 8, 1982. Photogravure. BEP.

20c black, yellow, magenta, cyan & ultramarine

CO 135D black omitted —
Quantity: unique.

The unique discovery copy occupies position 7 in a plate strip of 20.

International Peace Garden. June 30, 1982. Engraved, lithographed. BEP.

20c black (engraved); yellow, red, green & gray (lithographed)

CO 136 black (engraved) omitted 250.00
Quantity: 250-400 reported

Science & Industry. January 19, 1983. Engraved, lithographed. BEP.

20c black (engraved); yellow, magenta & blue (lithographed)

CO 137 black (engraved) omitted 1,400.00
plate block of 6 containing 2
error stamps & 4 normal stamps —
Quantity: 40

Transition multiples exist and sell for a premium.

Medal of Honor. June 7, 1983. Engraved, lithographed. BEP.

20c red (engraved); black, ocher, blue & green (lithographed)

CO 138 red omitted 275.00
as above, plate block of 4 —
Quantity: 320-400

Inventors. September 21, 1983. Se-tenant block of 4. Engraved, lithographed. BEP.

20c black (engraved); salmon (lithographed)

a) Charles Steinmetz b) Edwin Armstrong
c) Nikola Tesla d) Philo T. Farnsworth

CO 139 block of 4, black (engraved) omitted 375.00
as above, plate block of 4 —
as above, Zip block of 4 —
any single, black (engraved) omitted 95.00
Quantity: 200+ blocks of 4 reported

Streetcars. October 8, 1983. Se-tenant block of 4. Engraved, lithographed. BEP.

20c black (engraved); black, yellow, magenta, & blue (lithographed)

a) First Streetcar b) Early Electric Streetcar
c) Bobtail Streetcar d) St. Charles Streetcar

CO 140 block of 4, black (engraved)
omitted 400.00
as above, plate block of 4 —
any single (a-d), black (engraved)
omitted 75.00
Quantity: 120+ blocks of 4 reported

Although catalogue prices are based on the best information available at press time, readers should be aware that prices for error stamps fluctuate over time, and therefore, are advised to contact dealers active in the error stamp market for timely quotes when buying or selling.

AMERIPEX. May 25, 1985. Engraved, lithographed. BEP.

22c black, red & blue (engraved); gray & beige (lithographed)

CO 141 black, red & blue (engraved) omitted 175.00
Quantity: 700-800

CO 141A black & red (engraved) omitted —
Quantity: 4-5 reported

CO 141B red (engraved) omitted 2,250.00
Quantity: 2-3 reported

a) b) c) d)

Stamp Collecting. January 23, 1986. Booklet pane of 4. Engraved, lithographed. BEP.

22c black, bright green, purple, & dark blue (engraved); yellow, red, light blue & beige (lithographed)

a) American Philatelic Association
b) Youngster with Album
c) Magnifying Glass
d) Ameripex 86

CO 142 booklet pane of 4, black omitted 45.00
unexploded booklet of 2 panes,
black omitted 90.00
used booklet pane on first day cover 150.00
Quantity: several thousand

Engraved black was printed only on stamps a & d; therefore, absence of black on stamps b & c is not the result of an error. Refer to note following **IM 434** regarding first day covers.

CO 142A booklet pane of 4, light blue
(litho) omitted 2,350.00
Quantity: 4 booklets reported

CO 142B booklet pane of 4, beige (litho)
omitted —
Quantity: 2-5 reported

134

Republic of Texas

Texas. March 2, 1986. Photogravure. ABN.

22c black, red & dark gray blue

CO 142C red omitted 2,500.00
 Quantity: *20 copies reported*

CO 142D dark gray blue omitted —
 Quantity: 2 stamps, which occur
 in a plate block

The two error stamps, together with three color-partially-omitted stamps, were contained in the discovery pane of 50, which sold in May 1996 for $13,750.

Arctic Explorers. May 28, 1986. Se-tenant block of 4. Photogravure. ABN.

22c black, gray black, yellow, red, blue & gray

a) Greely b) Kane
c) Peary, Henson d) Stefansson

CO 143 block of 4, black omitted **LRS (6/97)** 11,550.00
 block of 4, black omitted a & b;
 c & d normal —
 Quantity: 4 blocks & 4 pairs reported

Sea Shells. April 4, 1985. Se-tenant booklet pane of 10. Engraved. BEP.

22c black, reddish brown & violet

a) Frilled Dogwinkle
b) Reticulated Helmet
c) New England Neptune
d) Calico Scallop
e) Lightning Whelk

CO 144 booklet pane of 10, violet omitted 700.00
 Quantity: 75-100+ reported

Presidents I. May 22, 1986. Souvenir sheet of 9. Engraved, lithographed. BEP.

22c dark blue (engraved); black, red & beige (lithographed)

CO 145 sheet of 9, dark blue omitted *3,500.00*
 Quantity: 5-6 reported

CO 146 sheet of 9, black marginal
 inscription omitted *2,000.00*
 Quantity: 6-10 reported

Presidents II. May 22, 1986. Souvenir sheet of 9. Engraved, lithographed. BEP.

 22c dark green (engraved); black, red & beige (lithographed)

CO 146A sheet of 9, black marginal
 inscription omitted 3,000.00
 Quantity: very rare

Presidents IV. May 22, 1986. Souvenir sheet of 9. Engraved, lithographed. BEP.

 22c dark blue gray (engraved); black, red & beige (lithographed)

CO 147B sheet of 9, dark blue gray omitted
 from left 6 stamps **LRS (1/94)** 2,240.00
 Quantity: reportedly unique

Navajo Art. September 4, 1986. Se-tenant block of 4. Engraved, lithographed. BEP.

 22c black (engraved); black, yellow, magenta & blue (lithographed)

 a) Navajo Blanket b) Navajo Blanket
 c) Navajo Blanket d) Navajo Blanket

CO 148 block of 4, black (engraved) omitted 375.00
 any single (a-d), black omitted —
 Quantity: 150-200 blocks of 4

Presidents III. May 22, 1986. Souvenir sheet of 9. Engraved, lithographed. BEP

 22c dark brown (engraved); black, red & beige (lithographed)

CO 147 sheet of 9, black marginal
 inscription omitted 2,750.00
 Quantity: rare

CO 147A sheet of 9, dark brown (engraved)
 omitted —
 Quantity: *very rare*

Pan American Games. January 29, 1987. Photogravure. BEP.

22c black, yellow, red, blue, & metallic silver

CO 149 metallic silver omitted 1,500.00
Quantity: 30 reported

All known examples are poorly centered. Transition multiples exist and sell for a premium.

Enrico Caruso. February 27, 1987. Photogravure. ABN.

22c black, yellow, magenta & gray

CO 150 black omitted *5,000.00*
Quantity: 10

Transition multiples exist and sell for a premium.

Girls Scouts. March 12, 1987. Engraved, lithographed. BEP.

22c black & red (engraved); black, yellow, magenta, cyan & green (lithographed)

CO 150A black, yellow, magenta, cyan & green (litho) omitted *2,500.00*
as above, plate block —
Quantity: 46, including unique plate block

Many contain stray flecks of lithographed color in places where they would not normally occur, such flecks believed to have been deposited by the tagging roller. Price is for stamp with such flecks.

CO 150B black & red (engraved) omitted *2,000.00*
Quantity: 50 reported

The error is very subtle. The omission of color occurs in only a few merit badges. It can be easily overlooked. Expert certificate recommended.

Wildlife. June 13, 1987. Se-tenant pane of 50. Photogravure. BEP.

22c black (2 plates), yellow, magenta & cyan

CO 151 any single, magenta omitted —
Quantity: unique pane of 50, see note

The discovery pane has been broken up and sold as individual stamps. Recent dealer prices have been in the $2,200 to $3,000 per stamp range. Expert certificate recommended.

Friendship With Morocco. July 17, 1987. Engraved, lithographed. BEP.

22c dark rose & black

CO 152 black omitted 275.00
Quantity: 175-200 reported

Lacemaking. August 14, 1987. Se-tenant block of 4. Engraved, lithographed. BEP.

22c white (engraved); ultramarine (lithographed)

CO 153 block of 4, white omitted 850.00
single stamp, white omitted 165.00
Quantity: 80 blocks of 4;
80 singles reported

When separated from se-tenant blocks, single stamps of this error are indistinguishable from one another.

New Jersey. August 26, 1987. Photogravure. BEP.

22c black, yellow, red, cyan & tan

CO 154 black omitted 6,500.00
transition pair, black omitted
Quantity: 4 reported

Transition multiples exist.

Constitution Bicentennial. August 28, 1987. Booklet pane of 5. Photogravure. BEP.

22c black, yellow, red & greenish gray

a) The Bicentennial
b) We The People
c) Establish Justice
d) And Secure
e) Do Ordain

CO 154A any single, greenish gray omitted —
Quantity: 1-3 singles of each reported

☛ Caution. Expert certificate necessary. The greenish gray is the background color on the stamps. No intact booklet pane is known at this time. Pairs and strips of 3 exist. A set of the 5 a-e (a pair and a strip of 3) sold at auction for $4,400 in February 1993.

CPA. September 21, 1987. Engraved, lithographed. BEP.

22c black (engraved); black, red, green & tan (lithographed)

CO 155 black (engraved) omitted 700.00
Quantity: 300-400 reported

Locomotives. October 1, 1987. Se-tenant booklet pane of 5. Engraved, lithographed. BEP.

22c black (engraved); black, yellow, red, blue & dark green (lithographed)

　　a) Stourbridge Lion
　　b) Best Friend of Charleston
　　c) John Bull
　　d) Brother Jonathan
　　e) Gowan & Marx

CO 155A booklet pane of 5, black omitted on e　　—
　　Quantity: *very rare, possibly unique*

CO 155B stamp (d), red omitted **LRS (1/92)**　　1,100.00
　　Quantity: 1 unused & 1 used reported

Honeybee. September 2, 1988. Coil. Engraved, lithographed. BEP.

25c black (engraved); black, yellow, magenta, blue, & beige (lithographed)

CO 156 black (engraved) omitted　　60.00
　　as above, used　　—
　　as above, used on cover　　100.00
　　Quantity: several hundred unused;
　　　20-50 used on cover

Cover listing is for contemporaneous use on commercial cover. Covers are known postmarked Midland, Texas during January 1990, and Midland, Texas during April 1990.

☛ Blocks and vertical pairs with engraved black omitted were purloined by employees at a paper recycling firm. They are printer's waste and are untagged. It is estimated that 150 may have been used on mail but no copies are known in collector's hands at this time.

CO 157 black (litho) omitted　　475.00
　　Quantity: 100+ reported

☛ Caution. Many copies exist with a few black litho dots, which although invisible to the naked eye, are visible under magnification. In order to qualify as a color-omitted error, a stamp must contain no trace of lithographic black. Copies with traces of lithographed black sell for a small fraction of the price of true 100% black omitted copies.

CO 157A yellow (litho) omitted　　1,000.00
　　Quantity: 50-60 reported

☛ Caution. Certificate necessary. Copies often exist with a few yellow litho dots, which although difficult to see with the naked eye, are visible under 30-power magnification. In order to be considered a yellow omitted error, a stamp must contain no trace of lithographic yellow.

Antarctic Explorers. September 14, 1988. Se-tenant block of 4. Photogravure. ABN.

25c black, gray black, yellow, magenta, cyan, brown & Prussian green

　　a) Nathaniel Palmer　　b) Lt. Charles Wilkes
　　c) Richard E. Byrd　　d) Lincoln Ellsworth

CO 158 black omitted　　1,400.00
　　single stamp, black omitted　　—
　　plate block of 4, black omitted　　—
　　Quantity: 2 panes (20 blocks and
　　　20 singles)

Madonna & Child. October 20, 1988. Engraved, lithographed. BEP.

25c black & red (engraved); yellow, red, blue, pale rose & metallic gold (lithographed)

CO 159 metallic gold omitted　　25.00
　　plate block of 4, gold omitted　　—
　　Quantity: few thousand

Although catalogue prices are based on the best information available at press time, readers should be aware that prices for error stamps fluctuate over time, and therefore, are advised to contact dealers active in the error stamp market for timely quotes when buying or selling.

Astronauts. July 20, 1989. Engraved, lithographed. BEP.

$2.40 black (engraved); black, yellow, red, blue & dark blue (lithographed)

CO 161 black (engraved) omitted 2,500.00
plate block of 4
Quantity: 60-80

☛ Caution. No black engraved cross hatching should be visible on the white area of the space suits.

CO 161A black (litho) omitted 3,250.00
plate block of 4
Quantity: *20-30 reported*

Bill of Rights. September 25, 1989. Photogravure. BEP.

25c black (engraved); black, red & blue (lithographed)

CO 162 black (engraved) omitted 325.00
Quantity: 200

Dinosaurs. October 1, 1989. Se-tenant block of 4. Engraved, lithographed. BEP.

25c black (engraved); black, yellow, magenta & cyan (lithographed)

a) Tyrannosaurus b) Pteranodon
c) Stegosaurus d) Brontosaurus

CO 163 block of 4, black (engraved) omitted
well centered block of 4 1,000.00
poorly centered block of 4 800.00
any single, a-d 175.00
Quantity: 75-100 blocks of 4 reported

Some copies of this error were discovered in postal vending machine packets in which the blocks had been folded along one row of perforations, and are, therefore, prone to separation. Price is for sound block with perforations that have not been folded. Folded blocks sell for less. Most blocks are poorly centered as in the illustration.

Christmas Madonna. October 19, 1989. Engraved, lithographed. BEP.

25c black & red (engraved); pink, yellow, magenta & pale gray blue (lithographed)

CO 163A red (engraved) omitted 750.00
Quantity: 50

Christmas. October 19, 1989. Booklet pane of 10. Photogravure. ABN.

25c black, yellow, magenta, red & cyan

CO 164 booklet pane of 10, red
omitted **LRS (6/97)** 7,150.00
Quantity: *very rare*

20th UPU Congress. November 19, 1989. Se-tenant block of 4. Perf 11. Engraved, lithographed. BEP.

25c dark blue (engraved); black, yellow, magenta & cyan (lithographed)

a) Biplane
c) Stagecoach
b) Delivery Truck
d) Riverboat

CO 165 block of 4, dark blue (engraved) omitted
 well centered block of 4 900.00
 poorly centered block of 4 700.00
 any single (a-d), dark blue omitted 200.00
 plate block of 4, dark blue omitted —
 Quantity: 60-80 blocks reported

Most copies of **IM 165** are poorly centered as in the illustration.

20th UPU Congress. November 27, 1989. Souvenir sheet of 4. Imperforate. Engraved, lithographed. BEP.

25c dark blue & gray (engraved); black, yellow, magenta & cyan (lithographed)

a) Stagecoach
c) Biplane
b) Riverboat
d) Delivery Truck

CO 165A souvenir sheet, dark blue & gray
 (engraved) omitted **LRS (12/99)** 6,875.00
 Quantity: 2 reported

Love. January 18, 1990. Booklet pane of 10. Photogravure. BEP.

25c black, red, blue & green

CO 166 booklet pane of 10, red omitted 1,850.00
 single stamp, red omitted 200.00
 Quantity: 20 panes of 10

Umbrella. February 3, 1990. Booklet pane of 10. Photogravure. BEP.

15c yellow, magenta, cyan, dark blue, green & buff

CO 167 booklet pane of 10, dark blue
 omitted 1,600.00
 single stamp, dark blue omitted 175.00
 Quantity: 75 panes reported

Wyoming. February 23, 1990. Engraved, lithographed. BEP.

25c black (engraved); black, yellow, magenta & cyan (lithographed)

CO 168 black (engraved) omitted 1,750.00
 as above, affixed to 4x5 card *400.00*
 used, black (engraved) omitted —
 Quantity: 80 mint copies, 10 of which
 are affixed to 4x5 cards; 1 used copy

Bobcat. June 1, 1990. Engraved, lithographed. BEP.

$2 black (engraved); black, yellow, magenta & cyan (lithographed)

CO 172	black (engraved) omitted	275.00
	plate block of 4, black omitted	1,200.00
	Quantity: 300-400 reported	

Many variations in the color of the green leaves occur on this issue. They are not color-omitted errors.

American Indian Headdresses. July 6, 1990. Se-tenant booklet pane of 10. Engraved, lithographed. BEP.

25c black (engraved); black, yellow, magenta, cyan & olive (lithographed)

a) Assiniboine
b) Cheyenne
c) Comanche
d) Flathead
e) Shoshone

CO 173	booklet pane of 10, black (engraved) omitted	*3,500.00*
	any single, black (engraved) omitted	*350.00*
	single (a) used on piece	—
	Quantity: *3 panes reported*	

Micronesia - Marshall Islands. September 28, 1990. Se-tenant pairs. Engraved, lithographed. BEP.

25c black (engraved); black, yellow, magenta, cyan & blue (lithographed)

a) Micronesia b) Marshall Islands

CO 174	pair, black (engraved) omitted	3,500.00
	single (a), black (engraved) omitted	900.00
	Quantity: 20 pairs, 20 singles (a) reported	

☛ Caution. Often with minute flecks of black. Examine carefully under 30-power magnification.

Lighthouses. April 25, 1990. Booklet pane of 5. Engraved, lithographed. BEP.

25c white (engraved); black, yellow, magenta & cyan (lithographed)

CO 169	booklet pane of 5, white omitted	75.00
	unexploded booklet with 4 panes	275.00
	any single used	—
	any single, used on cover	—
	Quantity: 500+ booklets	

Price is for pane with usual tab disturbance, which is not considered a fault. Cover listing is for contemporaneous use on commercial cover.

☛ Caution. Copies exist with white ink lightly applied or with white shifted to the bottom of the design. White ink must be 100% omitted in order to qualify as a color-omitted error.

Fawn. March 11, 1991. Photogravure. BEP.

19c black, yellow, magenta, cyan & dark gray green

| CO 170 | magenta omitted | 850.00 |
| | Quantity: *100 reported* | |

The non-omitted colors on CO 170 are misregistered.

Sunfish. December 2, 1992. Engraved, lithographed. SVS.

45c black (engraved); black, yellow, magenta & cyan (lithographed)

CO 171	black (engraved) omitted	500.00
	used, black (engraved) omitted	—
	Quantity: 100-200 reported; 2 used copies	

Sea Mammals. October 3, 1990. Se-tenant block of 4. Engraved, lithographed. BEP.

25c black (engraved); black, yellow, magenta & cyan (lithographed)

a) Killer Whale
c) Sea Otter
b) Northern Sea Lion
d) Common Dolphin

CO 175 block of 4, black (engraved) omitted 750.00
any single, black omitted 175.00
any single, black omitted, used —
Quantity: 100-120 blocks of 4

Fishing Flies. May 31 1991. Booklet pane of 5. Photogravure. ABN.

29c black, yellow, magenta, cyan & orange

a) Royal Wulff
b) Jock Scott
c) Apte Tarpon Fly
d) Lefty's Deceiver
e) Muddler Minnow

CO 175A stamp a, black omitted —
stamp b, black omitted —
stamp c, black omitted —
Quantity: each reportedly unique

Eagle. July 7, 1991. Engraved, lithographed. ABN.

$2.90 black (engraved); black, yellow red & cyan (lithographed)

CO 175B black (engraved) omitted —
Quantity: *20 reported*

Of the 20 reported copies, 3 are sound, the balance with faults due to mishandling.

Express Mail. June 16, 1991. Engraved, lithographed. ABN.

$14 red (engraved); black, yellow, magenta & cyan (lithographed)

CO 175C red (engraved) omitted —
Quantity: *very rare*

Editor's Note. The $10.75 Express Mail stamp of 1995 has been reported with cyan omitted, however we are not aware of any examples with cyan 100% omitted. Check under 30-power magnification.

Although catalogue prices are based on the best information available at press time, readers should be aware that prices for error stamps fluctuate over time, and therefore, are advised to contact dealers active in the error stamp market for timely quotes when buying or selling.

Note. Quantities for listings appearing for the first time in this edition are marked "new." They are tentative and subject to change.

World War II. September 31, 1991. Se-tenant block of 10. Engraved, lithographed. BEP.

29c black (engraved); black, yellow, magenta & cyan (lithographed)

a) Burma Road	f) Reuben James
b) Draft	g) Civil Defense
c) Lend Lease	h) Liberty Ship
d) Atlantic Charter	i) Pearl Harbor
e) Arsenal of Democracy	j) Declares War

CO 176 se-tenant block of 10, black
(engraved) omitted **LRS (6/94)*** 12,650.00
Quantity: 1 pane containing 2 blocks of 10

* The **LRS** price of $12,650 is for the intact pane containing two blocks of 10.

Comedians. August 29, 1991. Booklet pane of 10. Engraved, lithographed. BEP.

29c red & violet (engraved); black, red & violet (lithographed)

a) Laurel & Hardy
b) Bergen & McCarthy
c) Jack Benny
d) Fanny Brice
e) Abbott & Costello

CO 177 booklet pane of 10, red & violet
(engraved) omitted 750.00
any single (a, c or e) red
(engraved) omitted —
any single (b or d) violet (engraved)
omitted —
first day cover with strip of 5 (a-e),
red & violet (engraved) omitted —
Quantity: 100-150 booklet panes reported,
6 first day covers

Refer to note following **IM 434** regarding first day covers.

District of Columbia Bicentennial. September 7, 1991. Engraved, lithographed. BEP.

29c black (engraved); black, yellow, magenta & cyan (lithographed)

CO 178 black (engraved) omitted 125.00
plate block of 4, black omitted 525.00
Quantity: 1,000+

Christmas. October 17, 1991. Booklet pane of 10. Engraved, lithographed. BEP.

(29c) black & red (engraved); yellow, magenta, cyan & gold (lithographed)

CO 179 black & red (engraved) omitted *3,750.00*
Quantity: 9 sound copies; 1 faulty copy

Alaska Highway. May 30, 1992. Engraved, lithographed. BEP.

29c black (engraved); black, yellow, magenta, cyan & dark brown (lithographed)

CO 180 black (engraved) omitted
well centered 850.00
poorly centered 475.00
used on cover, black omitted *125.00*
Quantity: 220

Of the 220 copies, 100 copies are poorly centered as in the illustration and 120 copies are well centered. Cover price is for contemporaneous usage.

World War II. August 17, 1992. Se-tenant block of 10. Engraved, lithographed. BEP.

29c black (engraved); black, yellow, magenta & cyan (lithographed)

a) Tokyo Raid	f) Secret Code
b) Ration Stamps	g) Yorktown Lost
c) Battle of Coral Sea	h) Women in War
d) Corregidor	i) Guadalcanal
e) Aleutian Island	j) North Africa

CO 180A block of 10, red (litho)
omitted **LRS (10/94)** 6,050.00
Quantity: 1 pane containing 2
blocks of 10

Minerals. September 17, 1992. Se-tenant block of 4. Engraved, lithographed. BEP.

29c black (engraved); black, yellow, magenta, cyan & silver (lithographed)

a) Azurite	b) Copper
c) Variscite	d) Wulfenite

CO 181 strip of 4, silver (litho) omitted —
Quantity: 2 strips of 4 containing a-d

The strips of 4 of **CO 181** with color omitted are contained in blocks of 8 stamps that also contain 4 normal stamps.

☛ Copies with magenta (lithographed) omitted have been reported; however, we are not aware of any genuine examples.

Eagle & Shield. September 25, 1992. Pane of 17 plus label. Photogravure. Self-adhesive. Straight die cut. BCA.

29c brown (engraved); black, yellow, magenta & cyan (lithographed)

CO 181B brown (engraved) omitted 400.00
Quantity: 75-150 reported

Juan Rodriguez Cabrillo. September 28, 1992. Engraved, lithographed. SVS.

29c black (engraved); black, yellow, magenta, cyan, dark red & tan (litho)

CO 181C black (engraved) omitted *4,250.00*
Quantity: *8-10 reported*

Sports Horses. May 1, 1993. Se-tenant block of 4. Engraved, lithographed. SVS.

29c black (engraved); black, yellow, magenta & cyan (lithographed)

a) Steeplechase	b) Thoroughbred Racing
c) Harness Racing	d) Polo

CO 182 block of 4, black (engraved) omitted 1,250.00
any single (a-d), black omitted 300.00
Quantity: 40-48 blocks of 4

Garden Flowers. May 15, 1993. Booklet pane of 5. Engraved, lithographed. BEP.

 29c black (engraved); black, yellow, magenta & cyan (lithographed)

 a) Hyacinth
 b) Daffodil
 c) Tulip
 d) Iris
 e) Lilac

CO 183 booklet pane, black (engraved)
 omitted 300.00
 Quantity: 250+ panes reported

Individual panes usually contain a tab fault. Price is for pane with tab fault.

National Postal Museum. July 30, 1993. Engraved, lithographed. ABN.

 29c black & dark red (engraved); black, yellow, magenta, cyan, tan & dark blue (lithographed)

 a) Ben Franklin b) Pony Express
 c) Charles Lindbergh d) Stamps & Barcode

CO 184 block of 4, black & dark red
 (engraved) omitted —
 hz strip of 4, black & dark red
 (engraved) omitted —
 pair, black and dark red (engraved)
 omitted —
 Quantity: 8-16 blocks of 4, 2 strips of 4

Stars of the Silent Screen. April 27, 1994. Se-tenant block of 10. BEP.

 29c red & pale violet (engraved); black, red & pale violet (lithographed)

 a) Rudolph Valentino f) Zasu Pitts
 b) Clara Bow g) Harold Lloyd
 c) Charlie Chaplin h) Keystone Cops
 d) Lon Chaney i) Theda Bara
 e) John Gilbert j) Buster Keaton

CO 185 block of 10, black (litho) omitted —
 Quantity: 2 blocks of 10

CO 186 block of 10, black (litho),
 red & pale violet (engraved) omitted —
 Quantity: 2 blocks of 10

Garden Flowers. April 28, 1994. Booklet pane of 5. Engraved, lithographed. BEP.

 29c black (engraved); black, yellow, magenta & cyan (lithographed)

 a) Lily
 b) Zinnia
 c) Gladiola
 d) Marigold
 e) Rose

CO 187 booklet pane, black (engraved)
 omitted 325.00
 Quantity: 250-300 panes

Individual panes usually contain a tab fault. Price is for pane with tab fault.

Cranes. October 9, 1994. Se-tenant pair. Engraved, lithographed. BCA.

29c black & red (engraved); black, yellow, magenta & cyan (lithographed)

a) Black-necked Crane b) Whooping Crane

CO 188 pair, black & red (engraved) omitted *2,000.00*
single (a or b), black & red omitted —
plate block of 4, black & red omitted
Quantity: *30-40 pairs*

Love. February 1, 1995. Pane of 20 plus label. Engraved, lithographed. Self-adhesive. Straight die cut. BCA.

(32c) red (engraved); black, yellow, magenta & cyan (lithographed)

CO 189 single stamp, red (engraved) omitted *500.00*
Quantity: 22-42 stamps

Three error panes are reported to exist. One contains three color-omitted stamps as a result of a color shift in which the red that should have been printed on the top three stamps was shifted one row lower. The other two panes contain 19-20 stamps each on which red is omitted. One of the reported panes contains the plate number B2222; the other contains plate number B3333.

Richard Nixon. April 26, 1995. Engraved, lithographed. BCA.

32c dark red (engraved); black, yellow, magenta & cyan (lithographed)

CO 190 dark red (engraved) omitted 1,400.00
Quantity: *70 reported*

Transition multiples exist and sell for a premium.

Recreational Sports. May 20, 1995. Se-tenant strip of 5. Lithographed. BCA.

32c black, yellow, magenta & cyan

a) Softball
b) Bowling
c) Tennis
d) Golf
e) Volleyball

CO 191 strip of 5, yellow, magenta & cyan
omitted *2,500.00*
Quantity: *8-16 strips reported*

CO 192 strip of 5, yellow omitted *2,500.00*
Quantity: *12 strips reported*

Women's Suffrage. August 26, 1995. Engraved, lithographed. APU.

32c black (engraved); black, yellow, magenta & cyan (lithographed)

CO 193 black (engraved) omitted 425.00
plate block of 4 —
Quantity: *40-60 reported*

☛ Caution. This issue was prone to printing problems. Many varieties exist with colors partially omitted. Certificate recommended. Many copies of **CO 193** are poorly centered as illustrated. Price is for a poorly centered copy. Well centered copies sell for double.

148

Celebrate the Century 1900s. February 3, 1998. Se-tenant pane of 15. Engraved, lithographed. APU.

32c red (engraved); black, yellow, magenta & cyan (lithographed)

CO 204 pane of 15, red engraved omitted —
Quantity: *new, possibly unique*

Engraved red appears on only one stamp, the Gibson Girl. Engraved red was the only color used to print the Gibson Girl stamp. Its omission creates a blank stamp.

Holiday Wreaths. October 15, 1998. Se-tenant pane of 20. Lithographed. Self-adhesive. Serpentine die cut. BCA.

32c black, yellow, magenta, cyan, red & green

a) Evergreen Wreath b) Chili Wreath
c) Colonial Wreath d) Tropical Wreath

CO 205 block, red omitted *1,250.00*
strip, red omitted —
Quantity: *two panes reported*

The color red was used to print the denomination and salutation on stamps a and d; green was used on stamps b and c. Red appearing elsewhere on the stamps arises from magenta in the four-color process, not from the dedicated single-color red printing plate. The se-tenant designs vary in order of appearance from block to block within a pane. By virtue of the layout, each of the blocks of 4 contains plate numbers in its selvage.

Weather Vane. November 9, 1998. Lithographed. APU.

(1c) black, yellow, blue, red & dark blue

CO 206 black omitted *175.00*
plate block, black omitted —
Quantity: *100-150 reported*

Note. Quantities for listings appearing for the first time in this edition are marked "new." They are tentative and subject to change.

Editor's Note. Dummy simulations bearing the design of the 32c Flag Over Porch coil stamp, but lacking the "USA 32," were included as leaders in a refrigerator-magnet stamp dispenser sold at some Wal-Mart stores in the spring of 1999. They are not color-omitted error stamps.

Hat & H. November 9, 1998. Coil. Photogravure. Self-adhesive. Serpentine die cut. BEP.

(33c) black, red, blue & gray

CO 208 red omitted —
 strip, red omitted, plate No. 2222 —
 Quantity: 100 reported

On the discovery roll, the gray and blue portions of the design are shifted right as in the illustrated pair. **CO 208** can be collected as a single stamp or a pair. The listing is for a single stamp.

CO 209 black omitted —
 Quantity: *35 reported*

Of the 35 copies, 17 have normal die cuts between stamps and 18 possess trace die cut impressions analogous to blind perfs.

Refer to **IM 597** for listings of black omitted and die cut omitted examples.

Flag Over City. February 25, 1999. Coil. Photogravure. Self-adhesive. Serpentine die cut. BEP.

33c dark blue, light blue, red & yellow

CO 211 pair, light blue & yellow omitted *1,250.00*
 strip, as above, plate No. 6666 —
 Quantity: 95 stamps

The dark blue and red portions of the design are misregistered in relation to one another, separated by about one eighth inch. In addition, the design is shifted to the right resulting in die cuts appearing to be misplaced. Only dark blue and red digits appear on plate number strips.

AIR MAIL STAMPS

50th Anniversary of Airmail. May 15, 1968. Engraved, lithographed. BEP.

10c black (engraved); red & blue (lithographed)

COA 1 red omitted —
as above, used pair on piece
 LRS (82) 6,050.00
Quantity: very rare

☛ Caution. Dangerous fakes, including first day covers, exist. Expert certificate essential.

First Man on the Moon. September 9, 1969. Engraved, lithographed. BEP.

10c black, red, & dark blue (engraved); yellow, red, light blue, blue & gray (lithographed)

COA 2 red (litho) omitted 525.00
pair, one with red omitted 650.00
Quantity: 250-300

☛ Caution. Many copies exist with red shoulder patch omitted but with litho dots of red present in the visor and yellow area of the lunar lander. All traces of red must be absent in order for the stamp to qualify as a major error. Careful inspection under magnification is necessary. Also, note that the European standard for color-omitted errors differs from the accepted U.S. standard; the European standard requires only that the shoulder patch be omitted to qualify as an error. Price for copy with patch omitted, but other red litho dots present: $295.

USA & Jet. May 21, 1971. Engraved, lithographed. BEP.

21c black & dark blue (engraved); light blue & red (lithographed)

COA 2A black omitted **LRS (11/97)** 12,100.00
Quantity: 2

This error occurs as the result of a foldover at the bottom right of a pane yielding 2 black omitted stamps. The price listed is for the intact pane.

National Parks Centennial. May 3, 1972. Engraved, lithographed. BEP.

11c black (engraved); yellow, blue, orange & green (lithographed)

COA 3 blue & green omitted 925.00
as above, plate block of 4 —
Zip block of 4, blue & green omitted —
used single, blue & green omitted —
Quantity: 92 reported

Progress in Electronics. July 10, 1973. Engraved, lithographed. BEP.

11c black & deep red (engraved); black, red, brown, olive green & light violet (lithographed)

COA 4 red & olive green (litho) omitted 1,150.00
Quantity: 100

COA 4A olive green (litho) omitted —
Quantity: n/a

This error is visually similar to **COA 4** because the vermillion is nearly completely omitted, present only as small specks. The discovery examples are contained in a plate block of 4.

COA 5 COA 7

Wright Brothers. September 23, 1978. Vertical se-tenant pair. Engraved, lithographed. BEP.

31c black & blue (engraved); black, yellow, magenta, blue & brown (lithographed)

a) Wrights & Biplane
b) Wrights, Biplane & Hanger

COA 5 pair, black & blue (engraved) omitted 700.00
Quantity: 150 pairs reported

COA 6 pair, black (engraved) omitted —
Quantity: n/a

COA 7 pair, black, yellow, magenta,
blue & brown (litho) omitted 2,250.00
as above, plate block of 4 —
Quantity: 15 pairs

Transition multiples exist and sell for a premium.

Octave Chanute. March 29, 1979. Vertical se-tenant pairs. Engraved, lithographed. BEP.

21c black & blue (engraved); black, yellow, magenta, blue & brown (lithographed)

a) Large Portrait
b) Small Portrait

COA 8 pair, black & blue (engraved)
omitted 4,500.00
plate block of 4, colors omitted
as above on right pair —
Quantity: 5 pairs reported

Transition multiples exist and sell for a premium.

20th UPU Congress. November 28, 1989. Se-tenant block 4. Perf 11. Engraved, lithographed. BEP.

45c light blue (engraved); black, yellow, magenta & cyan (lithographed)

a) Spacecraft b) Hovercraft
c) Lunar Rover d) Space Shuttle

COA 10 block of 4, light blue
(engraved) omitted 900.00
block of 4 with hz gutter —
any single, a-d 200.00
Quantity: 60-80 blocks of 4

The Sikorsky 36c airmail stamp is known with the red engraved inscriptions omitted in varying degrees. However, red specks (visible under magnification) are present on all stamps seen to date, so it is not considered to be a true 100% color-omitted error. Nevertheless, it is considered a collectible variety: price $125 to $150, depending on the degree of red omitted.

Hinging. Prices for airmail color-omitted stamps are for never hinged copies. Hinged copies sell for less.

MIGRATORY BIRD HUNTING STAMPS

Canvasbacks. July 1, 1982. Engraved, lithographed. BEP.

$7.50 black (engraved); green, violet, pale yellow & orange

COWF 1	violet & orange omitted	*7,500.00*
	Quantity: 5 reported	

☞ Caution. Expert certificate necessary.

Fulvous Whistling Duck. July 1, 1986. Engraved, lithographed. BEP.

$7.50 black (engraved); yellow, pale blue, brown, gray green & light gray

COWF 2	black (engraved) omitted	3,750.00
	Quantity: 62	

King Eiders. June 30, 1991. Engraved, lithographed. BEP.

$15 black (engraved); black, yellow, magenta & cyan (lithographed)

COWF 4	black (engraved) omitted	7,500.00
	Quantity: *6-10 reported*	

Canvasbacks. June 30, 1993. Engraved, lithographed. BEP.

$15 black (engraved); black, yellow, magenta, cyan & tan (lithographed)

COWF 5	black (engraved) omitted	3,000.00
	Quantity: 120-150	

Transition copies exist with black partially omitted.

Refer to the section **Reverse Inscriptions Omitted** for additional migratory bird hunting stamp errors.

POSTAGE DUE STAMPS

Numeral of Value. June 19, 1959. Engraved, typographed. BEP.

COPD 1 single stamp, black omitted 275.00
 plate block of 4, black omitted —
 Quantity: several hundred

The red background for postage due stamps of this series were printed from common engraved plates. Denominations were added in black as demand required. When black is omitted, it is not possible to identify the denomination of an error, except in the case of pairs containing a normal stamp. Likewise, is it not possible to attribute black-omitted plate blocks to any specific denomination because denominations share plate numbers. Panes of postage due color-omitted errors usually contain a row of 10 pairs of one normal stamp and one error stamp. The balance of the pane consists of varying quantities of normal stamps and color-omitted stamps. Once the remaining color-omitted stamps have been detached from the pane, they are impossible to identify by denomination, and are listed above. Transition multiples also exist with black partially omitted from some stamps. They sell for a premium.

COPD 2 COPD 3

Numeral of Value. June 19, 1959. Engraved, typographed. BEP.

1c red (engraved); black (typographed)

COPD 2 pair, one with black omitted,
 one normal 500.00
 Quantity: 50+ pairs

Numeral of Value. June 19, 1959. Engraved, typographed. BEP.

3c red (engraved); black (typographed)

COPD 3 pair, one with black omitted,
 one normal 700.00
 Quantity: 40-60 pairs

Transition multiples exist for many denominations showing black partially omitted. They sell for a premium.

Numeral of Value. June 19, 1959. Engraved, typographed. BEP.

5c red (engraved); black (typographed)

COPD 4 pair, one with black omitted,
 one normal 1,500.00
 Quantity: 10 pairs reported

COPD 5 COPD 6

Numeral of Value. June 19, 1959. Engraved, typographed. BEP.

6c red (engraved); black (typographed)

COPD 5 pair, one with black omitted,
 one normal 1,250.00
 Quantity: 20 pairs

Numeral of Value. June 19, 1959. Engraved, typographed. BEP.

8c red (engraved); black (typographed)

COPD 6 pair, one with black omitted,
 one normal 1,000.00
 Quantity: 20 pairs

Hinging. Prices for postage due color-omitted stamps are for never hinged copies. Hinged copies sell for less.

STAMPED ENVELOPES

Prices are for unused entire envelopes unless otherwise noted.

Compass. October 13, 1975. Lithographed, embossed.

10c brown & blue (light brown paper)

COSE 1 brown omitted 125.00
 Quantity: n/a

Quilt Design. February 2, 1976. Lithographed, embossed.

13c brown & blue green (light brown paper)

COSE 2 brown omitted 125.00
 Quantity: n/a

Wheat Sheaf. March 15, 1976. Lithographed, embossed.

13c brown & green (light brown paper)

COSE 3 brown omitted 125.00
 Quantity: n/a

Mortar. June 30, 1976. Lithographed, embossed.

13c brown & orange (light brown paper)

COSE 3A brown omitted —
 Quantity: n/a

Tools. August 6, 1976. Lithographed, embossed.

13c brown & red (light brown paper)

COSE 4 brown omitted 125.00
 Quantity: n/a

Golf. April 7, 1977. Photogravure, embossed.

13c black, blue & yellow green

COSE 5 black omitted *800.00*
 Quantity: n/a

COSE 6 black & blue omitted *700.00*
 Quantity: n/a

Energy Conservation. October 20, 1977. Photogravure, embossed.

13c black, red & yellow

COSE 7 black omitted *200.00*
Quantity: n/a

COSE 8 black & red omitted *375.00*
Quantity: n/a

COSE 9 red & yellow omitted 275.00
Quantity: n/a

COSE 10 yellow omitted *200.00*
Quantity: n/a

U.S.A. July 28, 1978. Photogravure, embossed.

16c blue; black "Revalued to 15c" surcharge

COSE 11 black surcharge omitted 200.00
Quantity: n/a

Auto Racing. September 2, 1978. Photogravure, embossed.

15c black, red & blue

COSE 12 black omitted 125.00
Quantity: n/a

COSE 13 black & blue omitted —
Quantity: n/a

COSE 14 red omitted *125.00*
Quantity: n/a

COSE 15 red & blue omitted —
Quantity: n/a

Exists albino.

Veterinary Medicine. July 24, 1979. Photogravure, embossed.

15c gray-black & brown

COSE 15A gray-black omitted *650.00*
Quantity: n/a

COSE 15B brown omitted LRS (1/98) 990.00
Quantity: *5-7 reported*

Olympics 1980. December 10, 1979. Photogravure, embossed.

15c black, red & green

COSE 16 black omitted *200.00*
Quantity: n/a

COSE 17 black & green omitted *200.00*
Quantity: n/a

COSE 18 red & green omitted *200.00*
Quantity: n/a

COSE 19 red omitted *450.00*
Quantity: n/a

Exists albino.

Bicycle. May 16, 1980. Photogravure, embossed

15c blue & maroon

COSE 20 blue omitted 90.00
Quantity: n/a

Honeybee. October 10, 1980. Photogravure, embossed.

15c brown, yellow, dark olive green

COSE 21 brown omitted 120.00
 Quantity: n/a

Blinded Veteran. August 13, 1981. Photogravure, embossed.

18c red & blue

COSE 24 red omitted *250.00*
 Quantity: n/a

COSE 25 blue omitted *350.00*
 Quantity: n/a

The Great Seal
of the United States
1782-1982

USA 20c

Great Seal of the United States. June 15, 1982. Photogravure, embossed.

20c black, blue & red

COSE 26 blue omitted *150.00*
 Quantity: n/a

COSE 26A blue & red omitted —
 Quantity: n/a

Purple Heart. August 6, 1982. Lithographed, embossed.

20c black & purple

COSE 26B black omitted —
 Quantity: *possibly unique*

COSE 26C purple omitted —
 Quantity: n/a

Exists albino.

Paralyzed Veterans. August 3, 1983. Photogravure, embossed.

20c black, blue & red

COSE 27 black & red omitted *150.00*
 Quantity: n/a

COSE 28 black & blue omitted *150.00*
 Quantity: n/a

COSE 29 red omitted *350.00*
 Quantity: n/a

COSE 30 blue omitted *350.00*
 Quantity: n/a

COSE 30A black omitted *175.00*
 Quantity: n/a

157

USA 25. March 26, 1988. Photogravure, embossed.

25c red & blue

COSE 31 red omitted 75.00
 Quantity: 160+

Often with printed corner card "Magnificat High School."

Frigate Constitution. April 12, 1988. Typographed, embossed.

8.4c black & blue

COSE 32 black omitted —
 Quantity: *8 reported*

Love. September 22, 1989. Lithographed.

25c red, dark blue & pale cyan

COSE 33 dark blue omitted —
 Quantity: *5 reported*

Space Station. December 3, 1989. Lithographed, hologram.

25c ultramarine & multicolored hologram

COSE 34 ultramarine omitted 575.00
 Quantity: *8-10 reported*

Star & USA. January 24, 1991. Lithographed, embossed.

29c red & ultramarine

COSE 34A ultramarine omitted **LRS (5/98)** 750.00
 Quantity: n/a

COSE 34B red omitted *325.00*
 Quantity: n/a

Love. May 9, 1991. Lithographed.

29c rose red & dull violet

COSE 35 rose red omitted *350.00*
 Quantity: scarce

Star, USA & Bars. July 20, 1991. Lithographed.

29c dark blue & red

COSE 35A dark blue omitted *575.00*
 Quantity: n/a

COSE 35B red omitted —
 Quantity: n/a

Note. Quantities for listings appearing in this edition for the first time are marked "new." They are tentative and subject to change.

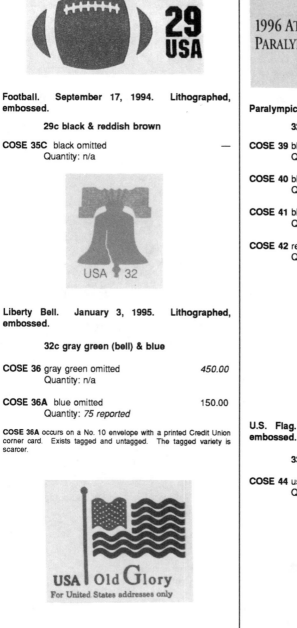

Football. September 17, 1994. Lithographed, embossed.

29c black & reddish brown

COSE 35C black omitted —
Quantity: n/a

Liberty Bell. January 3, 1995. Lithographed, embossed.

32c gray green (bell) & blue

COSE 36 gray green omitted *450.00*
Quantity: n/a

COSE 36A blue omitted 150.00
Quantity: *75 reported*

COSE 36A occurs on a No. 10 envelope with a printed Credit Union corner card. Exists tagged and untagged. The tagged variety is scarcer.

Old Glory. January 12, 1995. No. 10 business-size envelope. Lithographed.

G (32c) red & blue

COSE 37 red omitted *550.00*
Quantity: n/a

COSE 38 blue omitted —
Quantity: n/a

Paralympic Games. May 2, 1996. Lithographed.

32c black, blue, gold & red

COSE 39 blue & gold omitted —
Quantity: n/a

COSE 40 blue omitted —
Quantity: *2 initially reported*

COSE 41 black & red omitted *400.00*
Quantity: n/a

COSE 42 red omitted —
Quantity: n/a

U.S. Flag. January 11, 1999. Typographed, embossed.

33c blue, yellow & red

COSE 44 used entire, blue omitted —
Quantity: new, n/a

Federal Eagle. January 7, 2001. Lithographed.

34c bluish gray & gray

COSE 46 bluish gray omitted —
Quantity: new, n/a

AEROGRAMMES

Prices are for complete aerogrammes unless otherwise noted.

Jet Aircraft. May 1959. Inscription on reverse (type I, in 3 lines; type II, in 2 lines). Typographed.

10c red & blue (blue paper)

COAG 1 red omitted, type I —
Quantity: very rare

COAG 1A red omitted, type II —
Quantity: very rare, possibly unique

COAG 2 blue omitted, type II —
Quantity: scarce

Jet Aircraft & Globe. June 16, 1961. Typographed.

11c orange red & dark blue (blue paper)

COAG 3 orange red omitted 550.00
Quantity: n/a

COAG 4 dark blue omitted 750.00
Quantity: n/a

John F. Kennedy. May 29, 1967. Typographed.

13c orange red & dark blue (blue paper)

COAG 5 orange red omitted 450.00
Quantity: very rare

COAG 6 dark blue omitted 450.00
Quantity: n/a

Human Rights Year. December 3, 1968. Photogravure.

13c black, gray, brown & orange (blue paper)

COAG 7 black omitted —
Quantity: rare

COAG 8 orange omitted 450.00
Quantity: n/a

COAG 9 brown omitted 375.00
Quantity: n/a

U.S.A. January 4, 1974. Photogravure.

18c red, white & blue (blue paper)

COAG 10 red omitted —
Quantity: n/a

U.S.A. December 29, 1980. Photogravure.

30c red, blue & brown (blue paper)

COAG 11 red omitted 70.00
Quantity: 150

U.S.A. May 21, 1985. Photogravure.

36c black, blue, magenta & yellow (blue paper)

COAG 12 black omitted 950.00
used entire, black omitted —
Quantity: 3 reported, 1 used entire

POSTAL CARDS

Prices are for unused entire cards unless otherwise noted.

☛ Caution. Many postal cards were available from the Postal Service in large uncut sheets. It is possible to cut individual cards from such sheets with the stamp design appearing in virtually any position. Occasionally intentionally miscut cards are offered to the unsuspecting as errors. They are not errors and have no philatelic value.

FIPEX. May 4, 1956. Lithographed.

2c red & violet black

COPC 1	violet black omitted	600.00
	Quantity: n/a	

World Vacationland. August 30, 1963. Lithographed.

8c red & blue

COPC 2	blue omitted	—
	Quantity: n/a	

U.S. Customs. February 22, 1964. Lithographed.

4c red & blue

COPC 3	blue omitted	475.00
	used entire, blue omitted	—
	Quantity: n/a	
COPC 4	red omitted	—
	Quantity: n/a	

Social Security. September 26, 1964. Lithographed.

4c red & blue

COPC 5	blue omitted	750.00
	Quantity: n/a	
COPC 6	red omitted	—
	Quantity: n/a	

U.S. Coast Guard. August 4, 1965. Lithographed.

4c red & blue

COPC 7	blue omitted	450.00
	Quantity: n/a	

Weather Services. September 1, 1970. Lithographed.

5c black, blue, red & yellow

COPC 8	black omitted	750.00
	Quantity: n/a	
COPC 9	blue omitted	600.00
	used entire, blue omitted	—
	Quantity: rare	
COPC 9A	black & yellow omitted	—
	used entire, black & yellow omitted	850.00
	Quantity: n/a	

America's Hospitals. September 16, 1971. Lithographed.

6c black, blue, yellow & magenta

COPC 10	blue & yellow omitted	700.00
	Quantity: n/a	

Figurehead. January 4, 1974. Lithographed.

12c black, yellow, magenta & blue

COPC 10A black omitted　　　　—
　　　Quantity: *2 reported*

Nathanael Greene. Eutaw Springs, 1781

Eutaw Springs. September 8, 1981. Lithographed.

12c black, yellow, magenta & blue

COPC 10B yellow & magenta omitted　　　—
　　　Quantity: *2 reported*

Landing of Rochambeau, 1780

Rochambeau. July 11, 1980. Lithographed.

10c black, yellow, magenta & cyan

COPC 10C magenta & cyan omitted　　　—
　　　Quantity: *possibly unique*

Philadelphia Academy of Music. June 18, 1982. Lithographed.

13c dark brown, red & cream (buff paper)

COPC 11 dark brown & cream omitted　　950.00
　　　Quantity: *4 reported*

Olympics. August 5, 1983. Lithographed.

13c black, blue, yellow & magenta

COPC 12 black, yellow & magenta omitted　　—
　　　Quantity: *1 reported*

COPC 13 yellow & magenta omitted　　　—
　　　Quantity: n/a

Rancho San Pedro. September 16, 1984. Lithographed.

13c black, blue, yellow, & magenta

COPC 14 black & blue omitted　　　675.00
　　　Quantity: *5 reported*

Buffalo. March 23, 1988. Lithographed.

15c black, yellow, magenta & cyan

COPC 15 black omitted　　　—
　　　Quantity: n/a

Exists printed front and back.

COPC 16 black, yellow & cyan omitted　　—
　　　Quantity: n/a

COPC 17 black & magenta omitted　　　—
　　　Quantity: n/a

Yorkshire Packet. June 29, 1988. Lithographed.

28c black, yellow, magenta & cyan

COPC 19 black, yellow & cyan omitted —
Quantity: n/a

COPC 20 black & magenta omitted —
Quantity: n/a

COPC 21 black & cyan omitted —
Quantity: n/a

Settling of Ohio. July 15, 1988. Lithographed.

15c black, yellow, magenta & cyan

COPC 22 black, yellow & cyan omitted —
Quantity: n/a

COPC 23 black & magenta omitted —
Quantity: n/a

COPC 24 black & cyan omitted —
Quantity: n/a

Hearst Castle. September 20, 1988. Lithographed.

15c black, yellow, magenta & cyan

COPC 25 black, yellow & cyan omitted —
Quantity: n/a

COPC 26 black & magenta omitted —
Quantity: n/a

COPC 27 black & cyan omitted —
Quantity: n/a

AIR MAIL POSTAL CARDS

Virgin Islands. March 31, 1967. Lithographed.

6c black, blue, yellow & magenta

COAPC 1 magenta & yellow omitted —
Quantity: n/a

World Jamboree. August 4, 1967. Lithographed.

6c black, blue, yellow & magenta

COAPC 2 black & blue omitted —
Quantity: n/a

COAPC 3 blue omitted —
Quantity: n/a

COAPC 4 magenta & yellow —
Quantity: n/a

Angel Weathervane. December 17, 1975. Lithographed.

21c black, yellow, red & blue

COAPC 5 blue & red omitted —
Quantity: n/a

INVERT ERRORS

In this section, centers are described as inverted, without regard to the order in which the plates were printed. The visual relationship of design elements to one another is the most convenient way to describe an error: the inverted Jenny, the inverted candle flame, etc.

NOTE. Prices for classic errors vary widely according to condition and may be substantially higher or lower than prices listed.

Columbus Landing. 1869. Engraved.

15c brown & blue

IV 1	center inverted	*150,000.00*
	used, center inverted	*7,500.00*
	Quantity: 3 unused (1 with original gum, 2 without gum); 88-100 used	

Used copies almost always contain faults. Used price is for copy with faults; sound copies sell for premium of 100% or more, such as the nicely centered used copy that sold at auction for $30,800 in 1998. An unused copy with original gum sold for $247,500 in 1993.

IV 2	used, center double printed, one inverted **LRS (86)**	*20,900.00*
	Quantity: 3 used examples	

One copy is quite faulty and extensively repaired.

Declaration of Independence. April 7, 1869. Engraved.

24c green & violet

IV 3	center inverted	*100,000.00*
	used, center inverted	*10,000.00*
	used block of 4, center inverted **LRS (9/93)**	*569,250.00*
	on cover	—
	Quantity: 4 unused; 85-90 used	

Used copies usually contain faults; price is for copy with faults. Sound copies sell for a premium of 100% or more. The finest known unused copy sold for $258,500 in September 1993. Refer to notes following **IV 1** and **IM 35**. The copy on cover is unique. **IV 3** exists misperfed.

One hundred sets of plate proofs on card of the 1869 Series (15c, 24c, 30c & 90c) exist with centers inverted. The 90c value exists as an invert in proof form only. Market value per set of 4 single proofs is $10,000-$12,000. Plate blocks exist: 24c, two plate blocks of 8; 30c, one plate block 4 and one plate block of 8; 90c, two plate blocks of 8.

Eagle and Shield. May 15, 1869. Engraved.

30c red & blue

IV 5	center inverted	*100,000.00*
	used, center inverted	*40,000.00*
	Quantity: 7 unused; 36-40 used	

Almost all used copies contain faults; only 3 sound copies are known. Used price is for copy with faults: sound copies sell for 100% premium or more. One of the finest known unused copies sold at auction for $170,500 hammer price in 1991 and one of the finest used copies sold for $104,500 in 1998.

Steamship. May 1, 1901. Engraved.

1c black & green

IV 6	center inverted	5,000.00
	block of four **LRS (10/98)**	33,000.00
	used, center inverted	3,000.00
	used on cover	—
	Quantity: 250+	

Typically, unused copies are poorly centered, have disturbed gum and small faults. Price is for an example with typical small faults. Sound copies sell for a premium ranging from 100% to 300% or more.

Train. May 1, 1901. Engraved.

2c black & red

IV 7	center inverted	*17,500.00*
	intact block of 4 **LRS (89)**	203,500.00
	repaired block of 4 **LRS (10/98)**	148,500.00
	used, center inverted	*12,500.00*
	Quantity: 75-85 unused; 7 used; 2 blocks of 4 listed above	

Refer to price and condition note following **IV 6**. A select mint example of **IV 7** sold at auction for $60,000 hammer price in 1999. The finest known used example sold at auction for $66,000 in April 2001.

Antique Automobile. May 1, 1901. Engraved.

4c black & brown

IV 8	center inverted **NRI**	10,000.00
	block of 4 **LRS (6/00)**	132,000.00
	single, with **SPECIMEN** overprint	*5,000.00*
	Quantity: 97 without overprint,	
	100+ with **SPECIMEN** overprint	

Distributed by the Third Assistant Postmaster General, many were marked with the word "Specimen." Additional copies were traded by the National Museum for stamps needed for their collection. Most copies with "Specimen" overprint are centered toward the bottom.

Usually encountered with small faults or disturbed gum (from being stuck down to a Post Office archive book prior to dispersal). Price is for copy with usual small faults. Fault free copies, either unused or used, sell for a premium ranging from 100% to 150%. One of the finest known copies of **IV 8** sold for $27,500 in May 2000.

Dag Hammarskjold. October 23, 1962. Engraved.

4c black, brown & yellow

IV 9	yellow background inverted, used	
	on first day cover postmarked	
	October 23, 1962	*3,000.00*
	used on cover postmarked Cuyahoga	
	Falls, November 14, 1962	—
	pane of 50, signed per note below	—
	Quantity: 25-40 covers estimated	

☛ The discovery pane of 50 was signed in its margin by ten well-known philatelists, among them George W. Linn, Leo August and Ernest A. Kehr. So far as is known, it remains intact. After the discovery of the Hammarskjold error, the government reissued the stamp intentionally inverting the yellow. **IV 9** is identical to the re-issued stamp (issued November 16, 1962). Aside from the autographed discovery pane, the only positive way to identify the true error is by cover dated before November 16, 1962. First day covers exist postmarked either New York, NY or Brooklyn, NY. Of the first day covers, 22 are reported to be postmarked New York, NY. Covers also exist machine postmarked Cuyahoga Falls, Ohio, November 14, 1962, and notarized in the lower left corner by George W. Swartz, Notary Public.

☛ Caution. Counterfeit first day covers exist. An expert certificate is absolutely necessary for **IV 9** because of its similarity to the re-issue.

Washington Crossing the Delaware. May 29, 1976. Souvenir sheet of 5. Lithographed. BEP.

24c multicolored

IV 10	white (USA 24c) from 4th &	
	5th stamps inverted	—
	Quantity: very rare	

Note. The 24c and 31c souvenir sheets of the Bicentennial issue exist with perforations inverted in relation to the design.

Candle Holder. July 2, 1979. Engraved, lithographed. BEP.

$1 dark brown (engraved); yellow, orange & tan (lithographed)

IV 11	candle flame inverted	14,500.00
	as above, white vertical stripe	—
	block of 4, candle flame inverted	—
	Quantity: one pane of 100 located of	
	which 95 were purchased, including 8	
	white stripe varieties; the other 5	
	are presumed to have been lost in use.	

Copies of the 32c Nixon stamp with the lithographed portion of its design (Nixon's bust and the denomination) inverted in relation to the engraved (Richard Nixon) legend found their way onto the market in 1996, having been stolen by an employee of one of the printing plants. The employee has since been arrested, tried and convicted of theft of government property. The Postal Service ordered all copies seized; however, one or two copies are not accounted for.

AIR MAIL

Biplane. May 13, 1918. Engraved. BEP.

24c red & blue

IVA 1	center inverted	*125,000.00*
	block of 4, centers inverted	—
	center line block, centers inverted	—
	margin block of 4 with blue plate No., centers inverted	—
	Quantity: 100	

Prices for this stamp vary substantially according to condition. Each copy must be valued according to its merits. The listed price is only an average. Select copies have sold in the $125,000-$150,000 range during the past couple of years. An especially nice, lightly hinged, very fine copy sold at auction for $192,500 in October 1998; another sold for $176,00 in May 1999. Less desirable copies have sold for as little as $65,000.

POSTAL CARD INVERTS

Olympics 1984. April 30, 1984. Lithographed.

13c black, blue, yellow & magenta

IVPC 2 yellow & black inverted & to the left of basic design —
Quantity: 5 reported

HOLOGRAM OMITTED ERRORS

Earth. July 7, 2000. Circular pane of 1. Photogravure & hologram. SSP.

$11.75 multicolored & hologram

HO 1 hologram omitted —
 Quantity: *new, 3 reported*

Landing on the Moon. July 8, 2000. Souvenir sheet of 1. Photogravure & hologram. SSP.

$11.75 multicolored & hologram

HO 2 hologram omitted —
 Quantity: *new, 1 reported*

☛ Caution. Holograms are affixed to stamps with an adhesive. It may be possible to remove a hologram by dissolving the adhesive with a solvent. Therefore, caution is advised, and an expert certificate is strongly recommended.

REVERSE INSCRIPTION ERRORS

REVERSE INSCRIPTION OMITTED

YOUTHFUL HEROINE

On the dark night of April 26, 1777, 16-year-old Sybil Ludington rode her horse "Star" alone through the Connecticut countryside rallying her father's militia to repel a raid by the British on Danbury.

Reverse Inscription

Sybil Ludington. March 25, 1975. Photogravure. BEP.

8c multicolored, green reverse inscription

RO 1	green reverse inscription omitted Quantity: 100-150	200.00

☞ Caution. Green reverse inscription is printed in partially water soluble ink. Used copies without expert certificates should be regarded with suspicion.

GALLANT SOLDIER

The conspicuously courageous actions of black foot soldier Salem Poor at the Battle of Bunker Hill on June 17, 1775, earned him citations for his bravery and leadership ability.

Reverse Inscription

Salem Poor. March 25, 1975. Photogravure. BEP.

10c multicolored, green reverse inscription

RO 2	green reverse inscription omitted Quantity: 300+ reported	200.00

☞ Caution. Refer to note following RO 1.

FINANCIAL HERO

Businessman and broker Haym Salomon was responsible for raising most of the money needed to finance the American Revolution and later to save the new nation from collapse.

Reverse Inscription

Haym Salomon. March 25, 1975. Photogravure. BEP.

10c multicolored; green reverse inscription

RO 3	green reverse inscription omitted as above, used single Quantity: 400+ reported	200.00 —

☞ Caution. Refer to note following RO 1.

Olympics. May 2, 1996. Se-tenant pane of 20. Photogravure. SVS.

32c multicolored; black reverse inscription

RO 4	pane of 20, black reverse inscription omitted on the leftmost vertical row of stamps (positions 1, 6, 11 & 16) Quantity: unique	—

RO 4 is due to a shift in printing of the reverse inscriptions so that the description for "Decathlon" (the top leftmost stamp) is shifted right one stamp and appears on the reverse of the "Men's Canoeing" stamp (the second stamp from the left on the top row). Each of the 16 non-inscription-omitted stamps contains a shifted inscription.

MIGRATORY BIRD HUNTING STAMPS

TAKE PRIDE IN AMERICA
BUY DUCK STAMPS
SAVE WETLANDS
●
SEND IN ALL BIRD BANDS
●
SIGN YOUR DUCK STAMPS

IT IS UNLAWFUL TO HUNT WATERFOWL OR USE THIS STAMP
AS A NATIONAL WILDLIFE ENTRANCE PASS UNLESS YOU
SIGN YOUR NAME IN INK ON THE FACE OF THIS STAMP

Black Bellied Whistling Duck. June 30, 1990. Engraved, lithographed. BEP.

$12.50 multicolored

ROWF 1	reverse inscription omitted Quantity: 150	325.00

☞ Caution. The reverse inscription is printed on top of the gum. Beware regummed copies offered as inscription omitted copies. Expert certificate strongly advised. Beware other waterfowl hunting stamps offered as reverse inscription omitted errors. It is possible to emulate this type of error by washing gum off (along with the inscription) then regumming a stamp.

REVERSE INSCRIPTION INVERTED

Reverse inscriptions are normally oriented with the top of the inscription at the top of a stamp. Inverted inscriptions appear to be upside down when turning a stamp in the same fashion as turning the page of a book.

Blue Geese. July 1, 1955. Engraved. BEP.

$2 blue

RIWF1 reverse inscription inverted —
Quantity: *new, 1 mint, 1 used*

American Eiders. July 1, 1957. Engraved. BEP.

$2 yellow green

RIWF 2 reverse inscription inverted —
Quantity: 7-8

Labrador Retriever & Mallard. July 1, 1959. Engraved, lithographed. BEP.

$3 multicolored

RIWF 3 reverse inscription inverted —
Quantity: one reported

EFOs & OTHER UNUSUAL STAMPS

Tens of thousands of stamps exist with irregularities, such as misaligned perforations or color(s), paper folds or creases, over- or under inking, or other factors, that make them unusual in appearance. They are commonly referred to as EFOs (errors, freaks, and oddities). They are far too numerous to list or price individually. Even a reasonably modest discussion of EFOs could easily fill a book by itself. What follows is a generalized overview of the most commonly encountered types together with a few representative illustrations and some basic price guidelines.

Because so many EFOs are unique, and because no reliable population statistics exist for the rest, rarity is often not the primary factor in pricing. Visual appeal and topical appeal are most often the key elements in EFO pricing. The element of scarcity comes more into play in pricing non-unique EFOs, where a definite quantity is known. The best way to get a handle on EFO prices is to check dealer price lists for comparables, study prices realized from public auctions, and talk to EFO dealers and collectors.

EFO collecting is one of the most fascinating areas of philately. A growing number of collectors finds their peculiar appearance irresistible. And in a day and age where the Postal Service is flooding the market with hundreds of new issues whose primary—and often sole—purpose is to boost revenue, many find it appealing to collect the very items that the postal service goes to such great lengths to keep from the public—errors. There is something magical about owning the uncommon and the offbeat, about owning something few others own or choose to appreciate.

To the uninitiated the distinction between major errors and EFOs is not always clear or logical. Over the years, the way in which major errors were distinguished from other types of errors focused on how they were produced, major errors generally considered to be the result of a complete omission of one of the steps of production (e.g. perforations or color), the unintentional reversal of a sheet passing through the printing press (i.e. an invert), or the use of the wrong color ink to print a stamp. EFOs were generally considered to be the result of random flukes in production, e.g. misperfs, foldovers, misregistrations of color, smears, under- or overinking, odd shades resulting from ink-fountain contamination, etc., and not deemed as important or as valuable as major errors.

Before the 1960s major errors surfaced rarely—only a handful of inverts, a couple of color-omitted stamps, and precious few imperfs during the previous hundred years. Discovery of a new major error became a celebrated event, collectors prized them for their rarity and value, and stamp catalogues accorded them individual catalogue listings. By contrast, EFOs—although never common—turned up much more frequently, but were not accorded individual catalogue listings due to the randomness of their physical appearance and the sheer impossibility of trying to classify and describe each one of them. For years mainstream philately largely ignored EFOs, regarding them as little more than curiosities.

Since the late 1960s, hundreds of new imperforates and color-omitted errors have been discovered. The newfound abundance of major errors spawned a phenomenal rise in the popularity of error collecting and all types of error material—major errors and EFOs. EFOs have come into their own, now seriously studied, collected and appreciated by error enthusiasts.

Traditionally dividing line between a major error and an EFO focused on how an error was created, an approach that sometimes left gray areas. For example, until recently some did

not regard imperforates resulting from foldovers to be major errors because they were created in the same random fashion as freaks. More and more, the tendency is to classify errors by their physical appearance rather than by how they were created, which cannot always be known with certainty. Nevertheless, gray areas still exist. It seems that in the taxonomy of errors, there is always room for question about which phylum, class, order, family, genus or species an item belongs. Differences of opinion regarding nomenclature also exist, i.e. what should properly be called an error, a variety, a freak, and so forth. The foregoing is mentioned for the benefit of those new to the hobby, who may find all this confusing and difficult to understand at first. In the final analysis, definitions and classification should never be allowed to stand in the way of appreciating an error for what it is—something unusual, intriguing, and exquisite in its own right. And many EFOs are arguably as eye-arresting and fascinating as major errors. Beauty—as the saying goes—truly lies in the eye of the beholder.

MISPERFS

Misperfs (misperforated; also known as misplaced perforations; also used to refer to misplaced die cuts) and perforation shifts occur when stamps are misaligned with perforating or die cutting equipment or when part of a sheet of stamps (typically, a corner) has been folded over during production (see **foldovers**). They can occur on any perforated or die cut stamp: sheet stamps, coil stamps, and booklet panes. Misperforated commemorative stamps are generally priced higher than misperforated definitive stamps, and misperforated sheet definitives are generally (but not always) priced higher than misperforated coil stamps. Too many misperfs exist to list individually or attempt to price. Value is generally a function of topical appeal and degree of misperforation. Usually, the more visually striking (the more severe or unusual the misplacement of perforations) and topically popular an item, the greater its relative value.

Misperfs range from barely misaligned to dramatically misaligned, as illustrated by the two coil stamps above. The 20-cent flag coil is only slightly misperfed; the 22-cent flag coil is perforated nearly down the center of the stamp. Misperfed coils are most commonly collected in pairs or strips. Misperfed modern coil pairs, such as those illustrated, range in retail price from $2 to $5 for slightly misperfed to $10 to $20 per pair for those perforated down the center. Occasionally an older or scarcer item sells for more.

Misperfed commemorative stamps are generally scarcer than misperfed coils. Slightly misperfed modern commemoratives, such as the First Man on the Moon commemorative illustrated above, usually range in retail price from $15 to $25 per stamp depending on age and topic. The illustrated stamp trades nearer the high end of the range because aerospace is a popular topic. A similar perf shift on a less popular topic might sell more toward the lower end of the price range. Pairs and blocks are priced proportionately. Older (pre-1940) or rarer misperfs also sell for more.

Some stamps exist misperfed only slightly, shifting a legend or denomination from top to bottom or from one side to another, resulting in an outwardly normal appearing "change of design." This effect is illustrated by the Thomas Gallaudet stamp shown above. The

stamp on the far right is normal; the stamp on the far left is a changed design by virtue of the inscription moving to the opposite side of the stamp as a result of the perforation shift.

The Kennedy stamps of the Prominent Americans series illustrate another type of change of design. A normal 13-cent stamp is seen on the left; a "3-cent" variety is seen on the right, created by a very slight perforation shift. In most cases, a stamp with such a slight perforation shift would be unsalable, however, this "changed design" possesses eye-appeal and retails for about $10.

Misperfed "change of design" stamps are generally worth more than other slightly misperfed items in which no change of design occurs.

The Perry commemorative above is an example of a modest misperforation that yields a nice effect—you can read part of the design at top that normally appears at the bottom of the stamp. Again, pricing is a function of degree of misperforation and visual effect. This stamp has a retail value of $10 to $20.

Dramatically misperfed modern commemoratives such as the one illustrated above usually range in retail price from about $20 to $40 per stamp. Occasionally a rare or expensive item will command a price of as much as $125 or more per stamp.

Stamps with drastically angled misperfs, such as the illustrated 2-cent Liberty series definitive, whose appearance is striking (it almost makes you dizzy to look at it), retail for considerably more, as much as $75 to $100 per stamp.

Misperfs are sometimes collected as singles, however, multiples often reveal the misperforation more dramatically, as illustrated above by the block of Love stamps. Its perforations slant as a result of having gone through the perforator at a slight angle. The illustrated block sold at public auction for $66, or about $11 per stamp. Slightly angled misperfs tend to sell at prices similar to those for non-angled slight misperfs.

FOLDOVERS

As the name implies, foldovers occur when part of a sheet of stamps (most often a corner) is inadvertently folded during production, then subsequently trimmed, resulting in an odd shaped piece, often with an unusual perforation pattern (commonly known as crazy perfs). A

foldover can occur prior to printing and perforating, or it can occur after printing but prior to perforating. Foldovers often contain extra portions of selvage (known as appendages) that normally would have been trimmed off. Foldovers are occasionally responsible for creating a major error such as the imperforate error **IMA 6A** or the color omitted error **CO 1**. Major errors resulting from foldovers are rare. Usually a foldover results in an EFO. Each foldover is unique.

Foldovers are often collected in multiples, which are usually more visually striking and better illustrate an error. The 2-cent Liberty block appearing above is a good example of a foldover resulting in crazy perfs. Its retail value is $125 to $150. As with other EFOs, the range of value for crazy-perf foldovers varies and is a function of topical appeal and appearance.

Foldovers resulting in crazy perfs typically range in value from $10 to $150, with many retailing in the $20 to $50 range, such as the example illustrated above. Older examples and eye arresting examples sell for more, occasionally hundreds of dollars.

MISCUTS

Miscuts occur when the production sheets of stamps become misaligned with cutting equipment. Miscuts often occur on imperforate coil stamps, and mention is made of them in the listings for imperforate stamps. Dramatically miscut imperforate coil stamps usually sell for a premium. Slightly miscut imperforate coils do not. Miscuts also occur on perforated coil stamps. Generally, the more dramatic the miscut, the greater its value. Miscut pre-1981 coil stamps often occur with partial plate numbers or marginal markings. The greater the amount of partial number or marginal marking showing, the more valuable the item. Miscuts also occur on sheet stamps, and they occur on booklet panes, yielding portions of adjoining stamps or in some cases selvage or gutters. Miscuts often occur in combination with misperfs, yielding uncommonly large selvage, or in some cases, gutters and portions of adjoining panes. Slightly miscut perforated coils (showing 15- to 25 percent of the adjoining stamp) typically retail in the $15 to $25 a pair range; those drastically miscut (half each of two stamps), retail in the $50 to $75 a pair range.

Most collectors prefer to collect miscut booklets in the form of intact panes. Miscut booklet panes that result from a simple shift

often sell in the $15 to $50, depending upon the severity of the miscut. Slight miscuts sell toward the lower end of the range, dramatic miscuts toward the high end. The 5-cent Washington illustrated above is an example.

COLOR SHIFTS

Color shifts (also known as misaligned color or misregistered color) occur when one or more of the plates used to print multicolored stamps is out of register with the others, or when sheets are improperly fed on one or more of multiple passes through a press. Refer to sections on **lithography** and **photogravure** in the introduction for information on multicolor printing. Color shifts range from mundane to dramatic. Value is generally a function of topical appeal and appearance. Usually, the more visually striking (the more pronounced the misregistration of color) and topically popular an item, the greater its value. On rare occasions, color shifts occur in combination with misperfs. And on occasion, a color shift is mistaken for a misperf.

Color shifts generally range in retail price from $10 to $25 per stamp. Those with slight shifts sell toward the lower end of the range. Those with more dramatic shifts, such as the owl stamps illustrated above, sell toward the higher end of the range. Stamps with minute or barely discernable color shifts generally command little or no premium.

Occasionally, dramatic and visually striking color shifts, such as the honeybee coil illustrated above, sell for as much as $100 to $200. As with other EFOs, there are no hard and fast rules; price is a function of eye-appeal and demand.

GUTTER PAIRS & GUTTER SNIPES

Postage stamps are usually printed in press sheets yielding either four, six or more finished panes of stamps when trimmed apart. The spaces between panes on a press sheet are known as gutters. Gutter pairs and gutter snipes occur when press sheets are miscut so that a pane contains a portion of an adjacent pane, including the gutter separating the two. Gutter pairs and gutter snipes can also result from pre-trimming foldovers.

To be considered a full gutter pair, the pair must contain at least one complete stamp on either side of the gutter. Gutter pairs on issues available from the postal service in configurations that normally contain gutters (such as certain of the Farley sheets and modern uncut press sheets) are not considered errors. Pairs (or multiples) with full gutters between are rare and usually retail for hundreds of dollars, typically in the range of $250 to $750. The illustrated 3-cent Presidential is one of the more common full gutter pairs. It retails in the $125 to $150 range.

Items with less than a complete stamp on either side are known as gutter snipes and sell for considerably less, the price determined by the size of the incomplete stamp and the issue. The illustrated $5 postage due is much rarer than the 3-cent Win the War stamp. Some slight gutter snipes can be purchased for less than $25. Those with larger portions of stamps showing sell for more, usually in the $50 to $125. The illustrated $5 postage due pair retail in the $75 to $100 range. The Win the War pair, $45 to $60. Again, it's a matter of eye-appeal, and prices range broadly across the spectrum. Stamps showing only perforations from an adjoining pane (and no part of an adjoining stamp) are also called gutter snipes and typically sell for a dollar or so per stamp.

OPEN CREASES

Pre-production open creases result from paper bunching or folding over on itself prior to receiving a printed impression. Such stamps should normally be left in the largest multiple possible. Typically, the folded or creased portion of the affected stamp can be gently pulled apart revealing an unprinted (or open) area. The determining factors of value are: the size of the opening, the underlying catalogue value of the stamp, and the age of the stamp. Generally, the larger and more pronounced the crease, the greater its value. Ironically, open creases are more common on pre-1940 stamps than on later issues, and prices reflect this situation. Many open creased stamps fall in the $40 to $100 price range. However, a fair number sell for more than $100, especially mint examples and stamps with high underlying catalogue value, which can boost the price to as much as $1,000 or more. Mint examples sell for more than used examples of the same stamp. Of those illustrated above, the one on the left would be expected to sell for $100 to $125, while the one on the right would fetch $125 to $150.

ALBINOS & BLANK STAMPS

Albinos and blank stamps result from the omission of all printed colors. An albino stamp is generally understood to have a blind, intaglio plate impression embossed on its surface, which is often enough to permit identification of the stamp in the absence of its colors. A blank stamp results when all colors are omitted from a stamp printed by lithography or photogravure and no intaglio blind impression occurs. Blank stamps are usually impossible to identify unless attached to a normally (or partially) printed stamp of the same design. Blank stamps and albinos are collected in pairs or strips containing both normal (or partially normal) stamps and stamps with all color omitted. Blank stamps and albinos usually retail in the $75 to $300 range.

Albino impressions are much more common on stamped envelopes, where color is omitted

but the embossed part of the design remains. Pre-1960 albino stamped envelopes typically sell for $2 to $10 each. Recently issued albino stamped envelopes are much scarcer and sell for more, especially used copies.

MISCELLANEOUS

Smears, blobs and blotches are caused by excess ink, by cleaning solvent or other chemicals on a printing plate at some point during production. Solvent smears are usually collected in blocks, strips, or panes large enough to show the entire smear pattern.

Minor overinking smears (such as the one on the left) command only a nominal premium; heavily smeared stamps (such as the one on the right) usually sell in the $5 to $15 per stamp price range. Again, price is a function of eye-appeal. Ink blobs and blotches on stamps usually sell for more than smears. Again, it's a matter of eye appeal.

Underinked stamps (sometimes known as dry prints) are caused by too little ink being applied to a plate during printing. The stamp

on the left is normal; the one on the right is underinked. Those sufficiently underinked to be considered collectible typically retail from $3 to $15 per stamp depending on severity of the effect. The illustrated 2-cent Presidential retails about mid-range, $7.50 or so.

The two examples above are severely underinked and retail in the $10 to $15 per stamp range. Slightly underinked stamps have little value. On occasion, truly startling examples sell for as much as $50.

Offsets. The most pronounced examples are caused by a printing plate leaving a fully inked impression on an underlying roller when the press skips a sheet of paper. Subsequent sheets then receive normally inked impressions on the top side, as well as a reversed impression on the gummed side, where it has come in contact with the roller. The illustrated examples were created in this fashion. The first sheet going through after a skipped sheet receives the most vivid impression. Subsequent impressions fade as ink on the roller is exhausted, until after a few sheets there is no evidence that a skip ever occurred. Generally, the more bold and pronounced the offset, the greater its value. As with other EFOs, the price of offsets varies with the intensity of the offset image and topical appeal. Prices for roller offsets typically range from $25 to $100 per stamp, and can range higher depending on the item.

Offsets are occasionally simulated by normally printed stamps sticking together due

to high humidity. When pulled apart, they can give the appearance of an offset, however, they are not true offsets and have no philatelic value.

Imperforate Margins. Occasionally stamps occur with perforations omitted between the design and the margin. They should not be confused with stamps issued with natural straight edges. Although not considered major errors because the omission of perforations does not occur between stamps, imperforate margined stamps are, nevertheless, collectible. Usually, they're worth only a fraction of the value of an imperforate error.

Partial or Blind Perforations. Blind perfs are incompletely or partially impressed (or ground) perforations (or die cuts), often barely indented into the paper, giving a stamp the appearance of being imperforate. They are usually worth little, unless the perforations are so slightly impressed as to be barely noticeable. Occasionally, blind perfs are shifted into a stamp's design making their presence even more subtle and giving the item the appearance of being imperforate. Such dramatically blind-perfed stamps usually range in price from $5 to $20.

Plate Varieties. This term applies to a large class of small flaws that trace to the platemaking process or from damage to the plate during printing, which result in individualized flaws unique to one stamp or on an issued pane. Plate varieties occur more frequently on older engraved stamps than on modern engraved or photogravure stamps. Gripper cracks and double transfers are examples of plate varieties. Retail values tend to be modest, typically three to five times the retail value of a normal example.

Design errors, as opposed to production errors, typically exist on all stamps of an issue. Design errors consist of things such as the wrong number of stars on a flag or the misspelling of a name. Because all stamps of the issue contain the error, no premium is attached to the "error."

The Postal Service rarely attempts to correct design errors once issued. The 1994 Legends of the West issue, a se-tenant pane of twenty designs, which initially included the wrong portrait of Bill Pickett, is an exception. When the Pickett design error was discovered, the Postal Service ordered all post offices to return stocks of the error pane. The discovery and recall were made before the scheduled first day of issue, however, several panes reached public hands before the recall.

The Postal Service reprinted the pane with the correct portrait of Bill Pickett and released it in due course. Subsequently, it sold 150,000 panes containing the design error (the incorrect portrait of Bill Pickett, known as the "recalled" pane) by lottery. The recalled error pane is more valuable than the regular pane, only by virtue of the fact that it was released in limited quantity—150,000 panes—and because many collectors regard it as essential to completing a general collection of U.S. stamps.

Error collectors generally do not consider design errors to fall within the scope of the error collecting field. In philatelic vernacular, the term "error" almost always refers to a production error: imperforate, color omitted, invert, EFO, and so forth.

Our Handy Global Stamp Series

Krause-Minkus Standard Catalog of® Italy Stamps edited by Maurice D. Wozniak
More than 3,000 stamps issued in the Kingdom of Italy and Italian Republic are listed chronologically with more than 6,000 values given in the most commonly collected conditions. An informative introduction to stamp collecting makes this perfect for beginning and experienced collectors.
Softcover • 6 x 9 • 192 pages • 2,500 b&w photos
Item# ITA1 • $19.95

Krause-Minkus Standard Catalog of® Australia Stamps edited by Maurice D. Wozniak
Find information on every postage stamp from Australia and its territories - regular, commemorative and airmail - since 1902. Features more than 1,900 stamps in used and unused prices. Crisp black and white photos aid in stamp identification, and stamps are listed in easy-to-follow chronological order.
Softcover • 6 x 9 • 176 pages
2,100 b&w photos
Item# AUS1 • $14.95

Krause-Minkus Standard Catalog of® Israel Stamps edited by Maurice D. Wozniak
Key information on every Israeli postage stamp - regular, commemorative and airmail - is available. More than 1,500 stamps are listed and priced for used and unused stamps. Crisp, clean black and white photos of all stamps are available to aid in identification. Stamps are listed in easy-to-follow chronological order, with an accompanying table of tabs for specialty collectors.
Softcover • 6 x 9 • 208 pages • 1,500 b&w photos
Item# ISR1 • $14.95

Krause-Minkus Standard Catalog of® Great Britain Stamps edited by Maurice D. Wozniak
You'll find stamps from Scotland, Wales, Northern Ireland, and the Channel Islands in this single, handy volume. Stamps are illustrated and listed by Minkus number in chronological order, with philatelic data and current market prices in mint and used conditions.
Softcover • 6 x 9 • 480 pages
4,500+ b&w photos
Item# BGS1 • $23.95

To place a credit card order or to receive a FREE all-product catalog call

800-258-0929 offer PYB1

M-F, 7 am - 8 pm • Sat, 8 am - 2 pm, CST

Krause Publications
PO Box 5009
Iola, WI 54945-5009
www.krausebooks.com

Trusted Krause-Minkus Stamp References

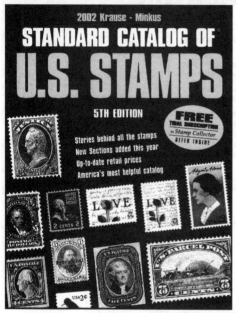

2002 Krause-Minkus Standard Catalog of® U.S. Stamps
5th Edition
edited by Maurice D. Wozniak

Beginning and expert collectors will find information here available in no other catalog. This fifth edition contains 10,000 listings with 25,000 market prices in used and mint grades, including rarities and errors. Learn the history behind each stamp with an explanation of who or what is featured. More than 5,800 clear photos make identification easy. "Decoding the Catalog" features help you differentiate similar stamps.
Softcover • 8-1/2 x 11 • 672 pages
5,800+ b&w photos
Item# SCM05 • $25.95

Krause-Minkus Standard Catalog of® Canadian & United Nations Stamps
2nd Edition
edited by Maurice D. Wozniak

This new 2nd Edition features more than 7,000 updated and revised prices, and 3,800 listings of all Canadian and UN stamps through 1999 - a 20 percent increase over the first edition. The collector-friendly format lists all stamps chronologically in the two most-collected grades of condition. Features detailed stamp stories, histories, an introduction to stamp collecting, tips on how to use the catalog, as well as special sections covering postcards and stationery.
Softcover • 8-1/2 x 11 • 368 pages
2,000+ b&w photos
Item# KMCU2 • $19.95

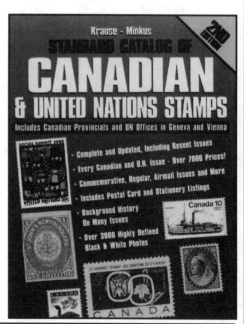

To place a credit card order or to receive a FREE all-product catalog call

800-258-0929, offer PYB1

M-F, 7 am - 8 pm • Sat, 8 am - 2 pm, CST

Krause Publications
PO Box 5009
Iola, WI 54945-5009 • www.krausebooks.com

Stamp Guides for Collectors

To place a credit card order or to receive a FREE all-product catalog call
800-258-0929 offer PYB1
M-F, 7 am - 8 pm • Sat, 8 am - 2 pm, CST

Krause Publications
PO Box 5009
Iola, WI 54945-5009
www.krausebooks.com

Shipping & Handling:
$4 for 1st book, $2 each additional, foreign orders are $20.95 for 1st book, $5.95 each additional.
Sales Tax:
CA, IA, IL, PA, TN, VA, & WI residents please add appropriate sales tax
Satisfaction Guarantee:
If for any reason you're not completely satisfied with your book purchase, simply return it within 14 days and receive a full refund, less shipping.

Retailers call toll-free 888-457-2873, ext. 880, M-F, 8 am - 5 pm